The Vanishing Path

The Vanishing Path: How to Be While There Is Still Time

By Miles Krassen

Edited and Adapted by Aubrey L. Glazer

FONS VITAE

First published in 2019 by
Fons Vitae
49 Mockingbird Valley Drive
Louisville, KY 40207
http://www.fonsvitae.com
Email: fonsvitaeky@aol.com
© Fons Vitae

Library of Congress Control Number: 2018966651
ISBN 978-1891785-962

Cover art: Elyssa N. Wortzman

To learn more about and support future publications
of *Panui*, see: www.lehrhaus.org/donate-topanui/
also, write to: alongourpath@gmail.com

PANUI

Printed in Canada

Table of Contents

It has been taught: Rabbi Shim'on said to the Companions, "How long will we sit on a single-based pillar? For it is written: *Time to act for YHVH – they have neglected Your Torah* (Psalm 119:126). Days are few and the creditor is pressing. A herald proclaims every day, but Reapers of the Field are few and at the edges of the vineyard, not noticing or knowing properly where the place is . . . Who is *the holy of YHVH?* Rabbi Shim'on bar Yochai, who is called *honored* in this world and in the world-that-is-coming."

Idra Rabba, Zohar III:127b, 145a

Once a seeker dreamt of a great treasure beneath a bridge in Vienna. So that seeker traveled to Vienna and stood near the bridge, trying to figure out what to do. This person did not dare search for the treasure by day, because of the many people who were there.

An officer passed by and asked, "What are you doing, standing here and contemplating?"

The seeker decided that it would be best to tell the whole story and ask for help, hoping that [the officer] would share the treasure with him. So the seeker told the officer the entire story.

The officer replied, "A Jew is concerned only with dreams! I also had a dream, and I also saw a treasure. It was in a small house, under the cellar."

In relating his dream, the officer accurately described that seeker's city and house. So the seeker rushed home, dug under the floorboards of their cellar, and found the treasure.

The seeker exclaimed, "Now I know that I had the treasure all along. But in order to find it, I had to travel to Vienna!"

***"The Treasure"*—Rebbe Nachman of Bratzlav**

All of your Companions are blessed by the *Fons Vitae* which you channel for us. For this we are forever grateful to be Reapers of the Field as we venture beyond the bridge that brings us home.

Aubrey, Elyssa, and Talya Sahara send heartfelt blessings of gratitude to our beloved teacher for caring, guiding, and inspiring our path.

How enriched are we to merit such a teacher like you who continues guiding us into these *Vanishing Paths*.

Blessed be our teacher, Moshe Aaron unto Ancient One of Days, *Amen Selah.*

אשרינו שזכינו למורה לתורת עה"ב כמוך
ברוך תהא מורינו משה אהרון לעתיק יומין ,אמן סלה.

אהרון להב ארגוונא שלם ,עשיאלה
וטליה סהרא (לבית נוריה)

Dedications

—anonymous

—Adriaan Finnerman

"Of all the teachers I have been blessed to study with— at rabbinical school and beyond—Reb Miles is the person I would call "my rabbi." Reb Miles's profound ability to speak words of Torah into a future orientation, his deep ontological spirituality, his extraordinary gift as a translator, and his modeling of the presence of an open God-channel all continue to inspire and awaken me. With enduring gratitude for my holy teacher. *Yeshar koach* and *zei gezunt!*"

—Rabbi Sarah Bracha Gershuny, *Congregation Nevei Kodesh*, Boulder, CO

"Brilliant beyond brilliant! For evolutionary Kabbalistic and Hasidic insights and practices, along with their utterly informed and inspired placement among the world's great wisdom traditions, Rabbi Dr. Moshe Aharon (Miles) Krassen has been a tremendously visionary and creative source for me over the past several decades. What a deep, precious, heart-felt, and life-enhancing blessing!"

—Hazzan Richard Kaplan, *The Shir Hashirim Minyan*, Berkeley, CA

"You have been my teacher since the *Shabbat HaGadol* retreat at *Elat Chayyim* in the immediate aftermath of September 11, 2001. With your gentle guidance, text study regularly balanced with niggunim (*Ein Od* in particular), that weekend was a life-raft. You were talking of the Force required to fully charge Shekinah's batteries so the new year could start, fully charged, and for that to happen properly the 'male' energies had to deep sleep . . . these were wacky, fascinating, feminist kabbalistic ideas that I hadn't yet encountered in my Jewish seeking; and I wanted to know much more. (A nod to Sarah Schneiderman here too!) New paradigm Judaism for the *ganze velt* . . . where what's useful from all the wisdom traditions is welcome in the weaving. Your very clear channel of Reception—coupled with your wisdom—fosters our passions and aspirations to transmit half as well as you receive."

—Ardele Lister

"From our first encounter, I knew with every cell in my body that I was in the presence of a true master, an embodiment of sapience in our world. If not for you Reb Miles, I would not be able to continue my work as a hazzan and ritual artist. Your perspective, grounded in tradition yet so far beyond conventional religious forms has transformed my understanding of Judaism and the religious impulse. I am forever indebted to you my teacher, my friend, my Rav."

—Hazzan George Mordecai

"With sincere gratitude for the abundant gift of awakened teachings leading to deep personal inspiration, with love . . ."

—Neil, Ilana, Zakkai, and Aliya Markowitz

"It is not permanent, since it does not exist at all.
It is not nothingness, since it is vividly clear and awake.
It is not oneness, since many things are cognized and known.
It is not plurality, since the many things known are inseparable in one taste.
(Shabkar Tsokdrug Rangdrol)"

—Rabbi Sam Feinsmith

"In gratitude for bringing new life into our broken world."

—Jeffrey Kessler

"Toward the One."

—Rafia, your faithful student and friend

"R' Miles identifies and guides us to the needed new paradigm."

—Jay *Zisha* Gold

"Thank you for the Torah of the future, brought down to nourish us all."

—Rabbi Josh Jacobs-Velde

—Elina Shcop and Mordecai Naseck

—Dr. Susan *Sara Leya* Schley

—Rabbi Julie Danan

Introduction:
A Hitch-Hiker's Guide to the Vanishing Path

When traveling into uncharted territory, every nomad needs a map. In your travels throughout the world, inevitably you have faced that dilemma before departing—which guide shall I take? *The Lonely Planet*[1] began as that "go-to" underground guide that immediately resonated with travelers who needed to get on the road without getting completely lost. You could pack your passport, a change of clothes and your credit card into your backpack, book the flight, pick up *The Lonely Planet* for your destination at the airport, read it on the plane, and be well-prepared to arrive and feel oriented—all within the course of the time it took to travel to your destination. And so that underground classic *The Lonely Planet* grew in popularity to the point where it is now so ubiquitous that whenever you take leave to hit the road, there are just another million nomads chasing the same place. Somewhere in that process, there emerged another attempt at returning to a more urgent layer of that nomadic urge that is now known as *Rough Guides*.[2] These are much less common guides, so much so that you will rarely find yourself at the same place with your fingers tucked into the same page as millions of others searching for that same place.

So as I travel to the outskirts of Sonoma County nestled in the redwood forests of Guerneville, I would be well advised to look at *Lonely Planet: San Francisco Bay Area and Wine Country Road Trips*[3] or *The Rough Guide to California*,[4] but would I find where I am really heading in advance? *Rough Guides* pride themselves on providing a more granular and nuanced understanding of the contemporary social scene. So even if *The Lonely Planet* hotel listings can be skimpy and uninspired, the historical and sightseeing information in tends to offer greater depth than others. I am much better off

---

1. Don George, ed., The Lonely Planet Travel Anthology: True Stories from the World's Best Writers (Oakland, CA: Lonely Planet, 2016).
2. The Rough Guide: USA (London: Rough Guides, 1992).
3. Sara Benson and Alison Bing, Lonely Planet: San Francisco Bay Area and Wine Country Road Trips (Oakland, CA: Lonely Planet Publications, 2015).
4. J. D. Dickey, Nick Edwards, Paul Whitfield, and Mark Ellwood, The Rough Guide to California (London: Rough Guides, 2008).

packing that original scroll on the road to rediscover my path.[5] Every time I return to this retreat in the redwoods, I discover different facets of my evolving path that could not be planned out in advance. In short, both *The Lonely Planet* and *Rough Guide* have something to offer—it really depends on what you are searching for. Let me share two contemporary exemplars.

A contemporary *Rough Guide* of the soul is *My Jewish Year* by stunt journalists Abigail Pogrebin and A. J. Jacobs.[6] While this outsider's report aspires to mass appeal, it strikes me that a very select readership will respond to this terse but topical approach to the Jewish calendar. While one would assume that anything written by a former 60 Minutes producer "going native" should be a rigorous review of what it is really like living a year by the Jewish calendar, the result is less than expected. What Pogrebin discovers are personal possibilities fused with universal implications, relegated here to remaining an amateur religious tourist. Her routes are circumscribed to traveling to synagogues and scores of rabbis and scholars—though none are Orthodox, Haredi, or Hasidic! Despite her numerous talents as a documentarian, her text will not necessarily resonate with seekers that are tone-deaf to mindfulness. While there is surely value in the ways Pogrebin revitalizes the tradition by getting up close and personal with eighteen holidays celebrated during the Jewish year, its depth has been run through a rough shot here with too much idiosyncratic sentimentality that loses any real precision or depth to the journey.

By contrast, a contemporary *Lonely Planet* of the soul is surely Rabbi Alan Lew's *This Is Real and You Are Completely Unprepared*.[7] In the beginning, the walls are tumbling down; in the end, stars are shining on the top of my head. This is the ticket stub that remains of a highly nuanced and ingenious insider's report that began as the go-to underground guide of the Bay Area when it was first published, immediately resonating with travelers who needed to get on the spiritual road without getting completely lost. You could pack your passport, a change of clothes, and your siddur, tallit, and tefillin into your backpack; seek a station on the calendar; pick up *This Is Real and You Are Completely Unprepared* and read it before the High Holy Days during the journey through *Tisha B'Av*; and be well-prepared to arrive and feel oriented through nine holidays—all within the course of the time it took to travel to your destination of Sukkot. And so that underground classic, *This Is Real and You Are Completely Unprepared* grew in popular-

---

5. Jack Kerouac and Howard Cunnell, On the Road: The Original Scroll (New York: Viking, 2007).

6. Abigail Pogrebin and A. J. Jacobs, My Jewish Year: 18 Holidays, One Wondering Jew (Bedford, NY: Fig Tree Books, 2017).

7. Alan Lew, This Is Real And You Are Completely Unprepared: The Days Of Awe As A Journey Of Transformation (New York: Back Bay Books Little Brown, 2018).

ity to the point where it is now about to be reissued in paperback, a sign of its ubiquity! Whenever I find myself between Av and Elul, I find myself encountering fellow pilgrims chasing the same place.

But clearly there remained unanswered questions and unchartered territory. So what about *A Hitchhiker's Guide to Europe?* While lying inebriated a field, contemplating the stars, Douglas Adams had a revelation to write a *Hitchhiker's guide not for Europe,* but for space. As it turns out, no one had yet imagined what it would be like to traverse multiverses and time periods after witnessing the destruction of the Earth to make room for a hyperspatial express route. Arthur Dent is the hapless visionary who leads the way while the planetary travel articles for *Hitchhiker's Guide to the Galaxy* are written by trusted friend, Ford Prefect.[8]

And so every traveler must discern what guide book suits their quest. By way of introduction, I want to suggest that the journey of the soul also requires a guide and each nomad in search of a path must discern what kind of guide best suits their quest. So when you decide it is time to take leave and journey toward your unique pathway of the soul returning home, it can boil down to whether you are inclined to traverse the pathways of *The Lonely Planet, A Rough Guide,* or *Hitchhiker's Guide to the Galaxy* of the soul.

To claim that this *Vanishing Path* is a kind of *Hitchhiker's Guide to the Galaxy* of the soul might strike some readers as arrogant, audacious, or even strange. After all, Krassen and I did not exactly wander around, getting into trouble, almost die multiple times, murder a whale and a bowl of petunias, steal a spaceship with an Infinite Improbability Drive, nor did we make sandwiches! And let's not forget that *Hitchhiker's Guide to the Galaxy* was banned at one school in the country to which I now return to—Canada—while Krassen resolutely remains in America! And yet, Krassen traverses multiverses and time periods after witnessing the ongoing destruction of the Earth to make room for his hyperspatial spiritual express route. Krassen is a kind of Arthur Dent—that hapless visionary who leads the way, while the planetary travel articles for *Hitchhiker's Guide to the Galaxy* are written by me, a trusted disciple, akin to Dent's friend, Ford Prefect, very much remaining alien to much of this hyperspatial spiritual express route by serving as a scholar and congregational rabbi, whose current spiritual express route merely crosses borders, from San Francisco to Montreal. And yet, along the way my soul continues to expand on its return to its home in the world-that-is-coming thanks to Krassen's *Hitchhiker's Guide to the Galaxy of the soul.*

In the beginning, concealment; at the end, darkness round midnight. Krassen's *Vanishing Path* is an iconoclastic *Hitchhiker's Guide to the Gal-*

---

8. Douglas Adams, The Hitchhiker's Guide to the Galaxy, (New York: Del Ray, 2017).

axy of the soul that seeks neither the roughness of a *Rough Guide* nor the popularization of a *Lonely Planet*. Krassen's *Vanishing Path* contemplates the Jewish calendar, from Purim to *Shovevim* (Tevet–Shevat) in fourteen stations. Even as the Vanishing Path in returns before the beginning to hover in origins, still there remains the all-too-human need for some kind of a map to hold onto. What Pogrebin's *Rough Guide* and Lew's *Lonely Planet* both assume is that a guide for the soul is one where the soul itself is an essence and home is a place of assured return. Building on the renowned critique of the study of religion and its subjectively assembled datum where map is never territory,[9] Krassen's *Hitchhiker's Guide to the Galaxy* of the soul incorporates updated wisdom from contemporary Hasidic and Haredi thinkers while remaining unconcerned with any apparent urgency of returning to nostalgia. For Krassen the soul is not an essence; rather, each person is a path. This has hyper-real implications for mapping out the vanishing path before us.

Krassen's *Hitchhiker's Guide to the Galaxy* of the soul where each person is a path contemplates a journey. That journey through the Hebrew calendar begins in Adar with Purim—why? The mystics teach that in the world-that-is-coming the only holiday on the Hebrew calendar that will remain will be *Yom HaKippurim*—celebrated as a day like Purim (*Yom Kippurim*)—a fast day is transformed into a feast day!

> Purim is so-called because of the name *Yom HaKippurim* [the Day of Atonement, literally, "the day like (=*k'*) Purim"] because in the future we will delight in that day [of at-onement] and transform it from [a day of] fasting to [a day of] delight [just like Purim] . . .[10]

And so the stations that ensue from Purim are as follows: from revealing concealments; from making the inner journey count to heroes making real the hidden Torah of the future; from seeing clearer through luminal darkness to deep love; from carving new tablets of the heart to correcting our corrections; from at-onement to acting within the shade of love; from rejoicing to kindling secrets lights; from insider's symposium to darkness round midnight. The arc of these *The Vanishing Path* is intended to stretch the soul well beyond the preliminary *Lonely Planet* map of the soul in *This Is Real and You Are Completely Unprepared*.

In the course of my preface that follows, you will learn about the difference between textures of time that mark these unique maps from "Liturgical Time" to "Institutional Time." While *This Is Real and You Are Completely Unprepared* is Lew's ingenious reflections on the refracted rays of

---

9. J. Z. Smith, Map Is Not Territory: Studies in the History of Religions (Chicago: University of Chicago Press, 1993).

10. Tikkunei Zohar, Tikkun, no. 21, folio 57b.

"Liturgical Time" that penetrate through the coarsely veiled foundation of "Institutional Time" in the synagogue that both he and I selflessly served in San Francisco, *The Vanishing Path* is Krassen's relentless pursuit of pristine and unadulterated "Liturgical Time" beyond any organization. In this sense, *The Vanishing Path* traces The Vanishing Path that provide the contours of a Möbius.

Imagine a twisted cylinder, that is, a one-sided surface with no boundaries, a veritable infinite loop—that is the Möbius strip! That image of a normal loop you are likely visualizing is one of an ant that could only crawl along either the top or the bottom, whereas this infinite loop of the Möbius strip has an ant crawling along it but that end would never reach an end. Rather than being merely one-sided, for these *Vanishing The Vanishing Path*, any nomadic ant crawling along it would wind along both the *bottom* and the *top* in a single stretch. It is precisely such simultaneous winding of bottom and top that captures the oscillation at hand: between concealment and revealment, between inside and outside, between past and future, between luminal darkness and the deep luminosity of at-onement, between carving out the heart to correcting corrections, between luminosity to the shade of love, between seeing the hidden sap of life to sweetening its midnight darkness. Each of us is traversing the infinite loop of the Möbius strip, like an ant crawling along it but that end would never reach an end. And when each *person is seen as a path, only then can* Krassen's *Hitchhiker's Guide to the Galaxy* of the soul be fully appreciated for what it is—an authentically Jewish *Vanishing Path* . . .

Aubrey L. Glazer
Panui
Guerneville, California
Tzom Tammuz, 5778

Preface: In Time to Love:
Along My Path to the Vanishing Path

by Aubrey L. Glazer

> "That which abides in thought yet cannot be grasped
> is called *Hokhmah*-Wisdom. What is the meaning of
> *Hokhmah*-Wisdom? *Hokh—mah* 'Wait for What.' Since
> you can never grasp it, *Hakeh*-'wait' for *mah*-'what.'
> 'What' will come and what will be. This is sublime, pri-
> mordial wisdom emerging from *'Ayin*."[1]

To wait for what will unfold requires patience and is, in a certain sense,
waiting for *nothing—no-thing* in particular. It is that search for sublime wisdom that brought me to this place. Here I am, sitting late into this
deepening darkness of night at Tassajara Zen Center, nestled in a mountain
valley, inland from the Big Sur coast in a remote part of the Ventana Wilderness, far, far away from the local, wired Zen retreats at City Center in San
Francisco and Green Gulch Farm in Marin. As the Tassajara stream rustles
by my cabin and the stars are dancing above to the symphony of crickets,
I am struck by the brilliance of this insight about the patience of waiting
in time as wisdom itself, and how it applies to my life, to all our lives. We
cannot know with certainty what will emerge down the path, even moment
to moment; and yet we trust that there is wisdom that will emerge from
waiting for what will unfold, so long as we are not too attached to it. Such
is a sublime wisdom of experience that takes time. Truth be told, *I have
nothing to really contribute* to these streams of deeper consciousness that
have been stepped into many times more than I would ever dare claim to
have traversed—and *yet, there is more to say* . . .

The book before you comes from a place of deep love and the need
to fulfill its eternal promise. Every student along the path to this sublime
wisdom seeks a teacher for guidance. There are many models of spiritual
formation that might define the master–disciple relationship. The relation-

---

1. R. Moses de Leon, Sheqel ha-Qodesh, ed. A. W. Greenup, trans. Daniel Matt (London, 1911), 23–24.

ship that has been most fruitful for me has been one of friendship, between partners engaged in loving study together, as one mystical master in the Hasidic tradition renders it: "Your greatest challenge should come from your most intimate mate. / It is the Ultimate Desire that one's help mate should come from that which challenges you most."[2]

It is truly a gift when you are able to find the time to wait for what will unfold with a partner. Often in my life, I have searched for that study partner in an intimate relationship, and too often I have failed. Pushing that kind of study relationship into the context of a life partnership perhaps is an unfair expectation. However, I am blessed to be in a place in my life where I have found that partner in Elyssa N. Wortzman, who is that helpmate who challenges me most—and for this am I forever grateful. But I also feel that one can be gifted with more than one helpmate, and in this way I have also been blessed. A few teachers have opened to me in this way through the years, especially Zvi Menachem Fox, as well as Elliot R. Wolfson and Shaul Magid. It is through their abiding friendships that they have also opened to me as study partners and challenged me beyond anything I might have imagined possible in such a study relationship with a teacher.

Beyond these helpmates, most spiritual seekers also yearn for a master. While the helpmate may challenge you deeply, it is often a challenge within a horizontal relationship. There is also, albeit rarely, another kind of relationship of master–disciple that offers challenges within a vertical relationship. Both of these relationships come from a place of love which, at its deepest core, as one philosopher remarks:

> . . . is a promise. The promise by constitution is an utterance that draws itself back before the law that lets it appear . . . the promise does not anticipate or assure the future: it is possible that one day I will no longer love you, and this possibility cannot be taken away from love—it belongs to it: it is against this possibility but also with it that the promise is made, the word given. Love is its own promise, eternity unveiled as law. Of course the promise must be kept. But if it is not, that does not mean there was no love, nor even that there was not love. Love is faithful only to itself. The promise must be kept, and nonetheless love is not the promise plus keeping the promise . . .[3]

Along my path, I have remained deeply skeptical of the vertical relation-

---

2. R. Mordecai Yosef Lainer of Izbicz, aka Izbica Rebbe (ca. 1860), Mai haShiloah, s.v. Genesis 1:18 (Brooklyn: Sentry Press,1973), 4b.

3. Jean-Luc Nancy, "Shattered Love," in The Inoperative Community, Theory and History of Literature, vol. 76, trans. P. Conner (Minneapolis: University of Minnesota Press, 1991), 100.

ship, and refused to submit to many opportunities to engage in the master–disciple relationship of *rebbe–hasid*, master–disciple. I have seen too many friends and colleagues become engulfed in demeaning, unproductive vertical relationships, usually a function of *B. G. S.* (Bad Guru Syndrome). Not me. I have held out. *And then* I fell in love with the promise of a teaching through two unique spiritual teachers. The love between a teacher and student holds before both "its own promise," and most teachers in a classroom setting are lucky to find one such student who sees this truth and is willing to pursue it. Just one student is enough. But it is a delicate relationship to cultivate, for the risk of its abuse is always in the offing. Yet the love that hovers between master and disciple in this relationship "is faithful only to itself," and at some point the relationship may subside. Such a dissolution in no way affects the power of this abiding love and its promise that must be carried forward. And so, this book is an homage to that love, an attempt to fulfill the eternal promise of that abiding love of "eternity unveiled as law," which I understand as spiritual practice.

This book is an appreciation of the wisdom that emerges from waiting for what has been and continues to unfold in the singularity of insights I have learned from two remarkable spiritual masters: Rabbi Alan Lew, of blessed memory (*o.b.m.*) and Reb Moshe Aaron Krassen, may he live years of distinction (*m.h.l.y.o.d.*). These two masters could not have been more distinct and divergent, and yet the promise of love could not have been stronger. By trusting that there is wisdom that will emerge from waiting for what will unfold, I have discovered a treasure that needs to be transmitted, and I see myself simply as a channel. While this book, *The Vanishing Path: Dance of Divine Time*, is the direct transmission of teachings from Reb Krassen, the inspiration to edit and write this book came from a love hovering in my brief encounter with Rabbi Lew, *o.b.m.* Moreover, I am continually moved by the testimonies of countless seekers from all walks of life who have and continue to be touched by the love at the core of Rabbi Lew's teachings. Each of them continues to read religiously his masterpiece in the spiritual practice of love, *This Is Real and You Are Completely Unprepared*, starting with the cycle that he sees as beginning on every 9th of Av. This may seem askew, but let me unpack this claim. To understand the balance of time and how its dance is always a dance in and out of time, I have dedicated significant time over the past decade learning from two masters while I myself remain a seeker.

This seeking began while I was a rabbinical student at the Jewish Theological Seminary, fluent in Hebrew but a yeshiva day school dropout who went to art school, then seeking a spiritual practice of meditation. While my undergraduate studies in French language and literature exposed me to critical thinking through the way meaning was conveyed in language, known as semiotics and hermeneutics, I had yet to really learn Jewish mysticism in earnest—but something continued to beckon me onward. As I was wandering in and out of the hallowed walls of 3080 Broadway, a name kept echoing—the meditating Zen-Buddhist rabbi, Alan Lew, *o.b.m.*

There is a wonderful story that I learned from Sherril Jaffe about the magical time she shared with her beloved, late husband, Alan, that echoed so many of my experiences, as she inimitably tells it:

> One day when we were walking down Broadway together, we ran into one of Alan's distinguished professors, and I complained to this old but very hale fellow that reading the Talmud had caused my husband's eyes to fail and carrying the heavy volumes of Talmud up and down Broadway between our apartment and the Seminary was causing his back to go out.
>
> "Nonsense," he said to me. "The Talmud never hurt anyone."
>
> I disagreed, but I couldn't really blame the Talmud for Alan's back, as he'd had back issues dating from before my time. A few years before we met, he'd told me, his back had gone out in the middle of a week-long Zen meditation retreat. It was so bad that he couldn't stand up, and he suffered that way for several days until his friends carried him to a faith healer, an old black lady living in a pink stucco house in Oakland who healed him instantly by laying on her hands, although, he said, she barely touched him.
>
> A few years later, when his back went out again, he returned to her, but found her sadly changed. She was now very old and suffering from dementia, and her treatments no longer worked.
>
> When Alan told me stories like this, it thrilled me to think that sometimes faith healers might actually perform such miracles, and it also frightened me a bit that not even a faith healer could save herself from the ravages of time. But for the most part, these stories Alan told me of his life mesmerized and uplifted me. They were always about the miracle and beauty of all life and never about the particular suffering of his particular back.[4]

What I learned from Alan through Sherril is how important it is to be mindful of time, of every moment. Whether by ravages or watermarks, time makes impressions on us, "like pulling up the covers when tucking in a child for the night" that I see now becomes a palimpsest. Those layers collect and never leave, if only we are present to them.

While Alan was already deeply committed to *Zazen* meditation before he entered the rabbinate, he felt at a certain point after ordination and work-

---

4. I am grateful to Sherril Jaffe from sharing this section of her forthcoming excerpt called The Death of Alan Lew (personal communication, June 5, 2018).

ing as a pulpit rabbi, when he met his mysterious teacher of Kabbalah and was studying with his disciple, Lenny, that while "it was one of the most intense spiritual places I had ever inhabited . . . it had come too late."[5] I was somewhat younger, disconnected in a different way, "not outside the window but in the window itself," already peering through the window of my Jewish life[6] with a penetratingly critical gaze and a burning curiosity about the limits of knowing. This insatiable curiosity left me cold when I dove into the only book on Jewish meditation in English at the time by Kaplan,[7] but led me to continue in my search for what lay at the limits of knowing by overdosing on the epistemology of French philosopher Michel Foucault,[8] a few marvelous French symbolist poets, like Baudelaire and Rimbaud to whom the occult and alchemy was not foreign,[9] and exposure to literary criticism of Kabbalah by Harold Bloom[10] and the mystical music of Leonard Cohen.[11] Somehow this eclectic curiosity peaked as I entered rabbinical school, returning to Jewish texts I had long abandoned now with the keys of Hebrew fluency to open them but with a true beginner's mind. So began my regular pilgrimage to explore the limits of knowing in Jewish meditation retreats in upstate New York at an experimental retreat center called *Elat Chayyim*. The contemplative spark was lit after attending a conference on a remarkable journey that poet Rodger Kamenetz took along with a multidenominational rabbinic emissary to engage in dialogue with the Dalai Lama.[12] What Kamenetz lacked in content compared with Kaplan, he made up with his poetic way of conveying his journey. Leaving home to return

---

5. See Alan Lew, One God Clapping: The Spiritual Path of a Zen Rabbi (Woodstock, VT: Jewish Lights Publishing, 2001), 265–71, esp. 270.

6. Lew, One God Clapping, 314–15: "We all have such a map. We all have such a key. And it waits to be discovered, not outside of us, but right there on the tip of our tongue, right there on top of our heart, not outside the window but in the window itself."

7. Aryeh Kaplan, Jewish Mediation: A Practical Guide (New York: Schocken Books, 1985). While Kaplan was a pioneer in popularizing Jewish mysticism, his appeal had reached its zenith before I discovered it, especially among Baalei teshuvah, which was not a worldview that ever resonated much with me on my search.

8. I have in mind the quasi-mystical deconstruction of knowledge in Michel Foucault, Les Mots Et Les Choses: Une Archéologie Des Sciences Humaines (Paris: Gallimard, 2015).

9. I have in mind the quasi-mysticisms present in Charles Baudelaire, Les Fleurs Du Mal (Paris: Flammarion, 2016); as well as in Arthur Rimbaud, Une Saison En Enfer (Paris: J. Corti, 1987).

10. I have in mind his delightful, little volume on Kabbalah and literary criticism from 1975, see Harold Bloom, Kabbalah and Criticism (London: Continuum, 2005).

11. This ongoing fascination with Leonard Cohen's mystic led to the writing of my recent book, Tangle of Matter & Ghost: Leonard Cohen's Post-Secular Songbook of Mysticm(s) Jewish and Beyond (Brighton, MA: Academic Studies Press, 2016).

12. Rodger Kamenetz, The Jew in the Lotus: A Poet's Rediscovery of Jewish Identity in Buddhist India (Northvale, NJ: Jason Aronson, 1998).

home only deeper really spoke to me.

Concurrent with his pioneering work in bringing *Makor Or*, a dedicated space for Jewish meditation, to his Conservative synagogue, Congregation Beth Sholom in San Francisco, Rabbi Lew was part of a West Coast zeitgeist dedicated to renewing the ancient, forgotten practice of Jewish meditation. So while Rabbi Lew was kindling the flames of the contemplative hearts in primarily Buddhist spaces with Sylvia Boorstein at Spirit Rock and Norman Fischer at Tassajara Zen Retreat Center on the West Coast, there was an equal force of renewal happening simultaneously on the East Coast in Jewish spaces with *Elat Chayyim*, as well as with the itinerant retreats of Institute for Jewish Spirituality (IJS), and the JCC of Manhattan in New York. While I was regularly crossing the coasts to attend silent retreats in the West Coast with Rabbi Jonathan Omer-Man at *Metivta*, I never made it to *Makor Or*, but always dreamed of it. In the meantime, while I remained based in the East Coast completing my rabbinical studies at JTS, I regularly attended any retreat offered in Jewish meditation and joined an early cohort of IJS. But my dream did not subside—someday I would meditate and learn from Rabbi Lew.

That propitious moment came after my ordination from JTS in 2000, when Rabbi Lew had already served with distinction at Beth Sholom from 1991–2006, and he was now enjoying the fruits of his labor as a freelance leader and teacher as rabbi emeritus. Here he was coleading a retreat for the Rabbinic Training Institute of JTS—an opportunity for Conservative rabbis to recharge their batteries and work on professional development that would be enhanced with some optional meditation. For this first time ever, I jumped at the possibility of formally joining my first real professional development related to Conservative Judaism, no less a retreat to meditate with Rabbi Lew at Pearlstone Retreat Center in Maryland! Our first encounter would be his last. As we entered this journey, I vividly recall taking a contemplative walk with Rabbi Lew and asking him what his current spiritual practice was all about. In the course of this walk through the forest of the Maryland countryside, the love that was hovering was palpable. He shared with me that inimitable passion in describing his current searching for ways to translate Reb Nachman of Bratzlav's *shfikut ha-nefesh* within Tahanun, that is, the "pouring out of one's heart" during the liturgical section of Supplication in daily prayer. He taught me on that walk that the most important practice to experiment with now was closing the siddur and opening the heart as you fall on your knees with your head on your left arm (or as I have adapted it, in child's pose) in Supplication. I had been struggling for many years with my practice of daily Tahanun, and found deep resonance in Rabbi Lew's neo-Hasidic recovery of this Supplication practice, which I continue to carry forward. Later during that same retreat, on another walk in the woods of Pearlstone Retreat Center, Rabbi Lew left this world on Monday, January 12, 2009 at age sixty-four.

That transition from nothing to something, and from something to nothing, is an illusory line we draw as humans, demarcating this world from the world-that-is-coming. I recall walking with Alan the morning before his last to discuss spiritual practices he was dedicating himself to recently. But there is something remarkable about that space in between something and nothing that marked our forest encounter. Again, I return to Sherril's recollection here that witnesses from afar how time is torn open, between this world and the next, all in a moment, a breath:

> The next morning, Alan rose early, as he always did. Every time in the Torah when it says someone rises early, something important is about to happen. Abraham rises early and saddles his ass on the day he is to take his dearest son to Mt. Moriah to be sacrificed. "The morning, which is the most memorable season of the day, is the awakening hour," Thoreau says. So Alan arose from his bed, dressed, drank a cup of coffee and led the morning meditation for the other rabbis. Afterwards, he *davenned* the spirited morning prayers in their company; then he went out for a walk on a country lane by himself.
>
> I do not know who found him, collapsed along the road alone, but it comforts me that he was never alone after that, not for a minute . . .[13]

That moment of being drawn together and torn apart remains emblazoned in my soul. I stood at that clearing in the wilderness that marked his taking leave again. Indeed, it was that love which he was able to channel into the practice of opening the heart it to this day!

Little did I know that just as this door was closing, another door was opening. As I sit, nestled in the majestic hillside of Tassajara Zen Retreat Center, spending the week on a meditation retreat with Dr. Daniel Matt and *Zoketsu* Norman Fischer, I return to this wisdom that will emerge from waiting for what will unfold. Our intention for the retreat is aptly entitled *About Nothing: Comparing Ayin in Kabbalah and Shunyata in Buddhism.* As I sit, meditate, contemplate, and learn with these master teachers, I continue to feel the presence of Rabbi Lew's absence. True, this space in Tassajara Zen Retreat Center resonates with his spiritual traces, as this was the original laboratory for his first experiments in Jewish meditation. I could not help but laugh when I heard from Joan, one of the retreatants back in the experimental days, now my congregant, how despondent Rabbi Lew

---

13. I am grateful to Sherril Jaffe from sharing this section of her forthcoming excerpt called The Death of Alan Lew (personal communication, June 5, 2018).

was on his return to the real world (that is, of San Francisco). When asked about how things went on that retreat Rabbi Lew responded, with a look of dismay: "Buddhists—9; Jews—0!" Back in that same place decades later, my smile emerged in the midst of this recent week sitting and contemplating no-thingness or *'Ayin* in Jewish mysticism. The irony of this response— "Buddhists—9; Jews—0!"—struck me. That is, Jews—*'Ayin!* There is a grain of truth in this irony that this next wave of Jewish seekers I was a part of were deeply into no-thingness, and perhaps at this juncture we were now the ones who had something to teach the Buddhists about nothing!

But there are more than residual memories of a bygone era spent meditating here. His students (many of whom are now my congregants) find themselves returning in pilgrimage to this glorious sanctuary nestled deep in the mountains in commemorative meditation to continue this work. They continue to speak of Rabbi Lew as if he was still very much alive and with us—*how?* It could not be better summed up than in this typical encounter. As I leave the *Zendo* meditation hall, I cross paths with the austere Buddhist priestess, Robin, who made an exception to allow me to wear my head covering while exploring the possibility of joining morning meditating in the *Zendo*. At this moment of meeting she was coming over to me to apologize. Full of compassion and caring, the priestess explains she did not know who I was and my relation to Rabbi Lew, *o.b.m.* She then shares her moving story of growing up in a secular humanist Jewish household in Long Island, eventually finding her spiritual path in Buddhism. The priestess recently was ordained by *Zoketsu* Norman at Tassajara Zen Retreat Center, where she has spent many seasons in monastic retreat. However, in my own journeying to this Zen Retreat Center that was the site of Alan's Jewish awakening, I intentionally decide to forgo the *Zazen* morning meditating in the *Zendo* for my own retreat within the retreat, returning to my Jewish meditation practice by the riverside. Every 9th of Av, this acting Buddhist priestess too returns to her Jewish bookshelf and begins reading, reflecting, and meditating on Rabbi Lew's once underground, now classic of contemporary scripture, *This Is Real and You Are Completely Unprepared.*[14]

The synergy shared constantly between Alan and Norman deserves further consideration as to why this book is now a classic of Jewish practice, as Norman notes astutely:

> In those days [of the seeking 1960s] a story was often told of a Jewish peasant who, looking elsewhere for a great treasure, returned home only to find it buried beneath the floor of his own house. This was taken to mean that Jews didn't have to look elsewhere (to

---

14. R. Alan Lew, This Is Real and You Are Completely Unprepared: The Days of Awe as a Journey of Transformation (New York: Little, Brown and Company, 2003).

Asian spiritualities) to find spiritual treasures; they could discover them hidden deep within their own tradition.

But Rabbi Lew told the story differently—in his version the treasure was not buried underneath the floorboards. It was hidden in plain sight, in the oven. Digging was not required. His approach to Jewish spirituality did not propose a quest for lost or neglected mystical knowledge. Instead he sought the rediscovery of what Jews already had but did not appreciate: the unseen depths of ordinary Jewish observance.

This Is Real is an astonishing and unexpected journey through the normative Jewish practice of the High Holidays, a journey that breathes drama and personal urgency into a tradition that many of us had dismissed as too faint to hold what we were feeling.

The ten years of committed Zen practice he did before he entered the rabbinate gave Rabbi Lew serious training in a grounded form of meditation. In applying that practice to the normative Judaism he passionately loved, Rabbi Lew was able to find the treasure hidden in plain sight. In *This Is Real*, the force of his personality and the skill of his pen make that treasure vivid.[15]

After having had the honor over the past three years of coleading Jewish meditation retreats with Norman (along with Rabbi Lew's disciple, Rabbi Dorothy Richman), I agree that *Makor Or* continues to focus on those "unseen depths of ordinary Jewish observance" as its sole path first articulated in the Bay Area of the 1990s. The quandary all seekers in search of a sustainable, inspiring spiritual practice is whether further layers along the path have come to light since that pioneering foray by Lew. I can call to mind no more vivid image to discern the nuances between Lew and Krassen here than what American poet Robert Frost called "The Road Not Taken" (1915): "Two roads diverged in a yellow wood, / And sorry I could not travel both / And be one traveler, long I stood / And looked down one as far as I could / To where it bent in the undergrowth . . ."

In reading the poem, we already know that the that the seeker has chosen to traverse the "road less traveled." After all, every "road less traveled" always initially strikes us as slightly grassier, slightly less trafficked. But pay attention to the poem here, because no sooner is this claim made than it doubles back, erasing the distinction as it is even being made: "Though as for that the passing there / Had worn them really about the same."

The poem invites us to recognize just how comparable are the two roads. Take another look, and see how—this time—that the roads are equal-

---

15. Norman Fischer, foreword to This Is Real and You Are Completely Unprepared (forthcoming, 2018).

ly untraveled, carpeted in newly fallen yellow leaves: "And both that morning equally lay / In leaves no step had trodden black."

The directness of Lew's Zen -refracted Jewish practice has another layer uncovered in Krassen's now-ness of these *The Vanishing Path*. The real discernment takes place at the fork in the road—to continue following the road more traveled, or to venture beyond into the road less traveled. The road well-traveled is represented by Lew's Orthopraxis-Egalitarianism, whereas the road less traveled is envisioned by Krassen as the Multi-Perspectival, Planetary-Gnostic Torah of the Future. The road more traveled is normative, institutionalized rabbinic Judaism that is vivid, direct, and alive in the oven of life, whereas the road less traveled disrupts normative rabbinic Judaism, channeling instead a more primordial, anarchic energy that is humbled into its own vanishing into the time that is coming now. Both paths are possible according to the Baal Shem Tov's reading of Psalm 27:1—pathway "road more traveled" (*derekh*) or byway "road less traveled" (*mishor*). It is precisely because of endless encounters like these the world over that I know in my heart of hearts that *The Vanishing Path* needs to be brought to light now . . .

Wearing Your Garment of Days

Sometimes you wear your heart on your sleeve—and like any garment it can tear off or open. In that process of making your inner world vulnerable to the outer world, the experience of life can feel like its threads are unraveling. The threads that sew one moment to another reveal in their stitching that there are many textures in time. Some moments are magical while other moments are nothing but drudgery. Each moment in each day serves as part of a fabric that interweaves into what the Zohar calls a "garment of days." As each of us is about to die, our inner stitching begins opening to experience higher dimensions of radiance through the pulsating stitches in this garment of days, such that the garment itself is woven out of one's virtuous days—sewing a moment of integrity to a moment of truth, stitching a moment of compassion to a moment of justice and so on, until an entire garment of days is woven. Such a glorious garment of days is merited and stitched together as accrued over eons. So how do we distinguish these textures, while woven within the warp and woof of such times? In what follows, I want to offer two stitches within a larger weave of my own journey that I hope will help others clarify their journey to truth.

Liturgical Time vs. Institutional Time

Being devoted to leading a religious institution requires time. The question is what type of time is given and what type of time is experienced? As clergy know, there is great difference between "liturgical time" and "institutional time." There is a notion of "liturgical time" that I have learned from scholars of Islam, like Henri Corbin, who rediscovered this temporality as a pristine channel returning the aspirant to the eternal. "Liturgical time" should be second nature to clergy, whose role is to create and perform rituals that guide seekers through this time-scape. And yet, most clergy who serve in American synagogues find themselves bedraggled with managing a calendar of "institutional time"—a time of dying days.

In rereading Rabbi Lew's *This Is Real and You Are Completely Unprepared*, I realize now why it is that this book has moved from being cult classic to the scripture of spiritual practice. What Rabbi Lew has managed is to write a manual of reflective spiritual practice that straddles "liturgical time" and "institutional time." I will unpack this claim in what follows as a way of honoring his contribution to this ever tenuous dialectic and as a way of attempting to rebalance those scales in my own journey.

"Liturgical time" is part of an eternal liturgy within the divine totality. As we settle deeper into this web of time, we witness the flow from end to end of the work of Creation and the work of Redemption as constituting cosmic liturgy. Standing in the shadow of Rabbi Lew, *z"l*, rereading *This Is Real and You Are Completely Unprepared* is a surreal process of reliving many parallels in what I am call "institutional time." When Rabbi Lew describes his "institutional time," he can paint it quite poignantly, for example: "Let me tell you about the best day I've had in a long time," where he goes on to describe each period of time that constitutes this "day," starting an early with heartfelt prayer at morning minyan, followed by four hospital visits, culminating with a windy wedding in Healdsburg—I know that rhythm of time intimately. But Rabbi Lew understood these moments in time as intertwined causally, between the young couple in Healdsburg standing beneath the wedding canopy and the four sick visits earlier that day, and within these stitches he heard a "resounding 'yes'" blowing through these universes that "included the despair of these four ladies and in fact transformed that despair." There is a real incompleteness we all feel throughout life as *Avaryonim*, fragmented beings in time, who are chasing after that completeness all our lives, "something so deep it can only be found in a whole community, in that shifting composite of need and lack and gift we create when we come together to acknowledge that we need each other." These fragments of time that mark us are in need of redemption by coming into a larger weave together. All these past moments and lost wounds Rabbi Lew reads poetically as part of our *Avar* or past make us *Avaryonim*—moments of time passed over.

And yet, we might jump to thinking that moments of time passed over are equivalent with history. While Edmund Burke (1729–97) claimed that "those who *don't know* history are destined to repeat it," George Santayana

(1863–1952) said "Those who *cannot remember* the past are condemned to repeat it." Rabbi Lew, unafraid of criticizing the latter, claimed: "I think that the great philosopher Georgy Santayana got it exactly wrong." Rabbi Lew goes on to suggest why from a spiritual perspective "history can become a formidable trap—a sticky snare from which we may find it impossible to extricate ourselves." The challenge of spiritual attunement to textures in time is to get out of the cycle of "recurring disaster" in our lives,[16] for it is "precisely those who insist on remembering history . . . [who] are doomed to repeat it."[17] This means that the memories of the past we hold onto so dearly must be let go of to make it possible to take hold of new experiences in time, because "forgiveness . . . means giving up our hopes for a better past."[18] And yet, when Rabbi Lew took this spiritual practice of individual forgetting of the past one holds onto to make space for forgiveness and then applied it to the group dynamic of the Jewish people in Israel/Palestine, it was the beginning of the end of his tenure in terms of synagogue "institutional time."

We live in a time now where Karl Marx was too right: "History repeats itself first as tragedy and second as farce."[19] Jewish Trumpism is alive and well in synagogues across America, even in San Francisco. The end of Rabbi Lew's synagogue "institutional time" was a tragedy; the end of my synagogue "institutional time" remains a farce.

That farce is best encapsulated by novelist George Orwell in his dystopian novel *Animal Farm*.[20] When pigs like Napoleon are running the farm, it is clear that synagogues are not only *treyf* but so is their leadership. Perhaps the only truing that will emerge in this ruthless and depraved situation of lay leadership is that just deserts of reincarnation will emerge sooner rather than later, to the point where sitting around a boardroom table, the rabbi can already be seen as presiding over an animal farm. Could one ever imagine leading a synagogue with pigs like Napoleon or Snowball, who increasingly quibble over the future of the farm? Their struggle with each other for power and influence among the other animals is a classic board scenario. Sit at a monthly synagogue board meeting and it quickly becomes next impossible to discern who is a pig and who remains human?!?

The pig as a symbol of greed, lust, and overindulgence is a perfect fit for the majority of synagogue leadership today. For our Sages, the major concern with the pig is that it pretends to be kosher, by sticking out its clo-

---

16. Lew, This is Real and You Are Completely Unprepared, 46.
17. Ibid., 47.
18. Ibid., 50.
19. Karl Marx, *The Eighteenth Brumaire of Louis Bonaparte* (New York: International Publishers, 1963), 1.
20. George Orwell, Animal Farm (New York: Penguin Books, 2018).

ven hooves (one of the two kosher signs)[21] as if to say, "Look at me, I am kosher!"[22] The very namesake for "pig" in Hebrew—*chazir*—is deceptive as it means "return,"[23] for he is trying to convince us that he chews his cud, and returns his food to his mouth as a kosher animal.[24] Thus, the pig is the animal par excellence that blurs the distinction between kosher and non-kosher, between ethical and corrupt.

Was Orwell not already envisioning a Torah of the world-that-is-coming? Even before Orwell, Judaism had to struggle with this reality of dissolving boundaries on a vanishing path. The Torah of the world-that-is-coming is of course not to be taken literally; rather, it should be understood that in the future we will eat *mashmanim*, as if eating pig was permissible![25] We must then dare to ask the Orwellian question and its inverse: Will pigs run synagogues? Will pigs eat humans and consume all that was once humane in the synagogue turning it into an animal farm? And yet as rabbis, both Rabbi Lew and I, we struggled with how to selectively forget in order to forgive, to let go so as to take hold of an ancient–new spiritual reality within liturgical time, always seeping into the present from the future now.

Dying Days

When Rabbi Lew's widow, Sherril, recounts to me moments leading up to the death of her beloved, frame by frame focusing microscopically on the time that loosens the plaque to clog his arteries leading towards his heart attack—I feel that unraveling of time too. Overall, in close to two decades of serving in a pulpit, and most recently, having walked in the shadow of Rabbi Lew by serving in his synagogue in San Francisco, I have come to see more clearly than ever the real distinction between that pristine, primordial "liturgical time" and the rest of that synagogue "institutional time"— the latter as utterly bedraggled with managing the time of dying days. Some deep death is afflicting American Judaism, to the point where the only type of synagogue leadership that continually bubbles to the surface is nasty, brutish, and short. The time clergy will spend in trying to cultivate ethical leadership with a moral compass invariably turns into a wasteland, usually after a brief first contract in what was once a long-term, covenantal relationship. That once sacred relationship between stewards of liturgical time has morphed into seeing the rabbi as something between a golf caddy and

---

21. Leviticus 11:3, ad. loc R. Avraham Azulai, Nachal Kedumin.

22. Genesis Rabbah 65:1; Genesis 36:24 ad. loc Rashi; see also Leviticus 11:4 ad. loc Kli Yakar, ibid., Rashi.

23. See Radak, Sefer Hashorashim (s.v. cheit, zayin, resh).

24. The pig is referred to by the euphemism "that other thing" (davar acher). Given its name is one of deception, the euphemism "that other thing" (davar acher) allows one to refer to him as something other than he really is in order that we not be duped.

25. Radvaz, Teshuvot 2:828.

a social worker. Just like a new model car that needs to be upgraded before any real maintenance is required, so too, the American synagogue leadership model prioritizes trading in the rabbi for something new every three years or less. It is a tragic farce of epic proportions that continues to accelerate, and the souls of those leading these communities are dying daily. And so I constantly here the concatenations of Reb Nachman's "Prayer for Dying Days" as dutifully recorded by his disciple, Reb Natan of Nemirov. It is a powerful prayer, lamenting the loss of "liturgical time" and the ability to make time count any longer, especially within "institutional time":

> O Compassionate One, overflowing, you know how days die, stiffening . . . turning cold when I lose my way, right to this moment, to this day.
>
> You know how I've drained the life from so many of days with such carelessness and anger. It's not enough that I haven't added zest to life through study and introspection, but I've also depleted any inspiration at all through my utter neglect and scorn of Jewish life . . .
>
> Be compassionate. Guide me. Redeem me, through the depth of your Compassion and Wonder. May I merit, through deeper attention, and intention, to mend and bring salve to these dying days . . . to revitalize and reprioritize and repair all the days of my life with deeper holiness. May my days henceforth be wholesome, holy and pristine, and become mended as I reconnect to your desire and will . . .

Like all of us, Rabbi Lew feared losing time to the abyss of nothingness at the center of the holy of holies, the center of being, the center of our lives:

> "Suddenly we understand why the Great Temple of Jerusalem was an elaborate construction surrounding nothing. There at the sacred center, at the Holy of Holies, a place we only entered on Yom Kippur, and then only by proxy, only through the agency of the high priest, there at the center, is precisely nothing—a vacated space, a charged emptiness, mirroring the charged emptiness that surrounds this world, that comes before this life and after it as well."[26]

This creative reading of the Temple that stands on a center of nothing, in ruins while it is in place is an example of Rabbi Lew's proclivity for translating the most provocative concepts of Buddhism into the heart of Judaism.

Time of Divine Mindfulness

Emptying space within a theistic tradition for a/theistic insights can be chal-

---

26. Lew, This is Real and You Are Completely Unprepared, 221.

lenging and often feel haphazard if not inauthentic. But in accepting normative, rabbinic theology of an omniscient, omnibenevolent, omnipresent deity, Rabbi Lew then needs to find a way to make this abstract, distant god feel more real and direct.

> "Indeed, the idea that God is aware of us, that God sees us and is mindful of us, is the very first assumption of this holy day. In its earlier biblical incarnation, Rosh Hashanah was called Yom Ha-Zikaron, the Day of Remembrance, the Day of Mindfulness. If God were not aware of us, this whole pageant of Teshuvah and forgiveness wouldn't make much sense."[27]

This kind of translation of theology into the lived time of direct experience marks part of Rabbi Lew's genius. But for Rabbi Lew, spiritual practice is not some magical panacea; it is a practice of deepening awareness of *what is*. "Spiritual practice won't change what happens. Rather, it will help us to experience what happens not as evil, but simply as what happens. Spiritual practice will help us to understand that everything that happens, even the decree of death, flows from God."[28] The whole journey of the high holidays is one of transformation, insofar as each of us is willing to look our dying days in the face and own them as part of the fabric of our being. "We are called to judgment every moment. Our response to every moment is a judgment on us, one that is continuously unfolding, and subject to continuous modification."[29]

On that final retreat at Pearlstone for the *Rabbinic Training Institute* (RTI), Rabbi Lew was continuing to courageously teach fellow rabbis serving primarily in synagogues that demanded "institutional time" cover over "liturgical time," that nonetheless:

> ". . . every moment is a rehearsal for our death. From the day we are born, we are engaged in the process of dying, not only because the larger arc of our life is moving in that direction, but because we experience death moment by moment."[30]

To bring such awareness of the preponderance of death that overshadows every living, breathing moment draws on teachings in Sufism and Buddhism. Rabbi Lew was convinced that the journey of the soul itself is what choreographs "this concatenation of ritual—this dance"[31] wherein "the soul

---

27. Lew, This Is Real and You Are Completely Unprepared, 137, compare with ibid., 11, 12.

28. Ibid., 14.

29. Ibid., 17.

30. Ibid., 17.

31. Ibid., 18.

has filled in this map with its own imperatives."[32] Such robust awareness of the subtleties of the soul positioned Rabbi Lew to be a healer through the moments of directly sitting with *what is*, rather than an ecstatic or apocalyptic mystic. That direct experience of the demonstrative *what is*, or *zot* in Zohar, is never evoked. And yet, Rabbi Lew draws on the ecstatic mystical presence of iconoclastic Indian poet-saint revered by Hindus, Muslims, and Sikhs, Kabir (1440–1518),[33] or Japanese Zen priest of the Soto lineage, like Shunryu Suzuki Roshi (1904–71), whose impact on the San Francisco Zen Center started as early as 1959.[34] Clearly, Rabbi Lew's garment of days could sometimes feel as comfortable as a homey quilt, even if all the squares did not quite fit together. Seeing the whole quilt still provides comfort to thousands who read this underground classic annually.

Time of Heart vs. Time of Soul

Longtime friend and meditation colleague of Rabbi Lew, Norman Fischer, wrote in his lucid preface to the new edition of *This Is Real*[35] that he considers this to be a work of true neo-Hasidism. Such a claim needs to be unpacked, in light of just how Rabbi Lew refers to the Hasidic teachings of Reb Nachman of Bratzlav, as well as mentioning the commentary of *Iturai Torah*,[36] and focusing momentarily on his own personal Rhiziner Hasidic lineage, traced to his great-grandfather, Reb Mordecai Shustick.[37] What constitutes neo-Hasidism is beyond the scope of these reflections, but it must be more than anecdotes about how this Rhiziner Hasid would always refuse to be caught in a family photograph. One could say that at its most basic level neo-Hasidism is the renewal of this pristine focus on the comportment of the heart, but what Rabbi Lew was focusing on in *This Is Real* actually tended to be the soul. This preference becomes all the more explicit in how Rabbi Lew misremembers or misreads Reb Shlomo Carlebach's teaching on having one heart versus two when he sang in Germany.[38] It is interesting that more recently, scholars of Jewish mysticism like Jonathan Garb point to this focus on the heart as a salient feature of modern Kabbalah.[39] Be that as it may, Rabbi Lew's concern with the soul as opposed to the heart can perhaps then be seen in a more classic rabbinic rather than a mystic light. These abiding concerns for soul-making remain a pillar of

32. Lew, This Is Real and You Are Completely Unprepared, 18.
33. Ibid., 246–47, 264.
34. Ibid., 162.
35. Norman Fischer, Foreword, in This Is Real and You Are Completely Unprepared.
36. Lew, This Is Real and You Are Completely Unprepared, 77.
37. Ibid., 137.
38. Ibid., 231–33.
39. Jonathan Garb, Yearnings of the Soul: Psychological Thought in Modern Kabbalah (Chicago: The University of Chicago Press, 2015)

rabbinic Judaism that the mystics of Kabbalah and Hasidism return to with great creative flare, but which Rabbi Lew choses to read as a roadmap for being present to the moment of *what is.*

While it may seem pedantic to care about the difference between "heart" and "soul" when we are really after what makes a human being tick—it does then bring to light the deeper question: What does it mean to be a human being relative to the individual's fragment or spark we call a "soul"? What I have learned from Krassen, by contrast, is the pressing need to develop the notion of person as path. Such a path is already sketched out in the enigmatic scriptural vision of Jacob's ladder. "A person is a path" ('*adam nikra 'ole v'yored*), as Yaakov Yosef of Polnoyye remarked in trying to understand the dynamism of Jacob's vision of a ladder with angels ascending and descending it. A human is a self-informing process for Krassen, rather than being an unchanging essence as soul for Lew. What distinguishes one person from another is a process. It is a process that is unique as each person is in-formed by different bits of information and thus take different forms. In that process there is a "co-creation of self" (*nokeikh mi'shelo*) without an essence. Just as the notion of the soul is outdated, so too is the cosmos.

Time of Divine Totality

What immediately will grab you in reading *This Is Real* in contrast to *The Vanishing Path* is the way the divine is conceived and addressed. "Divine totality" is used frequently within *The Vanishing Path* as an English way of better defining the Greek *Kosmos* or what we refer to as "cosmos," which in turn is a translation of the Hebrew '*Or Ein Sof.* More than just a syntactical issue is the question of whether there is more than one cosmos as plural as "cosmoses." For example, the sixteenth-century mystic Isaac Luria presents a mystical cosmology as an attempt to account for the cosmos, but when we read that chapter of Lurianic Kabbalah in Jewish mysticism, if we are honestly present, we quickly realize that it is an outdated vision of the cosmos that may no longer apply. It is a frivolous account of both the cosmos and the universe, but Luria could not necessarily distinguish between them. The cosmos is not created, but the Creator of worlds is eternal.

A totality that is eternal is the cosmos; and it is unchanging. Awareness is a quality of the cosmos, but *not identical with it.* This is a classic misreading that is carried over from Buddhism to Judaism. It leads us away from a way of *being human* that is most worth cultivating. The cosmos is the source of all the universes, of which there are *multiverses*, alternative universes that evolved beings of consciousness. That awareness is a function of the cosmos but it is *not identical with it.* Furthermore, it is not the most significant way of understanding the cosmos. Recent quantum physics is reaching us that the basic fabric of the cosmos is *information*.[40] While modern physicists until this point had come to see the cosmos as consisting of energy and matter, still this left many questions in its wake.

Cosmos as Pure Awareness and Mind

The cosmos is not only pure awareness, but also mind. Pure awareness and mind are distinct. The mind is dealing with intelligence and active thought that is co-creative, whereas pure awareness is just witnessing and creates nothing. Pure awareness of non-self in Buddhism is meant to enable one to reach enlightenment, whereas active, intelligent participation is taking place in the creative evolution of the *cosmos itself*. The divine totality is already the *all in everything*. So Hayyim Vital's instinct is important, to claim in Lurianic Kabbalah's classic *Etz Hayyim* that if the world did not exist, then god would not be god and all the divine names would not be true. The cosmos creates and is self-informing, whereby information becomes the essential element of reality. And so we are inspired to *in-form* ourselves and our world with this *in-formation*, becoming *co-creators*.

Cosmos as Evolutionary Project

The contemporary devotion of *avodah* is the support of the cosmos evolutionary project—to manifest a certain kind of universe and the evolutionary role of life on earth. Yet instead of being supports for the evolution of this world, we are destroying it at an accelerating pace. While mindfulness allows one to cultivate certain skills as a co-creator, it is not the goal of personal development. We need all kinds of skillful means. The harmonious development of the human by Gurdjieff suggests an integral approach of cultivating human beings that might *become normal*. What we consider normal is *abnormal*. So the meta-programming devotional work allows one to become attuned with the forces that make up our universe and help that universe become harmonious with the cosmos. True egocentricity is important to deal with, yes, but what are we really trying to create? It is no longer sufficient to merely create a *Boddhisatva*. We need to recover the model for a "self-perfecting human being" that might be a hybrid of the prophet (*navi*) and the devoted one (tzaddik). The *navi* must be empathic, channeling divine pathos in the face of injustice and appreciative of the universe itself, while the tzaddik is that person who has a good heart, good head, and more a master of embodied life.[41]

---

40. Jude Currivan, The Cosmic Hologram: In-formation at the Center of Creation (Rochester, VT: Inner Traditions, 2017).

41. The idea of the human potential movement of Esalen showed an understanding of mastery to be an effective person that at its core was constructive. The three Taoist centers of physical, emotional and intellect as points of mastery are taken up with Gurdjieff.

Cosmos as In-formation

The cosmos is more than a source that creates matter and emits energy randomly. *Or Ein Sof* as cosmos is information as light that produces holographic forms, whereas YHVH is more of a stepped-down model of the cosmos, but not the cosmos itself that can be an object of consciousness. The cosmos is all and everything immediate and thus can have no observer with anything outside of it. Since Buddhism made its way into the West with its critique of the mind, it has yet to take into account the healing power of therapy. A completely *empty mind* that is nothing but awareness is not sufficient to be a fully developed human being. It does not seem to be the case that if you fix your mind, everything will follow. The universe can be inside us, but we are finite and the universe is finite, whereas the cosmos is infinite. The divine totality is intrinsically intelligent, made of information, and these bits of in-formation combine in ways to build worlds of cosmic consciousness. It is a heightened ability to recognize and appreciate the information that the cosmos is creating—this creates a state of awe. Wise comportment begin from radical amazement of our co-creative calling to in-form the cosmos as divine totality.

Co-creative Calling of Master and Disciple

Early on in my search during the renaissance of Jewish meditation, unbeknownst to me, that co-creative calling of master to disciple emerged allowing the cosmos to in-form my path my deeply. Now as I continue my decades-long Jewish meditation practice, I realize just how much I was already becoming deeply attached to another teacher, who, years earlier, I had encountered at *Elat Chayyim*, coleading retreats with Sylvia Boorstein—his name was Miles Krassen. He was the trickster teacher with that wily smile, and he laughed while transmitting some of the deepest teachings of Hasidism I had ever witnessed.

These teachings of Reb Krassen have continued to nourish me, providing me with the hope that there is a world-that-is-coming that can still connect to that abiding love supreme that might still emerge in our own age within the Jewish path. It is a path at once planetary and gnostic. In due course, I will explain what this means.

From our first encounter where the promise of that love supreme hovered, I have never been the same. And so, as a god-lover, I have dedicated for the past decade a regimen of weekly private study and spiritual direction with Reb Krassen. And as the self-selecting few who find their way to Reb Moshe Krassen's cave, presently in Albuquerque, New Mexico, I hold multiple passports. I am ordained as a Conservative rabbi with renewal leanings and a neo-Hasidic impulse—where else in the world could I go but to the teachings of Reb Moshe Aaron?!? For the past three years, I have serendipitously also had the honor of serving as senior rabbi at the flagship contemplative synagogue in the Conservative movement, San Francisco's Congregation Beth Sholom. This was the site that for all intents and purposes birthed the Jewish meditation renaissance a few decades ago, when Rabbi Alan Lew, *o.b.m.*, envisioned an ancient–new space for contemplative Judaism, known as *Makor Or: Meditation Group* that eventually became a structural pillar in all senses of the new synagogue building. Along with his spiritual Buddhist buddy, *Zoketsu* Norman Fischer, they sought to breathe new life into a dying spiritual tradition of Conservative Judaism by adapting and importing aspects of Zen Buddhist meditation into the core practice of this community. Serving at Beth Sholom as senior rabbi, I have seen it as my calling to carry forward the legacy of the teachings and practice of Rabbi Alan Lew, *o.b.m.*, and I've been blessed to spend time coleading retreats with Norman with this mission in mind. Norman and I have often wondered aloud together: *what is the future path for this kind of contemplative work?* Norman is asking himself these questions, and he is responding with Everyday Zen and his tireless work at the San Francisco Zen Center while I serve at this boutique Conservative synagogue in San Francisco. Yet he and I both see that the floodgates of seekers that were arriving in throngs decades ago are no longer there. How will we carry these practices forward into the world-that-is-coming?

With his uncanny prescience, Rabbi Lew, *o.b.m.*, caught this catch-22 we now find ourselves in right from the opening words of his contemporary classic, *This Is Real and You Are Completely Unprepared*: "You are walking through the world half asleep . . ."[42] Norman encapsulates the shock of awakening, likened to satori in Zen, as he eloquently writes: "None of us, he tells us, is ready for the reality of our fragile lives. And yet, we can't avoid it. For Rabbi Lew, God is necessary, as real as our lives, and the High Holidays mark that potent time in the Jewish year when the God encounter is moving, mandatory, and heart-breaking."[43] This state of spiritual sleepwalking requires a guide, and it needs a path for seekers to traverse, lest we fall asleep for good. Dov Ber identified many stages of sleeping, ranging from nodding off to falling into a coma. At this hour, both Norman and I are convinced that the soul is comatose or what Dov Ber calls "*heiner felt*."[44] How tragic that the contemplative synagogue Rabbi Lew envisioned had fallen into desuetude until my return years later to attempt resurrecting it! The question Norman and I continued asking, from 2015–18 remained: *How might we awaken the comatose soul of this generation? How do you*

---

42. Lew, This Is Real, 3.

43. Norman Fischer, foreword to This Is Real.

44. Reb Arele Roth, Shomer Emunuim, vol. 2 (Jerusalem: Toldot Aharon, 5758), 374.

awaken souls who don't even know what the question is any longer?

The Vanishing Path is a journey in time to awaken us from our present comatose spiritual lives. Like the companions of the mystical fellowship of the Zohar, known as *Hevrayya*, Reb Krassen's Torah of the Future is calling us now:

> The voice retuned as before and said: / O high, hidden, concealed ones, open-eyed, roaming the entire world, gaze and see! / O low, sleeping ones, close-eyed, awake! / Who among you turns darkness into light, tastes the bitter as sweet before arriving here? / Who among you awaits each day the light that shines when the King visits the doe and is glorified and is called the King of all kings of the world? / Whoever does not await this each day in that world has no portion here.[45]

The cry for awakening is even more urgent than any existentialist cry in this moment "of supreme tension" where we are called upon to "leap into flight [of] an unswerving arrow, a shaft that is inflexible and free"[46]—yet as that very freedom is slipping away into the darkness where we have stopped thinking, this teaching of Reb Krassen calls out to every *RADLA* seeker, echoing the Zohar:

> A voice, the voice of voices awakened from above and below. / Open-eyed we were. / A wheel rolled from above to numerous sides, / The sound of a pleasant melody awakened: / Awaken sleepy, slumbering ones, with sleep in their eyes / [Who] do not know and do not look and do not see. / Impervious ears, heavy heart, they sleep and do not know. / The Torah stands before them yet they pay no heed, and do not know upon what they gaze, they see yet do not see. / The Torah sends forth voices: Look stupid ones, open your eyes and you will know. / Yet there is none who pays heed and there is none who inclines his ear! / For how long will you [remain] in the darkness of your desire, / Look to know and the enlightening light will be revealed to you![47]

There is a need to awaken from the mire of an unthinking existence, so full of hatred and cruelty below, while awakening the Tower of Song and its ecstatic angelic choir from immobility above,[48] as the Zohar teaches:

---

45. Zohar 1:4a (Matt revised).

46. Albert Camus, *L'homme révolté* (Paris: Gallimard, 1957).

47. Zohar 1:161b.

48. Aubrey L. Glazer, "Falling with Our Angels, So Human," in Tangle of Matter & Ghost: Leonard Cohen's Post-Secular Songbook of Mysticism(s) Jewish and Beyond (Brighton, MA: Academic Studies Press, 2016), 165–78.

"The awakening above is produced only in response to an awakening from below, for the awakening above depends upon the longing/desire of that below."[49] As the world—and especially America—falls deeper and deeper into a cataclysmic spiritual comatose of *"heiner felt,"* I have never felt so strongly this call of love emerging from Krassen for us to wake up again. From the aroma of infinity his Torah of the future beckons us now, the incense of his spirit gets each and every *neshamah* very interested to become aligned again with the balance of time.

Being Off-balance All the Time in Vonnegut's Hog Slaughterhouse

All this talk of mysticism can be exhausting. So, let us now rediscover where this recalibrating of time emerges from by entering into a sketch of this master's spiritual life. To do that: "You feel somehow marginal, somehow slightly off-balance all the time."[50] Being marginally off-balanced is what it takes to be a writer, according to Kurt Vonnegut.[51] To understand the balance of time through the teachings of Dr. Miles Krassen, aka Reb Moshe Aaron Krassen, we would do well in appreciating anew Vonnegut, as I learned repeatedly from Krassen. From writer to mystic to musician and back again, Krassen's journey was never a straight path, and so neither should anyone's be. So, it is fitting to begin to get to know Krassen through another iconoclast who continues hovering between an American cult figure and a serious writer and social activist born in Indianapolis, Indiana. Vonnegut figured as part of the latest generation in a German-American community that had flourished since its arrival in America before the Civil War. By May 1944, his mother, Edith, died from a sleeping pill overdose, and so Kurt found himself just few months later drifting on a troopship bound to fight the Nazi storm cloud shadowing Europe at the time.

Wandering the frozen chaos of the Battle of the Bulge, Hitler's last-ditch counterattack on the western front, Vonnegut along with his fellow POWs were billeted belowground in a hog slaughterhouse, which led Vonnegut to reflect in another novel that:[52] "But, as Bokonon tell us, any man can call time out, but no man can say how long the time out will be."[53] It is precisely this period of hiding in the hog slaughterhouse, known as *Schlachthof Fünf* (Slaughterhouse Five), that brought Vonnegut a new sense of time. It was on the night of February 13, 1945 that the slaughterhouse was the only

---

49. Zohar, vol. I 86b.

50. Kurt Vonnegut, Palm Sunday: An Autobiographical Collage (Dial: New York, 2011), 59.

51. November 11, 1922–April 12, 2007.

52. Kurt Vonnegut, Letters of Note: An Eclectic Collection of Correspondence Deserving of a Wider Audience, ed. Shaun Usher, vol. 1, Letter 125: 1944 (Chronicle Books: San Francisco, 2017), 340.

53. Kurt Vonnegut, Cat's Cradle (Random House Publishing: New York 2009), 248.

adequate bomb shelter in town when the central district of the city was incinerated by the British and American air forces. Eventually surfacing into a death-scape of smoke and rubble, Vonnegut along with his fellow POWs were forced at gunpoint to comb the smoldering wreckage for corpses, to the jeers of the by-standing civilians.

Vonnegut eventually emerged from his prison camp through an open gate as the Nazi war machine was defeated by spring. Vonnegut may not have known "how long the time out will be" for his existence, but he continued to live and write by "call[ing] time out." With his frostbitten Purple Heart, Vonnegut returned to the United States, and his wounds in time are likely what made him so intent to make up for lost time.[54] So when Vonnegut reflects on time, it matters, as he writes: "All time is all time. It does not change. It does not lend itself to warnings or explanations. It simply *is*. Take it moment by moment. And you will find that we are all, as I've said before, bugs in amber."[55] Poised to see the world from that off-balance horizon of what "simply is," one comes to see time and thus existence differently. Its flow, its texture, and its imprint on our every step through life—from the heights of ecstatic joy to the depths of loss and suffering. Knowing how to navigate these highs and lows, a soul can become "seasoned through time."

Finding Balance in Fleeting Time Through Ecclesiastes

Ecclesiastes also searches to find balance in time, understanding just how fleeting life can be and thus preached:

> [1] To every thing there is a season, and a time to every purpose under the heaven:
> [2] A time to be born, and a time to die; a time to plant, and a time to pluck up that which is planted;
> [3] A time to kill, and a time to heal; a time to break down, and a time to build up;
> [4] A time to weep, and a time to laugh; a time to mourn, and a time to dance;
> [5] A time to cast away stones, and a time to gather stones together; a time to embrace, and a time to refrain from embracing;
> [6] A time to seek, and a time to lose; a time to keep, and a time to cast away;
> [7] A time to rend, and a time to sew; a time to keep silence, and a time to speak;
> [8] A time to love, and a time to hate; a time for war, and a time for peace.

54. American National Biography, s.v. "Kurt Vonnegut," http://www.anb.org/articles/16/16-03912.html (accessed May 3, 2017).

55. Kurt Vonnegut, Slaughterhouse Five (New York: Dell, 1991, 1969), 86.

But the *telos,* the *tachlis* or purpose of life is often not as present as it could be from moment to moment, as the late great Hebrew poet Yehuda Amichai once wrote: "A man doesn't have time in his life to have time for everything. He doesn't have seasons enough to have a season for every purpose. Ecclesiastes was wrong about that."[56] While I agree with Amichai that Ecclesiastes did not really get every moment's purpose within the flow of time, I continue to wonder with Krassen about time. Ecclesiastes's interrogation continues:

[9] What profit has the one that works in that one labors?

[10] I have seen the task which God has given to human beings to be exercised therewith.

[11] He has made everything beautiful in its time; also He has set time (*olam*) in their heart, yet so that one cannot find out the work that God has done from the beginning even to the end.

[12] I know that there is nothing better for them, than to rejoice, and to get pleasure so long as they live.

[13] But also that every human should eat and drink, and enjoy pleasure for all their labor, is the gift of God.

Arguably, the first Jewish existentialist, Ecclesiastes, takes time seriously, even if, in the end, the Hebrew poet is right that this biblical gadfly got it wrong. As is clear from 3:1-8, Ecclesiastes contemplates the nature of existence from moment to moment, asking: Is life a series of moments? Or is life more than the sum of its disparate moments? If all there is nothing but this moment, then how does one create meaning beyond the abyss of nihilism? However, if the great Clockmaker "has made everything beautiful in its time," then it follows that being created in the divine image necessarily means that "God has also set time in their heart" (3:11). Reading Ecclesiastes in a way that invites us to realize "that each moment carries with it the chance to be something new"[57] opens up new pathways of appreciating such a neglected classic in the Hebrew canon.

Finding Time Set in the Heart Through Albert Camus

It is with this urgent sense of time set in his heart that Albert Camus challenges us in the vein of a modern Ecclesiastes, trying his precursor's pathways in time. Born in occupied French Algeria in 1913, it is unsurprising that Camus blossomed into a French novelist, dramatist, essayist, and existentialist philosopher of the first order, in large part due to the plight of

---

56. Yehuda Amichai, "A Man in his Life," trans. C. Bloch, in The Poetry of Yehuda Amichai (New York: Farrar, Straus & Giroux, 2015), 323.

57. Rami M. Shapiro, The Way of Solomon: Finding Joy and Contentment in the Wisdom of Ecclesiastes (San Francisco: HarperSanFrancisco, 2000).

French occupation during the Vichy collusion with the Nazis in France. Surely, Camus would have continued to carry forward the horrors of the occupation with him rather than succumbing to the current cowardly posture in France of denying its complicity in the *Val d'Hiver* deportations of French Jewry to the gas chambers. While there is no rational denial of the fact that 13,000 Jewish lives were rounded up and deported in 1942 at *Val d'Hiver*, there is a national forgetting that is already happening, even in the French Jewish community who wanted to vote Marine Le Pen into power,[58] much like the American Jewish community that voted Donald Trump into power. Never mind Jacques Chirac's groundbreaking 1995 apology for his government's historic complicity in the deportations, yet, when Le Pen claims in an interview that "I don't *think* France was responsible for *Val D'Hiv*," she is on a certain level right—after all, when was the last time we ever expected a political leader to *actually think*! Yet the disaster could not be greater or more urgent this time on a planetary level. Still, there is wisdom that will emerge from waiting for what will unfold . . .

The time of Camus's persecution was deeply imprinted on the nature of his thinking, so that his relentless interrogation of the human condition could only have emerged from the crucible of the French occupation of Algeria and the Nazi occupation of Paris. Inevitably, occupation imprints on the human experience and this experience causes a loss or privation of time. The challenge facing every existentialist from Ecclesiastes to Camus is whether life is worth living or the greatest display of freedom is the taking of one's own life through suicide. In *L'homme révolté*, Camus takes us through a breakneck history of philosophy on the question of time and death, from metaphysical revolt starting with the biblical Cain to modern German philosopher Nietzsche's death of god,[59] to its parallel in historical revolt from regicides to deicides its parallel in historical revolt from regicides to deicides,[60] to state terrorism that culminates in revolution.[61] (*Yet in America and France we thought that Camus's time had passed!?!*) But by the climax of Camus's breakneck history of philosophy, we reach a place of seeming balance, what he calls "*mesure et demesure*"[62] or "moderation and excess," which brings the existentialist once again to a precipice which he calls "thought at the Meridian." Camus envisions an off-balance view of time, whereby "revolt is an irregular pendulum searching for its most

58. Annabelle Azade, "Le Pen Beckons French Jews—and Some Respond," *Forward*, April 17, 2017, http://forward.com/news/world/369504/le-pen-beckons-french-jews-and-some-respond/ (accessed May 3, 2017).

59. Albert Camus, L'homme révolté (Paris: Editions Gallimard, 2016), 23–132. Compare with ibid., trans. A. Bower (Vintage: New York, 1956).

60. Ibid., 133–301 (my translations).

61. Ibid., 302–36.

62. Ibid., 363–72.

perfect and profound rhythm. Its irregularity is its very pivot point, bringing to light measure and limit which share the very principle of its nature."[63] Thought at the meridian for Camus is the ability to see "moderation as born of revolt and that it can only survive through revolt. It is a continual conflict, perpetually sustained and mastered by the intelligence."[64] The chaos of revolt is thus built into the order of time's creation. Even in a time where we have all but stopped thinking, where Camus counts most as a modern Ecclesiastes is in his willingness to think beyond nihilism. Such willingness to see beyond the abyss at "the Meridian of thought" is precisely how "revolt thus refuses divinity in partaking its battles and common destinies."[65] So Camus concludes his existential journey:

> Each tells the other that s/he is not God; here is the end of romanticism. At this moment, when each of us must fit an arrow to our bow and enter the lists anew, to reconquer, within history and in spite of it, that which s/he owns already, the thin yield of his fields, the brief love of this earth, at this moment when at last a human being is born, it is time to forsake our age and its adolescent furies. The bow bends; the wood complains. At the moment of supreme tension, there will leap into flight an unswerving arrow, a shaft that is inflexible and free.[66]

This darkening hour is indeed, for Krassen, the "moment of supreme tension" that necessitates such a "leap into flight [of] an unswerving arrow" through the Torah of the future now. Freedom by all means necessary demands that one becomes hopelessly hopeful as a helper to others so that this endangered freedom will remain unswerving. Such armory brings us back to the Hebrew poet Amichai, who concludes "A Man in His Life" by confronting the end of human time:

> He will die as figs die in autumn. Shriveled and full of himself and sweet, the leaves growing on the ground, the bare branches pointing to the place where there's time for everything.

I see in Krassen's Torah of the future time a real vision that Amichai was constantly pointing to but unable to reach until he died. Yet Krassen is still transmitting a Torah of the future now, where, in a sense, "there's time for everything"—a Torah for learning to die before we die, as the great Sufi masters would teach. To die before our death is meant to provide a path of living so that we do not die when we die. Herein lies the paradox known to

---

63. Ibid., 363.
64. Ibid., 372.
65. Ibid., 377.
66. Ibid., 377. Bower, L'homme révolté, 310 (with my slight emendations).

all mystics, especially the Sufis—how does one try to die to the attraction of living while remaining opened up to the beauty of life "where there's time for everything"?

Time for Everything in the Living One

If *after death* our outward senses cease, then what of those moments *in life* when outward senses cease—do our inward senses then open up? To help us open up to the attraction of living, what Sufis point us to is those moments that parallel the Hebrew poet "where there's time for everything." If God is beautiful and loves beauty, then the universe is but a mirror in which such beauty and grandeur can be admired. So, worship of life for the divine is the Living One, *al-Hayy* or *El Hay*. If this is known to be so, then the seeker yearns to emulate the Living One. After death, one voyages to the intermediary world where one experiences the reversal of inner and outer aspects. Thoughts once hidden in this world are now disclosed in the intermediary world. The transformation of the ego in Sufism is a form of realization. What one comes to realize is that even though the ego may still be inciting one's self to evil, the transformation leads to a kind of death to this tendency. In working to transcend the self, one passes through the temporality of imaginal colors like green, white, red, and black. These imaginal colors are for Shaykh al-Kashani seen as colors of death along the Sufi path. Sufi dervishes will sometimes don a black garment, upon having died unto self, yet beforehand other colors may have marked their time being at a different station or level along the path. The moment of green death is thus implied in the wearing of the patched garment made of discarded and worthless rags. Life in this state of deep devotional transparency is said to be blossoming into its green through abstemiousness and the blooming of one's countenance in the verdant grace of the inner beauty within which one can truly live.[67] Truly, living in the face of death and dying before you die is no small suite in the musical composition of life, nor is it sufficient to try to capture it in a codetta or a coda as the song of the soul keeps singing on.[68] Through this song of the soul that keeps singing, the echo of the Hebrew poet "where there's time for everything" resonates most strongly

---

67. William C. Chittick, The Sufi Path of Knowledge: Ibn Al-'arabi's Metaphysics of Imagination (Gulshan Books: Srinagar, Kashmir, 2009), xix; see also, "Sufis About Death," http://www.chishti.ru/sufi_death.htm (accessed May 3, 2017), with gratitude for my encounters with Ibrahim Baaje, Sufi Shaykh of the Chisti tariqa, o.b.m., as well as acknowledging the time Krassen spent with Shayke Ibrahim at Chochmat haLev in Berkeley through the years.

68. Aubrey L. Glazer, "Codetta: A Philosophy of Post-Secular Song in Light of Piyyut as a Cultural Lens," in Tangle of Matter & Ghost: Leonard Cohen's Post-Secular Songbook of Mysticism(s) Jewish & Beyond (Brighton, MA: Academic Studies Press, 2017), 228–37; ibid., "Coda: Burning Darker Beyond 'You Want it Darker,'" 238–46.

in all its verdant grace.

A Way Back Through Time-Swerve

While I have spent time diving deeply into these imaginal layers of time through *zikr* with the Jerrahi Sufi orders in Toronto and New York, as well as with *Chisti Pir* Ibrahim Baaje, *o.b.m.*, the nuances of these experiences did not fully align with me until another teacher showed me the way back through this "time-swerve."[69] That guide remains Elliot Wolfson, my first teacher of Kabbalah, who early on showed me through research, study, and friendship the importance of the imaginal through the scholarship of Corbin.

Given the texture of time we presently straddle, as well as the context of this *Spiritual Affinities* series, it is worthwhile to further appreciate the balance of time lived through the life of the scholar in Islamic mysticism, Henri Corbin.[70] Throughout his journey as an academic and spiritualist, Corbin continued to reflect on the intimate nature of time in the balance. As a French philosopher and orientalist whose interpretation of the Persian role in the development of Islamic thought is second to none, Henri Corbin studied with Étienne Gilson at the École *Pratique des Hautes* Études (Ve Section), receiving his degree in philosophy in 1925. Corbin also began to study Arabic and Sanskrit at the École *des Langues Orientales*, becoming an adjunct at the *Bibliothèque Nationale* in Paris and the following year received a degree in Arabic, Persian, and Turkish. In 1930, Corbin encountered German thought, especially the hermeneutics of Heidegger, which provided Corbin with the "hermeneutic key" (*clavis hermeneutica*). Coupled with this encounter was Corbin's discovery of Šehāb-al-dīn Abū Ḥafṣ ʿOmar b. Moḥammad Sohravardī (1155–91). It was his association with Louis Massignon that launched Corbin on this path, because Massignon gifted him a lithographed edition of Sohravardī's principal work, *Philosophy of Illumination*. So when Corbin and his wife went to Turkey by 1939 to discover the microfilms of the Sohravardī manuscripts hidden in the Istanbul libraries, again it was the texture of the darkening time of World War II that sequestered the couple there within the luminal darkness until 1945. Sohravardī's visions of luminal darkness continue to illuminate the ever-darkening reality of our times, reminding us that time always darkens before the coming of the greater light. So the coming light shall be glorious indeed!

Not that dissimilar from Vonnegut's being billeted belowground in a

---

69. Elliot R. Wolfson, Prologue: "Timeswerve/Hermeneutic Reversibility," in Language, Eros, Being: Kabbalistic Hermeneutics and Poetic Imagination (New York: Fordham University Press, 2004), vii–xxxi.

70. B. Paris, April 14, 1903, d. Paris, October 7, 1978.

hog slaughterhouse and emerging from the ashes more luminous, so too it was Corbin's study of Sohravardī and his involuntary exile that revealed to him "the virtues of silence and the discipline of the arcane."[71] Vonnegut's participation in the renowned meeting ground for Jungians and perennialists, known as the *Eranos* circle, drew him deeper into this path of the contemplating and writing on the *mundus imaginalis* between 1949 and 1978.[72] This heterogeneous society of international scholars that met annually in Switzerland allowed Corbin to develop more in-depth scholarly meditations on the imaginal layers of time.[73] In many ways, as a spiritual practitioner, Krassen's lineage is carrying forward the seeds that were planted in the *Eranos* circle, but from a place that is quite "off-balance."[74]

Time in the balance is not unique to Corbin and his reading of Islamic mysticism, but his articulation is quite nuanced. Time shares correlates in both Jewish and Islamic mysticism, given its shared root in Hebrew and Arabic as *ZeMaN*.[75] It is this *spiritual affinity* that allows the eternal promise of love to emerge again for me along my path in search of a spiritual practice that might convey glimmers of such love.

Arriving A/head in the Future Through Krassen's Vanishing Path

With the search for such practice in mind, I wonder: How is it possible to arrive a/head in the future now? And if so, what does Torah have to do with it and why point to its now-ness? These guiding questions continue serve as an introduction to the devotional thinking of one of the greatest mystical minds of our time that you have likely never heard of—Rabbi Dr. Moshe Aaron Krassen, aka Miles Krassen. The truth is that sometimes in life as

---

71. See Henry Corbin, The Voyage and the Messenger: Iran and Philosophy. (North Atlantic Books: Berkeley, California, 1998).

72. Steven M. Wasserstrom, Religion after Religion: Gershom Scholem, Mircea Eliade, and Henry Corbin at Eranos (Princeton, NJ: Princeton University Press, 2001).

73. On cycles of time in Mazdaism and Ismailism, the imam in Ismaili gnosis, and the relation between ancient Gnosticism and Ismailism, see Henri Corbin, Temps cyclique et gnose ismaélienne (Editeurs Berg International: Paris, 1982); idem, Cyclical Time and Ismaili Gnosis, trans. R. Manheim and J. Morris (Routledge: London, 1983). For the pioneering correlations of the mundus imaginalis with Kabbalah, see Elliot R. Wolfson, Through a Speculum that Shines: Vision and Imagination in Medieval Jewish Mysticism (Princeton, NJ: Princeton University Press, 1997), 8, 57, 62, 63n, 108; Elliot R. Wolfson, "'Imago Templi' and the Meeting of the Two Seas: Liturgical Time-Space and the Feminine Imaginary in Zoharic Kabbalah," RES: Anthropology and Aesthetics 51, no. 1 (2007): 121–35; more recently, see Elliot R. Wolfson, Giving beyond the Gift: Apophasis and Overcoming Theomania (Oxford: Oxford University Press, 2014).

74. Encyclopedia Iranica, s.v. "Henry Corbin," http://www.iranicaonline.org/articles/corbin-henry-b.

75. Henry Corbin, Temple and Contemplation, trans. P. & L. Sherrard (London: KPI, 1986), 59, 78–81, 109, 116, 157–58, 164, 192, 234, 268, 325, 331, 337–38, 375.

in love, you encounter remarkable souls that change you forever. I have found that being put off-balance and challenged to see the world, humanity, and the divine totality differently is what marks a true teacher. While neither I nor Krassen were billeted belowground in a hog slaughterhouse, yet something mystical came to pass and continues to happen every time I meet with Krassen. That marked my first experience, well over two decades ago on a Jewish meditation retreat in upstate New York, *Elat Chayyim* with Sylvia Boorstein and Rabbi Jeff Roth. It was Krassen's teaching couched in that laugh of the trickster that drew me in immediately. Moshe Aharon Ladizhiner remains for me a once-in-a-generation teacher and seeker, *Senex* and *Peur*, *Savah* and *Yenukah*. How such a teacher–seeker relates to the teaching of the calendar clearly requires some unpacking.

As a teacher, author, and scholar in the fields of comparative mysticism and the world's Wisdom traditions, and as a musician, Rabbi Miles Krassen, PhD, remains an enigma. Krassen completed his doctorate in religious studies at the University of Pennsylvania and received rabbinic ordination from the *P'nai Or Fellowship* under the auspices of Reb Zalman Schacter-Shalomi, *z"l*, but never felt beholden to the anarchic religiosity of Renewal.[76] Krassen serves as teacher and guide of a virtual community known as Planetary Judaism, an organization for disseminating evolutionary mystical Jewish teachings based on the spiritual insights of early Hasidism and Kabbalah.[77] He devotes himself to mystical studies and practice, and the teaching and training of teachers and practitioners of a new paradigm for inner development and self-transformation within the Jewish tradition.

Krassen has transcended and included his academic training as well as his published scholarship[78] by continuing to explore practicing and teaching inner Judaism for many years to private students and at summer retreats including *Elat Chayyim*, the *Aleph Kallah*, and *Ruach haAretz*. His classes and workshops are based on a deep fealty for traditional sources, familiarity with many non-Jewish wisdom traditions, and respect for the latest findings

76. Rabbi Zalman Schachter-Shalomi Collection, in Post-Holocaust American Judaism Collections (CU-Boulder) https://www.colorado.edu/jewishstudies/researcharchives/post-holocaust-american-judaism-archive/rabbi-zalman-schachter-shalomi-collection (accessed May 3, 2017).

77. See http://planetaryjudaism.org/ (accessed August 23, 2017).

78. Miles Krassen, Devequt and Faith in Zaddiqim: The Religious Tracts of Meshullam Feibush Heller of Zbarazh (Ann Arbor: University of Michigan Press, 1996); Isaiah Horowitz, The Generations of Adam, trans. Miles Krassen (New York: Paulist Press, 1996); Miles Krassen, "Book Review: Rabbi Abraham Isaac Kook and Jewish Spirituality," Shofar 15, no. 4 (1997): 126–27; Uniter of Heaven and Earth: Rabbi Meshullam Feibush Heller of Zbarazh and the Rise of Hasidism in Eastern Galicia (Albany: State University of New York Press, 1998); and Richard Kaplan, Invoking the Seven Beggars: Music and Teachings on Joy Based on Rebbe Nachman of Breslov's "Tale of the Seven Beggars" (New York: M. Krassen, 2004), sound recording.

of contemporary scholarship and science. Krassen's interest in mysticism and spirituality dates back to the 1950s, when he began studying yoga, Buddhism, and Taoism. In the 1960s, he became interested in Western Wisdom traditions dating back to Plato, the teachings of Gurdjieff, Sufism, Christian mysticism, and later, Tibetan Buddhism and Advaita Vedanta. During the 1970s, several providential experiences led him to discover the great, hidden depths of the Jewish mystical tradition and Hasidism. That discovery involved so deep an identification that to this day, although he continues to study and honor all wisdom traditions, his path remains centered in Hasidism and the Kabbalah. In the 1970s, Krassen's first Jewish teachers were Rabbi Shlomo Carlebach, may his memory bless us, and Rabbi Zalman Schachter-Shalomi, from whom he later received ordination in 1996. Under their influence, Krassen lived in Boro Park and studied at a local yeshiva. During that time, he was privileged to experience the teachings and spiritual practice of a number of great rebbes, especially Rabbi Shlomo Halberstam, the late Bobover Rebbe. As a result of these experiences, it soon became clear how many deep spiritual truths and methods for transformation had been preserved within Hasidism. Nevertheless, it was equally clear that these treasures were embedded in cultural forms and attitudes of an earlier period in human and Jewish history and needed to be situated within a new context and paradigm in order to guide us in our present state of development. In order to acquire the textual skills required to gain direct access to the treasury of Jewish mystical tradition, Krassen turned to the world of academic scholarship. Initially, he studied with Professor Lawrence Fine at Indiana University, where he received an MA in religious studies. He later became a student of Rabbi Dr. Arthur Green at the University of Pennsylvania, where he wrote a dissertation on the spirituality of early Hasidism. In the 1980s, Krassen was also a Lady Davis Fellow at the Hebrew University in Jerusalem. There he was privileged to study with leading scholars of Jewish mysticism and Kabbalah, including Professors Moshe Idel, Yehuda Liebes, Rachel Elior, and the late Rivka Schatz-Uffenheimer. After completing his doctorate, Krassen taught at Smith College and at Oberlin, where he served as associate professor of religion and director of Jewish studies. While at Oberlin, he wrote *Uniter of Heaven and Earth*, a study of mystical experience in early Hasidism, and *Isaiah Horowitz: The Generations of Adam*, an introduction and translation of a major portion of an important kabbalistic work of the seventeenth century. From 2004 to 2007, Krassen was professor of Judaic studies at Naropa University.

But as one peels away the layers of his time thus far presented, there is more than meets the eye—he would expect nothing less. And so as I peer through the latticework of Krassen's encounters, experiences, and teachings, I continue to encounter a paradox—a trickster-sage. Much like the painter Pablo Picasso, who began as a prodigy already mastering figurative art, the path of discovery and growth necessitated moving beyond these gifts by deconstructing them and in the process creating a new language. Like Picasso, Krassen also has had different periods, each with their own texture and shade depending on the decade. I see, however, a spiral path that continues evolving toward planetary Judaism through *RADLA* now.

At a young age, Krassen recalls seeing the future now, especially while watching football games with friends—the youngster could see the plays before they would happen. There were glimmers of yearning with scriptural *parsha* study in Hebrew school, but given these teachings were conveyed without any critical sense and no mythic structure, there was deep identification that may have led to a latent awareness of Torah but nothing explicit really remained. Perhaps this deeper awareness for seeing the future now really began to emerge when Krassen, at age twelve, became deeply intrigued in reading the *Pictorial History of Philosophy*.[79] It was then Krassen became mesmerized by the painting of a contemplative St. Francis of Assisi—the young boy was able to identify with this sense of the contemplative being outside of the city, apart from the world but in touch with something deep and sacred. "I felt somehow I was like him," remarks Krassen.

Coupled with a fascination for the contemplative life, Krassen was also outspoken at an early age. He recalls standing up for what seemed to be no particular reason to chastise his irascible classmates for chasing the teacher out of the class. Krassen was already gifted with an ability to speak in a certain way with a fearless air of authority to fellow students that was becoming manifest at that point. Experiences like this at a ripe age were indicative of his unusual way of being.

One might expect that the rite de passage of a bar mitzvah would provide a moment of deeper illumination for such a seeker. However, postwar American Judaism offered no such entry point to meaning—Judaism had become paralyzed in rote behavioralism and devoid of any moisture of existential meaning. And so his bar mitzvah was a doubly traumatic rite de passage, insofar as this Jewish coming-of-age ceremony coincided with his parents' divorce. While he found the ritual aspects of reading a Pentateuch selection in the Torah scroll and Haftorah from the prophets to be part of this rote behavior devoid of meaning, he did experience meaning—at the party! That was in large part due to his many Eastern European immigrant relatives who were there to celebrate. While the young bar mitzvah boy had no idea that these relative all came from the Hasidic world, he could feel that there was something very un-American about the way they would celebrate. Most of these relatives were from the Ukraine, not necessarily re-

---

79. Dagobert D. Runes, Pictorial History of Philosophy (New York: Philosophical Library, Incorporated, 1959).

ligious people, in a sense, still practicing without thinking about it or being reflective, but they had this quality of *simchah* that he never saw in ordinary American Judaism or life for that matter. These Hasidim could dance and get together to *farbreng!*[80]

That same intimacy of getting together began in his teen years with fellow beatniks as Krassen first began exploring Taoism and Buddhism. Attempts at living the contemplative life were rife and robust with one friend, a painter named Stu Sax, who was used to living according to the *I-Ching*.[81] Stu shared a Taoist amulet with Miles. Wearing this amulet— a symbol of Eastern spirituality— around his neck regularly, enraged his father's Western sensibilities. How could his Jewish son import this foreign spirituality?!? Meanwhile, despite all the paternal rage, Miles's mother was into *Transcendental Meditation*[82] and the *Maharishi*.[83] Reading Jewish beatniks like Jack Kerouac and Allen Ginsberg[84] led Miles into deeper readings in the Zen Buddhist writings of Alan Watts and D. T. Suzuki.[85] And so it comes as little surprise that while Krassen was actually attending class, in this case during biology class, he adamantly refused to dissect the frog. His refusal stemmed from being a Taoist, and Miles did not believe in killing other sentient beings. This was all part of a process of extricating himself from the Jewish ghetto (even while his father was trailing him to the café in his car). Krassen embodied an endless curiosity fused with the idealism of beatnik freedom. He celebrated life with a hedonism that was counter to the burden of the Jewish ghetto. This was Krassen's initial period of reading and thinking outside the Jewish world.

It was music or what one might even call musical thinking[86] that captivated the young Krassen at this point and not Judaism. Simply put, Judaism was not that meaningful nor could it even remotely have been considered a major interest at this point. Rather, music was Krassen's passion, as

---

80. Farbreng is a Yiddish term, common in the Hasidic milieu which means to gather and share celebratory teachings shared in fellowship, often round a table or tisch.

81. I-Ching, trans. James Legge, ed. and with an introduction by Raymond Van Over (New York: New American Library, 1971).

82. Transcendental Meditation (Springfield, MO: Gospel Publishing House, 1976).

83. Jack Forem, Transcendental Meditation: Maharishi Mahesh Yogi and the Science of Creative Intelligence (London: Allen & Unwin, 1984).

84. Jack Kerouac and Allen Ginsberg, Jack Kerouac and Allen Ginsberg: The Letters (New York: Penguin Books, 2014).

85. Alan Watts, The Way of Zen (New York: Random House Inc., 1999); Daisetz T. Suzuki and Richard M. Jaffe, Selected Works of D. T. Suzuki (Berkeley: University of California Press, 2015); see also, A. I. Switzer, and John Snelling, D. T. Suzuki: A Biography (London: Buddhist Society, 1985).

86. On musical thinking, see Aubrey L. Glazer, A New Physiognomy of Jewish Thinking: Critical Theory after Adorno as Applied to Jewish Thought (London: Bloomsbury Academic, 2012), esp. 45–74; 135–46.

he played jazz with a fake ID at fourteen years old in cabarets and bars. Through music, Krassen crossed boundaries, so that he was able to strike up friendships with African Americans, which was unusual in his insular Jewish community of Philadelphia. That insularity left little space for meaning-making. His maternal grandfather was trained in the Odessa Gymnasium, while his grandmother had a siddur to pray with at the local synagogue. And even though his paternal grandfather was from the renowned Hasidic shtetl or village of Tolne,[87] and his great-uncle was a rebbe from Zhitomir,[88] the young Krassen was never appraised explicitly of his illustrious Hasidic spiritual lineage. His great uncle lived in south Philadelphia and presided over the local Hasidic prayer space of the *Zhitomir shteibl* there. During his youth, while Krassen did attend the *Tolner shteibl* when he was young, there was no time spent at the *Zhitomir shteibl*.

At this point, Miles's father became quite unhappy with his son's interest in music—"How low- class!?!" And Hasidism—irrelevant!?! Why not do something worthwhile, his father badgered, like write a bestseller?!? While his father may have been highly discouraging of his prodigal son, he was never mean, rather just pushing him in other directions. And so a genuine interest in Hasidism emerged when Krassen was in his twenties. At that point, his father softened somewhat, quipping: "What would you want to be interested in that old stuff for?" For this elder, Hasidism was as irrelevant as his own elders, so why bother? It was only when Krassen was far away from Philadelphia, living in Bloomington, that his father would then share with him that his great-uncle, Yitzhak Lubarsky, was none other than . . . the Zhitomir rebbe! Krassen also learned from this distance that his father's favorite thing was to experience Shabbat with the Zhitomir rebbe—why? Because the Zhitomir rebbe and his Hasidim loved to sing and dance. In line with this love-hate relationship, Miles's mother had a very adversarial relationship with Judaism and resented with the way women were treated by the religion. The only one she liked, however, was this great uncle, Yitzhak Lubarsky, the Zhitomir rebbe—why? It was the Zhitomir rebbe who was singularly genuine and pleasant with her. She never felt judged or condemned. Miles has childhood memories of women coming over to the Zhitomir rebbe to see whether their chicken was kosher. This one was not kosher, but that one was—why? What was the difference between the chickens? The young Krassen soon learned that this was a poor woman, and she could not afford to buy another chicken! That story really touched

---

87. The spiritual leader referred to here is most likely the Tolner Rebbe of Philadelphia, Rabbi Moshe Tzvi Twersky, see http://tolnerrebbes.blogspot.com/2009/05/rabbi-yitzchok-twersky-tolner-rebbe-of.html (accessed June 14, 2017).

88. See YIVO Encyclopedia of Jews in Eastern Europe, s.v. "Zhytomyr," http://www.yivoencyclopedia.org/article.aspx/Zhytomyr (accessed June 14, 2017).

the youngster, this display of such openheartedness, lacking any judgment whatsoever.

While attending Northeast High School as a music major, Krassen cut most of the classes that bored him to sneak downtown to Center City, Philadelphia, and spend time in Logan Square Library. Krassen would spend the day roaming library, room to room, from music recordings to literature. He was especially interested in Russian novelists like Dostoyevsky.[89] After a few hours of this directed inattention, wandering from room to room in the library, Krassen would walk down to the museum to look at paintings. Once he was caught returning to his locker at school by the hall patrol who thought he was a student teacher—after all, he was sporting a goatee beard and a cravat, looking like a real beatnik. That led to a meeting with Vice Principal Hyman Boudich. At that disciplinary meeting, Krassen proceeded to sit down and launch a protest strike against student abuse—Krassen was then suspended. Boudich later apologized to his father for throwing Miles out of the high school, acknowledging that his son was a genius. The school could just not accommodate him. Notwithstanding his genius, Krassen was now officially a high school dropout.

This led to a choice: either pursue music or study great books. And so Krassen applied and received early acceptance at St. John's College, in Annapolis,[90] at sixteen years old. At that point, in his first year, he was reading *Theatetus*, and Krassen had a gnostic experience while reading the dialogue about knowledge. For it is there that Plato positions Socrates to discuss perceptions wherein one experiences "dreams and diseases, including insanity, and everything else that is said to cause illusions of sight and hearing and the other senses."[91] So even though Krassen's formation at St. John's directed his reading of this dialogue in a highly Aristotelean framework, where knowledge cannot be defined in terms of perception and that dreams threaten sensory-based knowledge, he was seeing things differently. At that point, Krassen experienced the dialogue in a way that could not be conveyed through language. It was a state of thought wherein dreams escape our ability to engage in rational inquiry intact, thus setting them apart from insanity and delusions. Krassen recalls experiencing an altered state

---

89. Fyodor Mikhaylovich Dostoyevsky, (b. November 11 [October 30, Old Style], 1821, Moscow, Russia–di. February 9 [January 28, Old Style], 1881, St. Petersburg), Russian novelist and short-story writer whose psychological penetration into the darkest recesses of the human heart, together with his unsurpassed moments of illumination, see Encyclopedia Britannica, s.v. "Dostoyevsky, Fyodor," https://www.britannica.com/biography/Fyodor-Dostoyevsky (accessed June 14, 2017).

90. "St. John's College: Annapolis Seminar Readings" (accessed June 14, 2017), https://www.sjc.edu/academic-programs/undergraduate/seminar/annapolis-undergraduate-readings.

91. Plato, Theatetus (157e).

of consciousness through Socrates's real intention, but found himself at a loss to explain his experience in the seminar. His mind flipped into a state of knowing that was precisely what Socrates was referring to—a conflation of knowing and *not-knowing*. This moment in understanding became very important to Krassen. Playing music remained part of his time at St. John's, yet the experience was mixed. Krassen felt it was too Aristotelian, insofar as most of the faculty was composed of many Jewish survivors from Frieburg and Marburg. Viktor Zuckerkandl,[92] a former music conductor, pianist, and phenomenologist, became Krassen's mentor, never feeling intimidated by this prodigy of a student yet making an impression through his kindness. While Krassen was studying with him in 1962, Zuckerandel still played piano, despite the Nazis having crushed his fingers. In his freshman year, Krassen studied Greek with Zuckerandel, who also introduced him to Ludwig Wittgenstein.[93] But, tragically, Zuckerandel died after that first year, and this loss affected Krassen's passion to learn, without a teacher encouraging him to be better. Another tutor took over—Douglas Allenbrook, a disciple of Boulange—and he befriended Miles. Krassen gravitated toward the philosopher-musicians with a phenomenological bent. In his final year, he studied Nietzsche and Wagner with Eva Braun, another Aristotelian, and it remained much too dry for Krassen's passion for gnosis. Finally, there was George Barry, another tutor who played fiddle and invited Krassen for sessions at his house. On graduating, Krassen was accepted to performing arts at Columbia after heading the Shakespeare troupe at St. John's, but he decided to go to study ethnomusicology at Bloomington in 1967. Barry would not support his choice to study ethnomusicology, rather recommending Krassen study religion or philosophy. At that time, as a graduate student, he received a Class 2-Student deferral from serving in the Vietnam War. At this point in his journey, Krassen came to truly appreciate the unique nature of the cosmopolitan Jew, like Zuckerandel and Allenbrook, who were truly displaced renaissance men of a bygone era.

From one generation of displaced musical thinkers to another, Krassen met Max and Barbara Kirshenblatt-Gimblett.[94] She was a pioneer in reviving lost culture that by now has become second nature to dumpster divers and artists living on the edge. Something remarkable was emerging after

92. Viktor Zuckerkandl (b. July 2, 1896, Vienna–d. April 5, 1965, Locarno), see Victor Zuckerkandl, "Man the Musician" (1975); The Sense of Music (Princeton, NJ: Princeton University Press, 1971).

93. Wittgenstein was born on April 26, 1889, in Vienna, Austria and legend has it that, at his death in 1951, his last words were "Tell them I've had a wonderful life"; see https://plato.stanford.edu/entries/wittgenstein/#BiogSket (accessed June 14, 2017).

94. Barbara Kirshenblatt-Gimblett, Robert R. Faulkner, and Howard S. Becker, Art from Start to Finish: Jazz, Painting, Writing and Other Improvisations (Chicago: University of Chicago Press, 2006).

the disillusionment of Woodstock and the Summer of Love, whereby in the 1970s, there emerged a revival of the instrumental and vocal folk tradition within the emerging klezmer movement. It was through musicians like Michael Alpert, Walter Zev Feldman, Hankus Netsky, Henry Sapoznik, and Andy Statman in the first wave of klezmer revivalists, whose fieldwork and re-creation projects laid the foundation for a resurgent interest in Eastern European Jewish music to which Krassen continues to find an affinity. And thanks to the YIVO Yiddish Folksong Project of the early 1970s, directed by Barbara Kirshenblatt-Gimblett, there was a thoroughgoing scholarly collection of songs from older folk singers that would transform a generation, including Krassen.[95] By contrast, Max became a different kind of mentor and, overall, Krassen was impressed by how this couple lived on the "wrong side" of town above a bar under the radar. They exemplified the life of the real artist he wanted to be. Even though their proclivity for dumpster diving initially freaked Miles out, Max, as a former green grocer assured him it was kosher and safe to eat—and of course it helped that Barbara was a great cook. So while they bonded, Max was mentoring Krassen to be an independent person he yearned to be. At that point, Krassen thought he was an artist who wanted to be a playwright and poet. In the spring of 1968, President Lyndon Johnson announced that he was not seeking reelection, so Krassen dropped out of ethnomusicology—it all felt inauthentic. So now losing his deferral as a student, Krassen was called in for induction to the military. Yet he had already prepared to fail, and was thoroughly unsurprised when he was met with the conclusion of his entrance exam:

> "Son, I have really bad news for you—you failed due to myriad psychological difficulties. You will not make it through basic training and it would be a waste of taxpayer's money—no potential to be a soldier."

After this rejection—he was not drafted into the US military—Krassen moved to the Lower East Side with friends who were exploring psychedelics, becoming part of a Gurdjieff group that presented him the challenge of self-transformation by really having to work on himself. During this period of 1968–70, Krassen would shuttle back and forth between Lower East Side and Woodstock. He did, however, return to Bloomington to complete his MA in ethnomusicology with a complete fellowship along with a job in the Archives of Traditional Music. While working at the archive, he was dubbing documentation for field collections. If any document came in to do with Appalachian or Celtic music, it was given directly to Krassen to dub,

---

95. YIVO Encyclopedia of Jews in Eastern Europe, s.v. "Study of Jewish Music," http://www.yivoencyclopedia.org/article.aspx/Music/Study_of_Jewish_Music (accessed June 14, 2017).

document, and catalogue. In the grand scheme of things for Krassen, this was really a dream job—listening to music from all over the world and getting paid to collect, catalog, and reflect on it. However, true to form as an unapologetic iconoclast, in his second semester, Krassen stopped attending classes, and once this was discovered, he was fired from the Archives of Traditional Music. From there he was accepted into the School of Library Science, with a full scholarship in Bloomington. After a year, Krassen quit even after getting perfect scores on all exams. Despite their requests to stay on, he lost interest. That moment was a crisis of *what next.*

From library sciences and archives it was not that far of a stretch to dystopian visions. By then, Krassen had begun writing a science fiction novel called *Ice Forest.* After sending a query letter with a writing sample to Lynn Carter at Ballantine Fantasy Series, Krassen was told if he completed the manuscript that they would be interested in pursuing it. And at the same time, Krassen sent a query to the main folk publishing company of interest, known as Oak Publications, who then immediately offered him a contract to write a book that became known as *Appalachian Fiddle.*[96] Apparently, his letter arrived precisely when Oak Publications was in a meeting about acquiring a book on Appalachian fiddling. Stone broke, Miles immediately turned away from his science fiction novel and went to work on this music book that was offered a contract and became a success, selling out over three thousand copies right away. It was such a classic that, to this day, he still receives royalties to subsist on from the very endeavor of ethnomusicology that he all but left behind. Next Miles offered up *Clawhammer Banjo,*[97] which was also successful. And, finally, Krassen was commissioned to write *O'Neil's Music of Ireland Revised,*[98] concluding with *Masters of Old Time Fiddling.*[99]

Little surprise that a mystic could be poised to play a mean fiddle, as the painting of Chagall reveals. Krassen's early immersion in the revival of old-time music can really be seen as another form of his path to wisdom. Krassen's time spent with traditional fiddlers he likens to an encounter with a kind of "Western wise-man . . . whose tunes were like incantations, a form of ancient wisdom that induced high feeling." What is critical to appreciate here is how for Krassen, style was a social entity, the common knowledge that formed the basis of community musical tradition. As a mystical ethnomusicologist, Krassen understood that individual style could have endur-

---

96. Miles Krassen, Appalachian Fiddle (Coopersburg, NY: Oak Publications, 1973).

97. Miles Krassen, Clawhammer Banjo (Coopersburg, NY: Oak Publications, 1974).

98. Miles Krassen, O'Neill's Music of Ireland: New and Revised (Coopersburg, NY: Oak Publications, 1976).

99. Miles Krassen, Masters of Old Time Fiddling: For Violin (Pittsford, NY: Castle Rock,1983).

ing significance, but only within this social nexus. Consequently, Krassen sought to explore in depth a single banjo tradition—the music of the Galax area and of southeastern West Virginia. All the current insights into mystical experience and its relation to social networks was already lived and intuited by Krassen decades ago.

For example, it was no coincidence that Krassen's *Clawhammer Banjo* featured contemporary photographs of rural scenes seemingly composed by circumstances from which someone had briefly withdrawn. On the back cover of *Appalachian Fiddle* there was a considerably more deliberate pose, with Krassen playing his fiddle on a stump beside a farmhouse, flanked on either side by a pig and an irascible goat, half out of the frame. These out of the frame images reflected an emerging symbolic currency circulating in the old-time music revival, wherein the revival was positioned not as an observer of tradition but as a part of a return to comprehensive traditional rural living. This movement in the 1970s paved the way for the ideological underpinning of "old-time" social enterprises, especially old-time music.[100]

Just as Krassen was attuned to the importance of apprenticing in music with a master, so too, Krassen made sure to attune himself to spiritual masters within his vicinity. Krassen knew well the elder brother of the Dalai Lama, Thuptin Norbu, while other of his friends were active with Pir Valayat Kahn[101] and his Sufi circle as well as others who were attached to diverse yogis. There was also the powerful presence of teacher Victor Donner, who was a disciple of Frithjof Schuon[102] and his tariqa of the Perennialist[103] who was also making an impression on Krassen, that is, until about 1975. It was that year where everything changed for Krassen—he was afflicted with tendonitis in his left arm. For a devoted fiddler, this was nothing short of traumatic as he practiced for hours a day. How would he go on without being able to play?!? However, it was this being of a different type, Rinpoche Thuptin Norbu, who made a lasting impression that may have planted a seed for seeing things otherwise during this traumatic period.

And so, a deeply pivotal moment emerges here in 1975: first, at a loss, Krassen found himself walking around the Little Professor Bookstore on Kirkland Avenue, and noticing this neglected book by Isaac Bashevis

---

100. John Bealle, Old-Time Music and Dance: Community and Folk Revival (Bloomington, IN: Quarry Books, 2005).

101. Pir Valayat Kahn, The Music of Life (New York: Omega Press, 1983).

102. Frithjof Schuon, Esoterism as Principle and as Way (New York: Quest Books, 1981); The Transcendent Unity of Religions (New York: Quest Books, 1984).

103. Huston Smith, "Is There a Perennial Philosophy?," Journal of the American Academy of Religion 55, no. 3 (1987): 553–66.

Singer:[104] *The Magician of Lublin.*[105] It was this title rather than the author that caught Krassen's attention. But he resisted reading it for one reason and one reason alone—because he was a Jewish author. But he could not overcome this resistance. In a state of enthusiastic *hitlabtut*, what was there to lose for seventy-five cents? Krassen began reading it and completely identified with the protagonist, who falls and injures his leg as an acrobat, and who is traumatized after being injured. He goes into a deep existential crisis, ultimately returning to his shtetl in Lublin and becoming a recluse in a hut doing. He spends the rest of his life in that hut, becoming known after so many years as a saint. Here was a moment of deep identification with the Jewish element, even though Krassen would resist it.

Secondly, even though Krassen seemed to have no explicit formal interest in Judaism, still he found himself reading everything he could about Eastern European Judaism, ultimately leading him back to Hasidism. His interest was most intensely focused on the Hasidic visionaries, the Baal Shem Tov,[106] and Reb Nachman of Bratzlav.[107] So, for example, a popular collection like *Souls on Fire*[108] touched Krassen deeply, notwithstanding its flawed holocaust theology, Miles deeply identified with these spiritual avatars.

All the while, Krassen continued serving as a Bloomington hotel night clerk on the midnight to dawn shift, ensuring the accounts were turned in by the morn. As fate would have it, Krassen's assistant was a Tibetan monk, sent to serve Thuptin Norbu. And so Krassen and Norbu would spend most of the night in spiritual conversations. Somewhere during that year, Krassen fell into a crisis of a lack of seriousness and commitment. If he did not practice something seriously, he would be a dilettante. So one night, when Krassen was not clerking, he stayed up all night and began praying before the bay window in his apartment with a clear view of the heavens saying: "I don't know who you are, but I'm at a total loss, but I need an answer?!? I don't know whether to be initiated as a Sufi and Buddhist!?!" And so in this state of limbo, Krassen experienced a lucid dream in conversation with

---

104. Isaac Bashevis Singer and Richard Burgin, Conversations with Isaac Bashevis Singer (New York: Doubleday Books, 1985).

105. Isaac Bashevis Singer, The Magician of Lublin: A Novel (New York: Macmillan, 2010).

106. Miles Krassen, Introduction: "Rabbi Israel Baal Shem Tov: Prophet of a New Paradigm," in Baal Shem Tov, The Pillar of Prayer: Teachings of Contemplative Guidance in Prayer, Sacred Study, and the Spiritual Life from the Baal Shem Tov and His Circle, trans. Menahem Kallus and ed. Aubrey L. Glazer (Louisville, KY: Fons Vitae, 2011), xiv–xxv.

107. Arthur Green, Tormented Master: A Life of Rabbi Nahman of Bratslav (Woodstock, VT: Jewish Lights Publishing, 1992).

108. Elie Wiesel, Souls on Fire: Portraits and Legends of Hasidic Masters (New York: Simon & Schuster, 2014).

Dalai Lama, where they exchanged a white scarf. Looking into each other's eyes, Krassen tells the Dalai Lama: "I'm sorry I have to be Jewish because of my father!" The Dalai Lama laughs and blesses Krassen. Krassen then awoke in a state of shock, and told his friend John Fewi, assistant to Thuptin Norbu, that this dream meant he was to be initiated as a Buddhist. Krassen disagreed—the dream meant he was obliged to follow the Jewish path.

Around this time, Krassen had already been hearing about the charismatic neo-Hasidic leaders, Reb Shlomo Carlebach, *z"l*,[109] and Reb Zalman, *z"l*,[110] both of whom had just moved to Philadelphia. These two ex-Chabad rabbis were renewing American Judaism through a neo-Hasidic lens all their own. The possibility of renewing the spirituality of American Judaism clearly influenced Krassen deeply, implanting seeds for the future at this point. After another stay with Barbara Kirshenblatt-Gimblett in the Lower East Side, Miles argued with Max (who was convinced Judaism was a mistake) while Barbara was encouraging Miles to pursue his interests in Judaism. Armed with all the Jewish paraphernalia he could amass in the Lower East Side, along with Hebrew primers from his father, and learning Talmud with Steinzaltz, Krassen embarked on a mission for Jewish learning. At that point Krassen realized the importance of having a teacher. So, while living in Bloomington, Krassen wrote to Reb Zalman asking advice for a teacher and sharing his visionary dreams. It was in the Leaves of Grass bookstore during the year of his NEA grant that Krassen happened on Reb Zalman's *Fragments of a Future Scroll*. Already having read this book, and being encouraged by the owner of the Leaves of Grass bookstore to pursue a deeper connection to the author, Krassen knew from these writings that he had to meet Reb Zalman. In those letters, Krassen confessed to Reb Zalman that he felt he himself was the reincarnation of a Hasidic rebbe. Henry Sapoznik, a banjo player and klezmer revivalist then called Krassen to let him know that he was also getting back into Judaism. The invitation was then opened to visit Henry and stay in his flat, in Flatbush, stopping off on

---

109. Natan Ophir, Rabbi Shlomo Carlebach: Life, Mission, and Legacy (Jerusalem: Urim Publications, 2014); Yaakov Ariel, "Hasidism in the Age of Aquarius: The House of Love and Prayer in San Francisco, 1967–1977," Religion and American Culture: A Journal of Interpretation 13, no. 2 (2003): 139–65. Compare with Sarah Blustain, "A Paradoxical Legacy: Rabbi Shlomo Carlebach's Shadow Side," Lilith 23, no. 1 (1998): 10; and more recently, see Sarah Imhoff, "Carlebach and the Unheard Stories," American Jewish History 100, no. 4 (2016): 555–60.

110. On his life and journey, see Shaul Magid, American Post-Judaism: Identity and Renewal in a Postethnic Society (Bloomington: Indiana University Press, 2013); on his manifestos for an American neo-Hasidism, see Zalman Schacter-Shalomi, Fragments of a Future Scroll: Ḥassidism for the Aquarian Age (Germantown, PA: Leaves of Grass Press, 1975); more recently, idem and Netanel Miles-Yepez, Foundations of the Fourth Turning of Hasidism: A Manifesto (Boulder, CO: Albion-Andalus Books, 2014).

the way to see Zalman at a *shabbaton* in his house at Emlin Street in Mount Airy.

That invitation uprooted Krassen instantaneously from Bloomington to Emlin Street, where he found himself immersed in that transformational Shabbat. There with Reb Zalman, they jammed higher and higher together with his fiddle and Reb Zalman's accordion all through that Shabbat, playing Hasidic niggunim. This was just before Danny Siegel was given ordination by Reb Zalman. At that time, Reb Zalman gave Krassen a number to call—Rabbi Meir Fund, who lived around the corner from Supposnik— "Would you like to meet Reb Shlomo Carlebach?" This seemingly simple question then led to years of immersive study in Dovid Deen's traveling yeshiva for "lost Jews," and spiritual seekers and freaks of all kinds in Boro Park that began after attending a Bobov wedding there. For Krassen, studying the magnum opus of Chabad Hasidism, the *Tanya*, took place for the first time in this context with Dovid Deen, but it did not draw him in to seek out Deen as his real teacher.[111] Krassen did not really feel at home in this setting, but remained and was paired in *hevruta* study with a certain prodigal Muncazer Hasid named Hayyim, who was doing therapy with Erich Fromm, and was clearly already off the path or what today has become a literary subgenre known as OTD.[112] Krassen was in a hurry to get the necessary text skills to open this sacred literature on his own, so to speed through that process, he was paired with Hayyim. Yet Hayyim disabused Krassen of all his naïve ideals of belief in "Torah true Judaism" that he may have brought in with him. While they would spend all morning learning Talmud, in the afternoon, they would go to learn Wittgenstein at Community College of New York in the Lower East Side.

This schizophrenic existence ultimately led to deep disillusionment with the Boro Park scene, as to whether there was any longer the possibility of upholding his naïve belief. Alan Kauffman, a fellow fiddler in the imminent New York Old music scene, was also a part of the Boro Park yeshiva milieu and equally disillusioned. And so a crisis moment emerged: Had Krassen really done the right thing by throwing himself back into Judaism? Then he met the editor of the main folk music forum called *Singout Magazine*! At that point, meeting editor and later Zen Roshi, Alan Senauke, invit-

---

111. For a different impression on the charisma of Dovid Deen as a teacher for Baalei teshuvah in Krasen's extended circles of affinity in Boro Park in that period, see Shaul Magid, "My Teacher's Son: A Memoir of Heresy Is Marked By a Father's Unnerving Piety," in http://www.tabletmag.com/jewish-arts-and-culture/books/190205/shulem-deen-dovid-din (accessed August 22, 2017).

112. OTD refers to going "Off The Derekh (Path)"; see Ezra Glinter, "Ex-Hasidic Writers Go Off the Derkeh and Onto The Page," Forward, May 27, 2014, http://forward. com/ culture/198622/ex-hasidic-writers-go-off-the-path-and-onto-the-pa/ (accessed August 23, 2017).

ed him to take a flat in his building in Park Slope. This allowed Krassen to transition back into the music scene, having become very disillusioned with Judaism while the music scene in New York was very rich. Krassen began writing liner notes for Shanakee Records for a number of the Irish music albums they released. Simultaneously, Supposnik brought Krassen to the Martin Steinberg Center for the Jewish Arts on the Upper West Side, run by Jeff Obler. The project that drew Krassen in was for the study of klezmer music, but research was not sufficient. While the klezmer revival could be said to have started with the band Klezmorim run by Martin Schwartz in Berkeley, something was also afoot in this klezmer revival in New York. And then, even further disillusioned, Krassen left the New York scene to return to Bloomington.

The next day, in the Indiana University newspaper there it was—a lecture being advertised in the newspaper on Hasidism by Professor Lawrence Fine. Krassen asked himself at the time, wondering:

> "What the hell was going on here!?! I left Bloomington after searching for Jews who knew of the Baal Shem Tov, the Kotzker or Reb Nachman—I was bereft! And the day I return, here is more Hasidism!"

Despite his disillusionment, and his default status as a graduate student in ethnomusicology, Krassen showed up, the only attendee, and listened intently to Larry's lecture. Miles's father showed up as well in Bloomington to help his son in supporting him in completing his graduate studies. Krassen then considered becoming a therapist with an MSW, but perusing his records of incomplete graduate studies they turned him down, thinking he was not serious enough. In returning to the bookstore, Krassen found himself in the religion department, he decided to enroll in the study of religion—after all, studying Hebrew and Aramaic would not hurt and needed no bureaucratic permissions. He took courses with Victor Danner on Sufism, Norbu on Buddhism, Fine on Jewish mysticism, and Henry Fischel on biblical Hebrew and Aramaic, and after the first semester, Krassen was the top student in every class he took. After one semester, he was asked to switch his major to religion with a full scholarship. He also picked up Weinrich's *College Yiddish*, and read Satmar's *Der Yid* and *Der Forwards* to improve his Yiddish, which he heard as a child but never understood. Not only did it not hurt, but also there was actually nothing he did not thoroughly enjoy. Studying in this way was an open doorway. Seeing the works of the Tolner rebbe, Dovidele Tzernovsky, especially made him salivate. Just trying to read the opening page, called the *sha'ar blatt*, took hours, but he knew he had to get deeper. Now nobody was looking over his shoulder, trying to control his mind and his behavior. Despite the oppression of Boro

Park, he could not find real meaning and was far from convinced that that *Baal teshuvah* movement was more reactionary than liberating. Bloomington provided that liberation, and only required attending and passing classes—what form of Jew was irrelevant.

Larry Fine, a student of Alexander Altmann, was tremendously kind and humble—these qualities of a teacher deeply touched Krassen. Every independent study he could get credit for, Krassen took with Fine. Starting with reading Zohar, Krassen moved through the mystical corpus of Kabbalah, reaching into some Hasidic literature. Krassen understood that Hasidism could not be penetrated in a meaningful way without this background in Kabbalah. After two years, Krassen completed his MA in Religious Studies, but there was no PhD program yet. Another crossroads emerged— *what next?*

Larry Fine called up Art Green, who was teaching at Penn, to get Krassen to continue with his PhD. Fischel wanted Krassen to study with the other Tolne rebbe, Isadore Twersky, at Harvard. Fine's conversation with Green seemed to be the tipping point: "Come to Philadelphia and see me." Krassen went and they talked for a few hours, and within that conversation Green asked him about what he was doing for Pesach. Krassen was reading Hasidism and Mordecai Kaplan—and so there was a meeting of the minds. He had to take the GRE and if he scored high enough, there would be a full scholarship. Krassen was accepted along with Seth Brody, of blessed memory, and Elliot Ginsburg. Those years Miles was a teaching assistant and began by studying *Kedushat Levi* in Art's sukkah, and mostly independent studies in Hasidism with a touch of Zohar and Talmud. After two years, Krassen had completed all the coursework for his MA and PhD, and then he passed comprehensive exams. It was Art who introduced Miles to all the Israeli academics in mysticism, like Moshe Idel, Rachel Elior, Rivka Schatz-Offenheimer, and Yehudah Liebes while he was studying there as a Lady Davis Fellow. Krassen stayed on for two years in Israel, befriending an old Boro Park ex-pat, Menachem Kallus, and Nehemia Polen. He made trips to *Meah Shearim* for sacred books known as *seforim* as well as the bookstore run by Kallus's cousin, aptly called The Hidden Corner or *Pinat haNistar*. The mystical group, known as *Argaman,* used the bookstore for meditation. This interested Krassen, insofar as it was an approach to Kabbalah that had much more resonance with esotericism, even though in Israel it became more of a *frum*, ultra-Orthodox group. The universalist aspects of Kabbalah and practice are what drew Krassen in further.

Would Krassen stay in Israel? A certain measure of disillusionment remained there for him. Avraham Flek was willing to support Krassen, but he left. "You're Jewish, ever heard of the Baal Shem Tov?" He drank some *Shelovitz* and told Hasidic tales. Miles was also writing for Haninya Goodman's newsletter on Kabbalah, but in the midst of the Gulf War, Krassen turned a decisive corner—he could no longer accept the tenets of Orthodox Judaism. The attempts at harmonization remained, but the tenets fell away as invalid. But Miles met Jeff Roth to become his student in Zohar, and also reconciled with Reb Zalman.

He returned to West Mount Airy, then to Emlin Street, where he was next door to Art Green and Zalman Schacter-Shalomi. They studied Zohar together. These early morning study meetings would oscillate between meticulous, literary analysis of the text with Art as opposed to ecstatic meta-level journeying with Zalman. In 1988, Krassen was married to an Italian woman he met in Israel named Giovanna Rosette. She had been living in Israel for a number of years and then returned with Krassen to Mount Airy. Lacking clarity about the depths of this love, Krassen decided that their love affair had to pass the muster of his mother. And so Miles and Giovanna happened to get married. But the love did not last.

At this time, Krassen was beginning to work through a translation of the *Peri Eitz Hadar*, which was enabled by a Rockefeller grant for *Shomrai Adamah* headed by Ellen Bernstein. Krassen was teaching Hasidism and meditation in the neighborhood. Sitting in the *Zendo* alternating with chanting led to altered states, and so Krassen sought to find a Jewish expression of this hybrid practice.

In the meantime, Krassen was still in the process of completing his PhD at Penn, on Rabbi Meshulam Zeibutz of Mebarashe's book of Hasidic mystical literature, called *Yosher Divrai Emeth*. Miles's choice emerged from a conversation with Art Green that very often something from the *Yosher Divrai Emeth* made an impression on him, even in English translation. As a concise *sefer*, the *Yosher Divrai Emeth* presented the possibility of mastering it, leading to *Uniter of Heaven and Earth*. The emphasis on *devekut* or *unio mystica* was a means of establishing a direct connection with the divine. This served as a source of guidance; in contrast to other Hasidic books, it was well written in a discursive, comprehensive presentation predating the *Tanya*.

Hananya Goodman, editor of the Kabbalah newsletter, was looking for a translator of the *Shenai Luchot haBrit*, focusing only the *Toledot Adam* section, and Krassen was more than qualified and ready to step up to the task. At the same time as the scud missiles were falling in Israel during the first Persian Gulf War, Smith College opened up a one-year appointment as assistant professor from 1992–93. While Krassen was teaching there, a position at Oberlin opened up, which provided more stability as a tenure-track position. Krassen took a one-year sabbatical in Berkeley during the 1995–96 schoolyear, where he substituted for Danny Matt, who was touring with *The Essential Kabbalah*. Returning to Oberlin, in his joint appointment in religion and Jewish studies, Krassen was granted tenure. Krassen connected with the Hillel rabbi, Shimon Brand, where they studied together every Shabbat. His creative halakhic outlook was inspiring to Krassen. The other relation that impacted Krassen was James A. Morris, an expert in Ibn al-Arabi. His office neighbored Krassen's. A certain kind of student was collecting around Morris and Krassen, and the department was becoming very suspect of such gurus.

To the shock of all, a year after receiving tenure, Krassen resigned. This was another moment of repudiation that recurred throughout his career. Academe was an attempt to hold things together, but it was never Krassen's real interest. It was related but not salient to Miles's real interest—spiritual search and practice. So Krassen wandered to Cleveland, where he spent time in a *Chabad shteibl, Tzemakh Tzedek* run by Rabbi Tazin, where Susanna Heschel also hovered from nearby Case Western University. Krassen connected deeply to *Chabad niggunim* in the dark, yet he was disappointed by the depth of interconnected study. It was a place of lost authenticity that meant something to Krassen, who could really understand the teachings. Whenever Krassen would ask a question there was never a satisfying discussion, just more sentimental, old-world Hasidism.

Krassen was really beginning to really enjoy teaching on retreat at *Elat Chayyim*. Krassen felt like he finally was teaching like a rebbe, and he was tired of masquerading as an academic when, at the heart of things, he was a mystic. This was the moment of our first encounter that I will never forget. So, after resigning from Oberlin, Krassen moved back to Philadelphia to do freelance teaching, living comfortably in a Center City co-op around 2000. At the same time, Reb Zalman resigned from Naropa University, and Hazzan Richard Kaplan called Krassen to gauge his interest in succeeding Reb Zalman. On speaking to Zalman about it, Miles wondered whether he really wanted to be there. Krassen was done with academe, but the spiritual environment was exactly what he wanted. Krassen moved to Boulder to work on what he considered a great experience in his spiritual evolution.

Both in Tucson and Albuquerque, Krassen has most recently committed himself to exploring *Rain of Blessing*, shifting into Gaian modes of Planetary Judaism. It is Jewish only insofar as it is the Judaism that ends Judaism. It is a critique of Judaism that moves from the monotheistic to the Gaian planetary mode. In terms of the spiritual approach, his kindred spirit is Jesuit eco-theologist Thomas Berry. It is this genuine search to sketch out a post-mysticism of Timothy Leary and Robert Anton Wilson, who understand evolutionary biology as a fulcrum with the recognition of the evolutionary nature of human existence, questioning and repudiating anything that is not an immediate part of life, of *being human*. Given that existence is in a transitional period, there are stages of Judaism's unraveling, where it is not necessarily becoming something else, but those who are part of it are becoming something else. There are treasures that remain preserved within Judaism that have power to contribute to finding the way. Now it is a matter of finding those The Vanishing Path. It is a reformulating the way that is irreducible and cannot be reduced to rules. Within this treasure house, there are certain clues along this way. Since this way has no name, one can be within the forms of Judaism and find this way. What has to go is any attachment to the dogmatic principles of Judaism which are in conflict with the finding of the way in its unknowability.

Yet transcending and including, at times negating for the sake of creating, has a broad scope, and it is embraced by most schools of Hasidism including Chabad, Bratzlav, Zlotchov, as well as Young Turks like R. Yitzhak Maeir Morgenstern, and by practitioners of many world religions, such as Kashmir Shaivism, Vedantana Buddhism, Thomas Merton, Idries Shah, Krishnamurti, even spanning into American novelists like Phillip Roth and Kurt Vonnegut. His appetite for knowledge is insatiable—daily, this is really the only consistent pathway Krassen continues to traverse. As my teacher, colleague, friend, and rebbe for over a decade and counting, I have even learned how such The Vanishing Path toward this Torah of the future encompasses and repudiates everything, including the best fair trade, organic coffee roasters on the planet—how else could one appreciate his Planetary Judaism without the right dosage?! And so, how fitting these words were transmitted in a Jerusalem café. After all, as Krassen was quick to remind me, Gurdjieff is said to have met with his five closest disciples every day at an appointed hour at a café in Moscow. How apt that Ouspensky, the disciple seemingly the least equipped to *grok* the master in the end was the one who transmitted the greatest kernel of his legacy. May these words serve as a worthy sketch toward that ineffable path at once hidden in plain sight while vanishing before our very eyes. . .

How to Make Time Count

The human desire to make time count is perennial. Yet how can time really count if it is constantly in flux? Try as one might, cycles can never ultimately capture the fleeting quality of time. Yet as the philosophers see it, the time of eternal recurrence[113] is an archetypal attempt at constructing cycles we call the calendar. Each month returns within a seemingly eternal pattern of recurrence from year to year, and years from jubilee to jubilee and so on. In general, our understanding of time and its manifestation in

---

113. For more on eternal recurrence, see Aubrey L. Glazer, "Coda: Burning Beyond 'You Want it Darker,'" in Tangle of Matter & Ghost: Leonard Cohen's Post-Secular Songbook of Mysticism(s) Jewish & Beyond (Brighton, MA : Academic Studies Press, 2017), 238–47.

the Gregorian calendar, is influenced in the West by the chronology of the archetypes of *Kronos* and Kairos. *Keva* and *Kavvanah* . . .

But to be in time to love and to truly understand making time count through the calendar requires a re-appreciation of family time embodied the *Senex-Puer* archetypes. At first blush, *Senex-Puer* archetypes could not seem further from the question of time, and yet, the Wise Elder and the Youth profoundly affect textures of time. I turn to James Hillman's interpretation of *Senex* as a temporal path-mark, which is instructive, insofar as:

> The *senex* emblem of the skull signifies that every complex can be envisioned from its death aspect, its ultimate psychic core where all flesh of dynamics and appearances is stripped away and there is nothing left of those hopeful thoughts of what it might yet become, the "final" interpretation of the complex as its end. The end gives the pessimistic and cynical reflection as counterpart to *puer* beginnings.[114]

As humans continue longing for superior knowledge, systems and habits give way to strong feelings about time, the past and death, and so the *Senex* archetype is symbolized not only by the skull but also in a much more familiar and domesticated tool of the timepiece.[115]

And so, not surprisingly, the cold, distant, withdrawn *Senex* view is that possibility of abstraction that gives way to presenting principles of form, anatomy of events, plots and episodes rather than connections, interrelations, or the flow of feeling. We shall return to this flow of feeling embedded within the Hebrew psyche's sense of time shortly, but the *Senex* view draws downward, inward like the pull of gravity into subjectivity.[116] The *Senex* imagery is manifest in the form of the calendar as an effort to isolate cosmic systems and geometric diagrams, especially in the structured mandala where Saturn is in the penultimate concentric circle, no longer recognizable as symbolizing the Wise Elder:[117]

And so already, we see just how much of a certain paradox there is regarding time. While the *Senex* mind moves us to embrace wholeness through integration, arrival at such a goal is determined by *Senex* fantasies of depression, suffering, introversion, and imagination of the kind that turns us away from the world. Yet at the same time, to retain such stability through the ordering of time, there is a stress on numbers as archetypal

---

114. James Hillman, Blue Fire (New York: Harper & Row, 1989), 209.

115. Hillman, Blue Fire, 208.

116. Ibid., 209.

117. C. G. Jung, "Integra Natura," in The Red Book, https://www.loc.gov/exhibits/red-book-of-carl-jung/redbookandbeyond/Assets/rb0014_enlarge.jpg (accessed February 6, 2017).

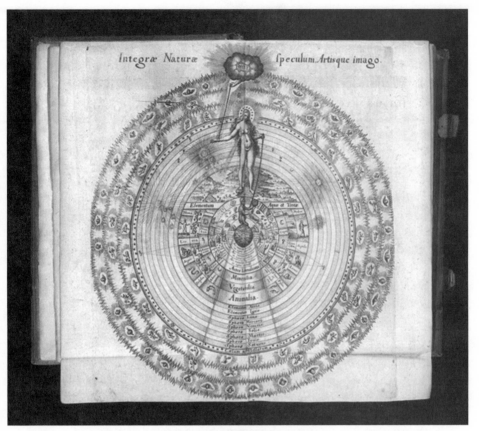

Figure 1. Alchemist Zodiac Wheel, *Integra Natura*.

root structures as a balance of opposites that belongs to *Kronos-Saturn*.[118] Here the power of the imagination is key, and should not be dismissed as a usurping heir replacing the Wise Elder, rather, *vis imaginativa*. If indeed "only *senex* has the sense of time needed for the seasons and their chronic repetition,"[119] then *Puer* is that necessary potency of creativity and drive that pushes against the stultified myth of eternal recurrence. This stands in opposition to the cold, distant, withdrawn *Senex* view of abstraction that gives way to principles of form; it is precisely at this pressure point that *Puer* view overcomes the loneliness and the affectionless objectivity of the calendar.

To merely view *Senex*-consciousness as "cut off from the feminine"[120] is to miss the deeper texture of the feminine correlated to Kronos, including

---

118. Hillman, Blue Fire, 209.
119. Ibid., 211.
120. Ibid., 212.

his mother (Demeter), his wife (Hera), and his daughter (Hestia), as well as Kronos's female counterparts in Lua, Dame Melancholy—all manifest "the unpleasant, even maleficent, aspects of the anima."[121] *Senex* femininity is akin to the dark side of the mother archetype, wherein earthiness of goddesses is intertwined with an excess of pneuma. And when this *Senex* state threatens to stultify, and the oscillation emerges so that the *Puer* state is reawakened by reconnecting to the child within oneself, eliciting a sudden ebbing and flowing again of unconscious emotions.[122]

And so, evident here in the dialectical tension between *Senex-Puer*, between the kabbalistic symbols of *Savah-Yenukah*, there appears to be an ontological image of two levels of being and two structures of consciousness.[123] *Senex-Puer* and *Savah-Yenukah* really symbolize the two simultaneous levels of being on which we live and oscillate, moving from one to another, so that there are not periods of time but moments of consciousness.

Senex or *Savah* is that archetype of the imaginal elder, longing for superior knowledge, imperturbability, magnanimity; intolerance for that which crosses one's systems and habits; ideas and feelings about time, the past, and death; obsessive memory ruminations; omniscient, omnipotent, eternal, a ruler through abstract principles of justice, morality, and order, an attachment to words yet not given to self-explanation in speech, benevolent but enraged when his will is crossed; removed the feminine (wifeless) and the sexual aspect of creation, up high with a geometric world of stars and planets in the cold and distant night of numbers; views the worlds from the outside, without heart, from such depth of distance that he sees it all upside down, and to this view the structure of things is revealed; he sees the irony of truth within words; gives abstract architecture and anatomy of events, plots, and graphs, presenting principles of form rather than connections, interrelations, or the flow of *Puer* and *Yenukah* archetype.

Puer and *Yenukah* is that archetypal aspect of the soul that seeks and calls to the spirit, primordial golden shadow, affinity for beauty, angelic essence, messenger of the divine, Messiah; ecstasy and guilt are part of the pattern of sonship; everyone should recognize the Great Mother in his actions and take flight from her relatedness into lofty abstraction and impersonal fantasy, still the viceroy is the son filled with the animus of the goddess, her pneuma (*neshamah*), her breath, and wind; viceroy serves the Great Mother best by making such divisions between his light and her darkness, his spirit and her matter, between his world and hers.

Is the Hebrew psyche of *Savah-Yenukah*, which sees time beyond chro-

---

121. Ibid.
122. Ibid., 213.
123. Ibid., 214.

Figure 2. Zodiac Wheel, *Beit Alpha*.

nology, constantly disrupting and critiquing it,[124] so different from *Senex-Puer*? One would be hard pressed, at first glance of the synagogue floors in mosaic at *Beit Alpha* in the Galilee of Israel[125] to see such a distinction! Take some time, a simple moment, and see what is at the center of this Hebrew Zodiac! Notwithstanding Helios, the sun god in the center, ancient Jewish astrologers were not in the least vexed by these early images of the cycles of time and their convergence with glyphs known to most in the Greco-Roman world as astronomy. While sages like Rabbi Akivah suggest

124. On completing this preface, I was pleasantly surprised to discover a wonderful analysis correlating post-Jungian archetypal psychology and Zohar; see Jonathan Benarroch, "Sava-Yanuka and Enoch-Metatron as James Hillman's Senex-Puer Archetype: A Post-Jungian Inquiry to a Zoharic Myth" [in Hebrew], in The Exegetic Imagination: Relationships Between Religion and Art in Jewish Culture (Jerusalem: Magnes Press, 2016), 46–71.

125. See Figure 2 above. Beit Alpha mosaic, Galilee, Israel, https://upload.wikimedia. org/wikipedia/com- mons/9/96/Beit_alfa01.jpg (accessed February 6, 2017).

that "the Israelites do not depend on the zodiac,"[126] he and his colleagues were versant enough in astronomy to know what not to depend on. What's at stake in this stage of rabbinic Judaism is the concern that some other knowledge of the ways the divine works in the world might impede on conviction in the one, unique Creator of the Universe. Nothing could be further from the truth, but sometimes truth is buried, and all that remains is a veneer of living with peace.

Awareness of the cycles of becoming is a concern that emerges from contemplating the created world. If one begins seeing creation from its multiple angles, then fractal patterns begin to emerge, and from the vantage point of so many angles we encounter *Sefer Yetzirah*. This discrete book of mysticism is a "divine *ars poetica.*"[127] By attributing the authorship of *Sefer Yetzirah* to Abraham, the ancestor of what becomes the religion of Judaism, there is an embrace here of a non-kabbalistic treatise that becomes a vade mecum for the Kabbalah.[128] As the first philosopher and ideal mystic, Abraham, much like Krassen, is a veritable iconoclast deconstructing and reimagining the world through its elemental parts, dwelling in the sacred energy of divine letters, phonemes, and words. Given its strange and startling style, one notices how *Sefer Yetzirah* makes an "attempt to account in Hebrew and within the context of Jewish thought for a way of thinking and experiencing the world that Hebrew culture and the Hebrew language could not yet accommodate."[129] In this sense, *Sefer Yetzirah* really exemplifies what Krassen is transmitting as a Torah of the Future now. Consider this next representation of this earlier glyph, here revealed in *Sefer Yetzirah*.

Notice a deeper correlation between each month, its astrological sign, its associated tribe, and the permutation of the divine name. What is instructive here is mystical shape of the godhead that is always in a state of becoming. Each month the divine name is seen as both center and circumference, radiating out from its singular origin to the circumference of its plurality each month. That is, each month there is another permutation of the divine name that dies and is reborn within the monthly texture.[130]

Notice that YHVH, the configuration of the divine name we are most familiar with, is aligned with the month of *Nissan*, Aries, and the tribe of Judah—for this is the month with the strongest associations to redemp-

---

126. See the Talmudic source, bShabbat 156a, *Ein mazel l'yisrael*. After all, if the divine totality has the power to choreograph the constellations, from place to place so as to change their influence, then what is there to worry about astrology?

127. Peter Cole and Aminadav Dykman, The Poetry of Kabbalah: Mystical Verse from the Jewish Tradition (New Haven, CT: Yale University Press, 2012), 37.

128. Cole and Dykman, The Poetry of Kabbalah, 38.

129. Ibid., 39.

130. Abraham the Ancestor, Sefer Yetzirah (The Book of Creation), trans. Aryeh Kaplan (York Beach, ME: Weiser, 1997).

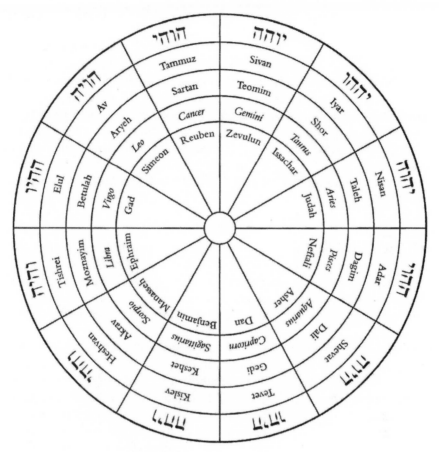

Figure 3. Zodiac Wheel, *Sefer Yetzirah.*

tion.[131] The Hebrew archetypal view of calendrical time—at once of being and becoming, of *Savah* and *Yenukah*—absorbs Near Eastern mythologies, but then depersonalizes the persona of each of the warring gods into a singular deity with a plurality of extensions each month.

To make time really count is to see how time hangs in the balance, off-balance to be re-balanced—so one needs to experience the teaching of time in the time of the true teacher. And so what follows is more or less what I

---

131. Is redemption correlated to metallurgy and smelting universal bonds between tribes? A recent theory suggests that the cult of YHVH as god of metallurgy originated among semi-nomadic copper smelters between the Bronze and Iron Age; see Ariel David, "Jewish God Yahweh Originated in Canaanite Vulcan," HaAretz, April 11, 2018, https://www.haaretz.com/archaeology/.premium.MAGAZINE-jewish-god-yahweh-originated-in-canaanite-vulcan-says-new-theory-1.5992072 (accessed June 11, 2018). Thanks to Kathy Fields-Rayant for sharing this fascinating source with me.

heard and experienced face-to-face with my teacher, Reb Moshe Aharon Krassen, as he was opening a portal in time to a few fellow seekers in what he called an *Or RADLA* initiation that took place at the *Naropa Institute* in Boulder, Colorado, November 2016.[132] By gathering in this place and time with other students and seekers devoted to the teachings of Krassen, I found myself surrounded with friends from around the world, especially close to my heart, my dear friend, Cantor George Mordecai. We both have been intent upon making time count, especially having felt as if we were billeted belowground together in a hog slaughterhouse for six years, imprisoned in the same seminary walls together. So, we were both intrigued as usual when Miles began his discourse, off-balance as usual, from the strangest time-space continuum...

Friendship as Time Off-balance

How do you elevate your friend through chastisement? It is part of our sacral devotion to point out to friends if they are *off*, and it is an obligation to tell them, as we read in Reb Nachman.[133] Even though it is a great obligation to care what others are doing, nevertheless, not everybody is really qualified to correct others. Rabbi Akivah doubts whether in his own age anyone was qualified to criticize others, and so, if such a great rabbinic leader doubted the possibility, what does it say about us? If you tell your friend that he or she is not on the level, then not only is it unproductive, not accomplishing anything, but actually it makes someone smell bad. If you try to criticize someone, not only do you not make it better, you make the situation stink. Saying "that stinks what you did"—it actually makes it stink, causing a stench and damaging the soul of the one you are criticizing, making them weaker not better. This causes a stench rather than making the soul more beautiful. When you hurt someone else, it reduces the quality of the divine flow coming into the world. For it is the soul that can pull in the divine flow, so when the soul is hurt, the flow is impeded. That soul is no longer able to channel its flow, and in a planetary sense, you are hurting the whole world. The divine flow depends on those souls and now cannot make its way into the world, and your stench is impeding their entry into this world. The soul, according to rabbinic tradition, as the *neshamah* is related to the olfactory senses, smelling out the situation. So what is it that the soul enjoys and not the body? It is incense, and this is why good incense gets the *neshamah* very interested. So, unless your soul is of a certain elevation, it is not a good idea to criticize others, and that damages the planetary balance of divine flow from souls into this world, and all the parts

---

132. Or RADLA, refers to the "Light of the unknown beginning," a primordial moment in the unfolding of infinite light into the finite world of perception.

133. Liqqutei Moharan Tinyana, no. 8.

of creation depending on that soul for this divine soul will not receive it. But when you have someone who is really qualified, then it has the opposite effect. The person who can do it is the person who can make it smell better so that another person does not get hurt, embarrassed, or humiliated, lest they stand out and feel uncomfortable. The only way you can really do it is by making the situation smell better. The chastisement needs to be on the level of Moses, who brings up the issue of the Golden Calf, doing it in such a way that he made the Israelites smell good. Rather than saying, "What idiots you are!" it was mentioned, but it was mentioned in a spicy way that adds fragrance. This is a quality of *Hod*, or splendor, insofar as the aroma is enhanced. It was a matter of the divine coordinates, giving the mapping of their sojourns, passing through the coordinates of their *neshamah*, teaching us what happens when you pass through certain coordinates of *Olam*-Space and *Shanah*-Time where things happen. It's about pointing out what happened without judgment. To get to the world-that-is-coming, you have to be on the level of Moses; you cannot make others smell bad. As we move to the new paradigm, we have to do this on so many levels, being in a situation as W. I. Thompson suggests, moving from the national to the noetic qualities. It is like a multinational corporation. When Americans lose jobs, who cares about specific people? They only care about bottom line. So we have a situation that is a function of globalization. Now you can say all those people stink, let's go and yell at the corporations, but that is not going to help us. What will help us is if we can see another way that would be of benefit to the maximum number of people in the planet. This is not going to work—this is going to precipitate a crash of the paradigm. But it creates a situation where too many people have too little and too many people have too much, which leads to a paradigm crash. That's "the little that hold[s] a lot"; the elite that has everything is not going to work. We need the other "little that holds a lot," which is the *sekhel*, and there is no sense in that, because they themselves are not going to survive, and the world is going to smell so terrible that no one will stand it. We have to go to the level of Mosaic-messianic consciousness, use the light of *RADLA*, and see the world-that-is-coming, to see what everyone really needs so that every gets what they need and it can be a world of glory and splendor (*hod v'hadar*).

Regarding being priests and becoming a holy nation, we learn from Reb Nachman[134] that this is the lineage we have to *become*. In the old paradigm, priests were determined by biological Judaism, but in the new paradigm priests are determined by what they *would do* in the world-that-is-coming. A real *cohen* or *cohenet* is related to the Abrahamic consciousness—and what is Abraham but the embodiment of priestliness that is a quality of love? The place of this love is the mediating sphere of *Yesod*, which is

---

134. Liqquatai Moharan, no. 34:7.

associated with Love and Peace. The place in the body which is the covenantal—the lower *Dan Chen*, the point in the lower abdomen, relating to
the revelation of *Da'at*-Intuition—you want to raise to the heart with the
center in *Yesod*. Doing things from the *kishkes*, from *Yesod*, that's this quality of being real—which is the secret of Hasidism. You cannot get it in your
heart if you cannot get in your *kishkes*.[135] Otherwise, it has no depth to it.
There is the surface of the heart and the depth of the heart—so you have to
go through the capacity of *Yesod* as tzaddik.

To do this, you need three things. First, you need to have the hook up
and communication with the Source of All Life— this is what prophetic
consciousness really means: that I'm in the communication with the place
of *RADLA* life, giving me guidance, and that I'm talking to God. The first
person I met who was actually doing that was Reb Zalman, *o.b.m.*; I had
never seen anybody just standing there, talking to God as if it was nothing
at all. He was a master of that, doing it his whole life. That's the way he
lived his whole life. Reb Zalman was a very earthy guy, from his earthiness
to what is beyond time and space, the place of *RADLA* life, the *Tiferet* of
Yetzirah, the *Ata*-You when everything is non-dual. Through your earthiness you can create a connection to the source of the effluence that is coming down. When you connect to it at the highest level, there is no content
at all. That's very high and beautiful but it's not enough if you are doing
the work of the world-that-is-coming. We are dealing with the "glory and
splendor in which She is enshrouded";[136] you have to go up and get it and
then bring it down, and when it gets to your heart you have the *Ata*-You—
an embodied god as a real *Ata*-You that you can talk to. When you connect
to the light of *RADLA*, through the interface point of "the little that holds a
lot," allowing it to come deeper into your heart, it becomes an *Ata*-You that
you can relate to from your personal experience. Then you can arouse and
awaken this *Yesod* sphere, so this sphere can speak to the heart, bringing
it understanding. The interiority of the heart is not accessible unless you
stimulate through what you feel in the *kishkes*. Bratzlav, which our lineage
is directly connected to, means "heart of flesh" (*Basar Lev*), so I'm going
teach you how to soften up your heart, to connect the *Yud* and *Vav*.

The second important practice is that we have to relate to each other,
like angels, getting something special from each person, each spark, each
light, so that the only way you will get the light that someone else has to
share is to have these heartfelt conversations. You have to talk about the
way you are getting influenced from the way the light of *RADLA* is coming through you. This is part of the getting everyone together in the art of
envisioning the world-that-is-coming. Everyone has different colors and

---

135. In Yiddish, *kishkes* literally means the belly or gut.
136. Proverbs 31:25.

different pieces, to get what the other person has—but there is no way it all comes down in one person. Somebody else has some piece of it more than you do, no matter who you are. In this way, it is the other person's point of view that matters.

It is in the sharing of these points that this love is expressed. When you are giving and receiving your point of view through the transmission that comes through, you are a *cohen*. The *cohen* is the one who receives, while the one who gives is the tzaddik. You have to a be *cohen* to someone else's tzaddik, and that will then cause your heart to sparkle and shine, so that one heart stimulates the heart of another person.

The third point is that all the points together form a network that connects to a source that unites them all. That's why it is so important that we have a lineage that connects us to something we are all part of. That's what lineage holding and consciousness is about. So, the lineage source is the collective soul, the network that forms a tabernacle from all the points of individual hearts, brought together and held together to create this full stature. The lineage establishes the point of view and what it's all about. If you don't have a lineage, you don't have a Torah. The lineage is what is projecting the Torah of the world-that-is- coming, and, if you have this Torah, then each one receives the specific way that he or she gets in his or her heart, becoming a tzaddik for others, but you have to have a blueprint. When we see the main characteristics of the Torah of the world-that-is-coming then we can contribute to it, as we know what we can do. Then each individual can do his own connecting, his own *Tefillah*, his own prophetic connection to "the little that holds a lot."

The *RADLA* lineage holds it together, regardless of the shortcomings, and then the love that holds this lineage will override whatever errancy that may arise. With these three components, you are connected to the lineage which draws the collective light of interconnectivity. Therefore, whomever is connected to the lineage your heart will be stimulated by, and through the work we do with each other, tzaddik/et and *cohen/et*, each person can help each other's heart to shine. And also the work you do on your own, however you do that, it will also keep your heart alive. The lineage of the Torah, the relationships we have with each other, increases the capacity of each heart to contribute to the realization of the paradigm shift, and the inner work you do on your heart all contributes to it. In that way one can have a real heart that feels. That is what it means to be a "holy nation"; we want to be an organization that performs the priestly duty that manifests the basis of the parable of the world-that-is-coming. To be able to set ourselves at the tzaddik point in the *kishkes*, really rooted in the abdomen, where awareness is housed, where our real being comes from, raising up and bringing down to there, which is the letter *Vav*, the capacity to connect above and below. We are not to just bliss out in *RADLA* that is beyond thinking and the mind, but to also have the connecting *Vav*, so that what comes in, comes through the light of *RADLA*. The connecting *Vav* needs the *Yod*, so that impulse comes from the tzaddik, to make an effort to stimulate the heart. The heart has so much loving in it, so that when the heart is warm the spring cannot resist it, drawing down the light of *RADLA*. Love is irresistible, the beloved cannot resist being loved. But how do you get there? Prayers that come from the heart and that arise through the stimulation through the three points of the lineage, of each person being a tzaddik by virtue of being a *cohen*, and by one's own micro-process of being so full of longing that God cannot resist you. *It is in such waiting, so full of longing, for what will unfold that the promise of love finds it way home . . .*

Aubrey L. Glazer
Panui
San Francisco/Guerneville, CA
16th of Tevet[137]–New Month of Tammuz, 5778

---

137. 16th Tevet is the anniversary of the passing of Rabbi Alan Lew, o.b.m. (d. January 12, 2009/5769).

Chapter 1
Positive Power of Concealment in Purim

1.0 Compassion and Re/membering—*Shabbatot* Preceding Purim

It's very lovely, and such a wonderful opportunity, to absorb the energy of Adar. There's a saying in the rabbinic teachings, that if you really want something to succeed, you should plant some "ADR" in it. (Actually, they are talking about planting *EDeR* [Cedar] which has the same letters as *ADaR* only with different vowels.) Sometimes that's understood as "you should do your planting in Adar"—which conveniently comes at about the right time for people in a lot of places to do their planting, but it's strange the way the blessed sages teach that you should plant Adar *in* something.

1.1 Remembering Compassion

The energy of Adar is really very special, and when you come to the month of Adar there are always extra-special Torah readings, in keeping with the energy of the month. Before you get to Purim, you have two special readings each Shabbat before you come to Purim: you have *Shabbat Shekalim*, and then you have *Shabbat Zachor*: the Shabbat which is called "shekels" and the Shabbat which is called "remember."

To get to Purim you have to get the energy of shekels, and the energy of remembering. "Shekels" means money—namely, you have to get the energy of spiritual capital. In the old days, people paid a certain tax, in shekels: you had to pay your dues, basically. This matter of spiritual capital really means tzedakah, or charity: when you give something to other people. In other words, money basically means compassion.

First of all, you have to have a Shabbat of compassion, of caring, of being willing to give to people who need, because that's a very direct expression of sharing the quality of the tzaddik, the righteous person—how we can make ourselves closer to the model that I believe the Creator has in mind for us. The divine hope is for us is to become tzaddikim in this world. We have a verse which is proof for that: "All of God's people are tzaddikim."[1] So everyone who comes into the mold, the form that God really wants for him or her, comes into some kind of a tzaddik model. Each

---

1. Isaiah 60:21.

one is different from the other, because there's not just one mold—but everyone has his or her place to fill within the totality of being.

So before you can get to Purim, you have to have *shekalim* and you have to have *zachor*. You have to have compassion, to be a sharer, to be able to give something righteously, to share of what you have with others.

1.2 "Amalek" Means That Which Attacks Us at Our Weakest Point

And then the Shabbat that comes right before Purim is called *Shabbat Zachor*, the Shabbat to remember. But what are we supposed to remember? We are supposed to remember "*zecher* Amalek." We are supposed to remember Amalek, a people in the biblical story who are infamous for attacking the Israelites when they were at the weakest point. They sneak up on the Israelites when they have been decimated by all kinds of problems of life, and they attack us from the rear. Amalek sneaks up from behind and attacks the weakest people who are struggling to keep up. They don't attack Moses and the leaders; they pick off all the weak people—the most vulnerable parts of ourselves.

We have to understand what this memory is, what we have to *zachor*. In the Torah it says, "Remember to blot out the memory of Amalek—don't forget."[2] Don't forget to remember. And that's the end of the special reading that we have for this Shabbat. *Don't forget to remember that we have to blot out every bit of Amalek. It is the quality of Amalek that sneaks up on us. What gets us in our weakest place and brings us down where we are most vulnerable.* We have to remember to watch out for a sneaky power that holds us back from reaching our potential—that holds us back from becoming tzaddikim, the people that can enter the "Holy Land."

We have one *parsha* or portion of Torah, *Shekalim*, that deals with money, that deals with tzedakah, that deals with giving. This is the side of compassion, the side of the heart, the side of caring, the side of sharing—all of those attributes that we need to have in order to be prepared to reach the highest of the high. And another that cautions us to be careful—not to become too self-assured.

1.3 Purim Has Eternal Significance and Is as High as Yom Kippur

There's a rabbinical pun that equates Purim with Yom Kippurim, because Yom Kippur is literally *Yom ki-Purim*—a day that is *like* Purim. It's a pun, you see; the word *k'* in Hebrew means "like," so *Yom HaKippurim* is a day *like* Purim. Everybody already knows that Yom Kippur is the highest day of the year, but if Yom Kippur is like Purim, then Purim must also be as high as Yom Kippur. So Purim is very, very special in its own way; it's different from Yom Kippur, but it's every bit as high, even though we often don't

---

2. Deuteronomy 25:17.

think of it as one of the most holy of the holy days.

But, in fact, it's such a powerful time that when the sages were reflecting on what would be on the other side of the messianic age, what the world would look like, what Judaism would look like, they claimed we would still have Purim. The other holidays we maybe wouldn't need, once there was a paradigm shift represented by the idea of a messianic age, but Purim is eternal. *Purim has an eternal validity, an eternal significance.* And that's how high it is. It's something that's unconditional—regardless of the construction of whatever paradigm we might find ourselves living in, there would still be Purim.

So how do we get to the place where we could have our share of Purim in this particular year? We need to go through tzedakah, through compassion—through all the aspects which have the power to give us the means of opening our heart in this world, through caring and sharing; and we need to remember something, to remember to blot out Amalek—that power that sneaks up on us and overcomes us. That's the side of wisdom. We have a compassion side, and we have a wisdom side.

What do we need to know to protect ourselves from our vulnerability? To put these two things together—this Shabbat of spiritual capital, of tzedakah, of "paying our dues," of sharing what we have, and the Shabbat of realizing, of absorbing what it is that we need to remember. If we could bring these two sides together, we could have what we need to prepare for Purim.

1.4 Haman, Amalek, and the Counteractive Mordechai Force

If we look at the question of Amalek in rabbinic literature, the rabbis basically equate Haman and Amalek. The enemy of the book of Esther, Haman, is an incarnation of Amalek, who represents this same problem that can overthrow us—that can come between us and bring us down—and maybe even have a possibility of destroying us, at least for a time.

When you think about this story, Haman represents the archenemy of the Jews in the book of Esther, and is an aspect or representation of this Amalek quality. And you have to think very carefully about what the antidote to Haman is, which is called Mordechai haYehudi, Mordechai the Jew. If you take the name Mordechai, you can calculate its meaning according to the numerology known as gematria. That is to say, take each letter of the name, convert it into a numerical value, and add them all up, because very often, the secrets of the Torah are revealed in these associations, in the gematria, which give you a possibility of recognizing relationships between things that are not obvious. The power of the name Mordechai is concealed, but we will rediscover it later on.

The name Mordechai is the garment that's holding something inside it. So you could say that the name Mordechai is a *kissui* or a "covering."

Mordechai is the concealment of something that's very precious. And it's well known that when the rabbis talk about Adar, one of the main topics that comes up is that the divine is basically absent in the book of Esther—God doesn't play a direct role. So this is really a teaching about concealment, and how within concealment—which we might think of as something which is not so positive—actually, if you look at it in a very deep way, assuming we know the great secret of life, we can begin to see concealment in a very positive way.

1.5 Positive Power of Concealment

Within concealment comes the possibility of everything that has still yet to manifest. It's precisely in concealment, where you can't find something that in fact, you *can* find something. It's only that what is there *is not what you know.* But take, for example, the present moment, like this one, right now: even if we are very present at this moment, there's more concealed in this moment than we know. *Regardless of what we can see, how much more is concealed in this moment!* This moment has the entire past and the entire future, because this moment could not be here unless every other moment preceded it. This moment doesn't stand alone—it's a link between the past and the future, and it comes partly because of everything that preceded it. It's connected to everything that came before it. *Everything that came before it is in fact concealed within this moment,* however it looks. But we don't see that. Our conscious mind does not know everything.

We might think that however we are experiencing this moment is all that there is, but so much more is happening. We can't even begin to know everything that's *in this moment.* And if that's true of the past, all the more so it's true of the future. We don't know what the future holds; but its entirety, all of its possibilities, are contained in this moment. So this very moment is a teaching on concealment.

1.6 Dangers of the Concealment of Concealment—"Deep Sleep"

But that concealment is not necessarily a bad thing. The only thing that makes it a bad thing—and here I'm referring to the Baal Shem Tov's great teaching on concealment that I like to remember at this time—concealment is not so bad; it's *concealment of concealment that's the problem. If I know that there's concealment, then that's OK. Even if I don't know exactly what's concealed, at least I know that something is concealed: there's much more there, there's much more depth.* Reality is not really limited to whatever I think it is. And of course the real meaning of concealment, what it always comes down to in the deepest sense, is that "God" *is within every concealment. Concealment makes it seem like God isn't present, but as long as we know that it's concealment—and the Baal Shem Tov taught this over and*

over again—as long as we recognize that we are dealing with concealment, we are very close to gilui *or revelation.*
We are very close to finding something more.

1.7 Problem: When We Forget There Is Concealment

The concealment of concealment means I don't even know there's conceal-ment; and if I don't even know there's concealment, that's called deep sleep. Deep sleep or forgetfulness, *shikcha*—a kind of amnesia.

And that deep, deep, deep possibility that we might really fall asleep—and of course, we know that we are falling asleep all the time, but that's not really so bad as long as we can wake up. But it's only really bad when we fall asleep so deeply that we can't—God forbid—wake up again. Sometime people can fall into a state of such deep sleep that it is impossible to wake them up any more. That's really the big risk: you don't want to fall asleep without being aware that you're falling asleep. Because that's when you find that you can't wake up.

Do you ever find yourself in a dream in which you realize that you're dreaming? Very often you then wake up. When you see that you're asleep, *there's already something awake there.* But there can be a state where ac-tually you can't awaken yourself. It's very difficult to awaken. And that's the concealment of concealment. You get into a state where you can't even recognize that something isn't right because you're so asleep. You might feel that something's a little off; and when something's a little off, then you're vulnerable. But *when I fall into the concealment of concealment, I won't even look for a way to wake up. I don't even know that there is such a thing as waking up.*

1.8 Power of the Story to Awaken Us from Deep Sleep

Now Rebbe Nachman of Breslov addresses this problem in the book of his collected teachings known as *Liqqutei Moharan.* He has a special teaching about the protagonist of the Zohar, a second-century *tanna* named Rab-bi Shimon bar Yochai. Rashbi, as he is also known, is kind of the "Guru Rinpoche of the Jews."[3] Rashbi is the ultimate enlightened master, and he has all of these great powers. And in that lesson, where Rebbe Nachman teaches about Rashbi, he suggests *there's only really one antidote to this problem of the concealment of concealment, and that is powerful stories.*

These powerful stories come from a place of greatest potency, deeply concealed within the subconscious mind. In Kabbalah, it is represented by an archetypal personification of consciousness and divine energy that is called *Atik Yomin*, the Ancient of Days, and sometimes called the Holy An-

---

3. Guru Rinpoche is Padma Sambhava, the founder and foremost teacher of Tibetan Buddhism.

cient One. This dimension of consciousness is named after a vision in the book of Daniel,[4] where there is a character, the Holy Ancient One or *'Atik Yomayah*, who is described as having the quality of *hadrat panim*—a very beautiful countenance. *It is of such beauty that it can break through even deepest sleep. It's just so incredibly, overwhelmingly beautiful that it can break through every level of concealment.*

So there is a power, according to Reb Nachman, that has the power to break through even the deepest sleep, even the sleep which is the concealment of concealment: the Ancient of Days—and that's the power of Mordechai.

1.9 Power of *Rav-Chesed*—Unconditional Love in Mordechai the Storyteller

Mordechai the Jew has precisely that power. Mordechai the Jew is a storyteller, because if you read the book of Esther you'll notice that there's a verse in there that says that Mordechai "told [*higeed*] this story"[5] to Esther. Mordechai told Esther a story.

What story did Mordechai tell Esther? He told her who she was. And there's no more profound story than being able to tell someone who he or she is—that's a real wake-up story! Now imagine if you could meet someone who could tell you the story of who you are: that would be a very fortunate thing. No matter if you were in the concealment of the concealment, such a story and such a storyteller could wake you up instantaneously.

Esther has this concealment because what's concealed from her is who she really is. She doesn't know who she really is. Mordechai is also a concealment. What does Mordechai tell Esther? He tells her that she's Esther. And Esther means *hester*—*hester panim* means "the hiding of the face." It means "concealment."

1.10 Esther as Concealment of Shekinah

Esther herself is a concealment. That's what Mordechai reveals to her. She's a concealment. She's a concealment of Shekinah. That's what Mordechai reveals to her, that she herself is a concealment of the Shekinah, of the Divine Presence Itself. Esther is the Shekinah, and she's called Esther because *EsTeR* is the same root word as *hEsTeR*, which means concealment.

So we have *hadrat panim*—the revelation of the beauty of the divine countenance; and we have *hester panim*—the hiding of that beauty. Esther conceals that beauty. Nevertheless, she is that beauty, and that's why once she knows who she is, she's able to be very powerful. And Mordechai—who can tell the story that can transform Esther into who she really is—has

---

4. Daniel 7:13.
5. Esther 3:4.

the power of the *hadrat panim*—the beauty of the holy countenance that can reveal the Holy Ancient One, the *Atik Yomin.*

The secret of Mordechai can be revealed. If you take each letter of the name of Mordechai and calculate the gematria, you will find it totals 274. And the number 274 is exactly the same gematria as *rav-Chesed*—Great Love. This utterly unconditional love is the Love Supreme. Mordechai has the character of great *Chesed.* He is the concealment of great *Chesed*—utterly unconditional love! What's hidden in *Mordechai* is the quality of the *Atik Yomin*: the great power, the overwhelming power, of the highest of the high—utterly unconditional love, which is the Love Supreme!

Now when we refer to the highest of the high, recall that there are many spheres of divine consciousness, some more manifest, some less so. *Chesed* is the name for one of those spheres or *sefirot.* And it means, basically, unconditional love. That's pretty great in itself. But even greater than that is *rav-Chesed*, the power and quality that comes from *Atik*, from the Holy Ancient One, the deepest depth of the subconscious mind: the ancient of ancients, the ancient of days, the beginning of everything.

1.11 Mordechai as Love Supreme

So what is it like there? What is the nature of the energy from which everything comes, the *Atik Yomin*? The secret is indicated in the name of Mordechai, and the secret is not mere *Chesed*—but *rav-Chesed*: the ultimate form of love—a Love Supreme. The ultimate form of love is usually called *rachamim. Rachamim* is translated sometimes as "mercy," but maybe "compassion" is a better term. English does not really capture the meaning of *rachamim*, which is so far beyond even unconditional love that it is absolutely pure in its good intention and its goodwill. *It's so absolutely all-embracing. It's before any distinction whatsoever. It's not based on any distinctions whatsoever between any kind of thing and any other thing. It's just completely spontaneous beneficent energy and flow.*

So that's the quality of Mordechai haYehudi, Mordechai the Jew. So why is he called "the Jew"? The rabbis say that that's because *Mordechai is what a Jew really should be. A Jew should be a channel of this* rav-Chesed, *should be a channel of* rachamim. That's what a Jew ought to be.

Mordechai, who reveals the concealment of Esther, is able to defeat Haman, who is Amalek, the one whom we are told—on the Shabbat before Purim especially—we should remember to blot out the memory of.

Apparently, we can learn from this that we need to become like Mordechai, if we are going to somehow overcome the power of Amalek, which is the power that imposes the concealment of the concealment, the power that makes us so asleep that we forget that we could even wake up, that we could remember God, that we could have 'emunah.

Even if you have concealment, concealment requires *'emunah*, requires conviction, because you just can't really know what it is that is hidden; all you can know is that *something is hidden*. But what it is . . . you have to wait and see. You have to wait and see what is going to be revealed.

1.12 Why Haman Chose the Month of Adar

This is a very deep teaching, because the rabbis teach that Haman planned to do everything that he could to undermine the Jews precisely in the month of Adar. *Adar is the month of concealment, so Haman was looking for the precise moment when the concealment would be at its greatest.* This shows us that Haman is Amalek, because Amalek is sneaking up when the Israelites are trying to get out of Egypt, and they have to go through all these obstacles and dangers trying to get to the Land of Israel, trying to merit entering into the holy land. And there is this force which is constantly looking precisely for the most vulnerable place in which to strike and knock them down.

Haman chose the month of Adar—why? The rabbis give two reasons. First, basically there was a miscalculation. Haman thought that Israel was more asleep than they really were. Haman thought that they had really reached the ultimate level of the concealment of concealment, but in fact they were not in so deep; they were only in concealment itself, albeit deeply asleep. The second reason, which maybe is even more interesting, is that Moshe Rabbeinu died in the month of Adar. And so Haman knew that it was the month of the death of Moshe, and he figured he would prevail if there were no Mosaic consciousness. This follows a principle in the way the rabbis look at the meaning of the calendar: when something very significant in the sacred story, the story of the Israelites, happens at a certain point in the year, then the significance of that event always colors the energy of that time of the year. And so the month of Adar is the time of the year when Moshe Rabbeinu left the world. Nobody knows where he's buried, and the location of his grave remains a mystery, which means that Moshe Rabbeinu is in concealment. He's buried in deep, deep, deep concealment.

And because the energy of Mosaic consciousness was in such deep concealment, Haman thought that meant there was no channel for Torah to come into the world during the month of Adar. So Haman surmised he would be able to get the Jews into the concealment of concealment because the energy of Mosaic consciousness wasn't there and therefore the Torah can't come down into the world. And the energy of Torah is precisely the channel that connects what is hidden to what is revealed. So the connection—what awakens, what can lead to the revelation of what's concealed—is the Torah itself, when there's a vessel that can reveal it. So Haman thought that precisely the month of Adar would be a good time to undermine the Jews because the power of Moshe, that energy of Mosaic consciousness, simply is absent, concealed.

1.13 Ever-present Power of *Rav-Chesed* Greater Than Torah

But Haman forgot something when he was calculating this, and that was: Mordechai haYehudi. There's a higher power even than the channel of Torah, even though the channel of Torah can reveal the most concealed of all powers. And that power is always there. That power is *rav-Chesed*. That's the power of *rav-Chesed*, of the Love Supreme! *Concealment is necessary for the revelation of new ancient Torah!*

And the power of *rav-Chesed* in concealment—the power of concealment itself—*the power that Mordechai had, was that he could make a story eternal. He could make an awakening story eternal*—because it's really the story of new Torah. The *story of new Torah is that everything new that manifests comes from concealment*, because what we know already gets stale, even if it was good at the time. Whatever it was, it gets worn out. Without the concealment, we couldn't bring anything new in; there would be no manifestation.

So it's precisely when something comes that covers us up that we have the most precious opportunity to discover more than has ever been revealed yet. And that's why the mystery of *'emunah*, the ability to connect to something concealed beyond the limits of the conscious mind, is so deeply connected to concealment.

1.14 Power of Dreaming Connects to a Deeper Wakefulness Than Waking Life

There is something even deeper here. We have a verse that says: "When God brought back the captives of Zion [*shivat Tzion*]—we were like dreamers [*hayinu k'cholmin*]."[6] If we hadn't been dreamers, we wouldn't have been able to be redeemed. For dreaming is sleeping; it's the preciousness of sleeping, the preciousness of the concealment, of the places where we don't know. It's precisely in these places—the paradox is: there's more God in the concealment than there is in what's revealed!

If we have a moment that feels like revelation, we are very happy—and we should be very happy. The energy when something is revealed—we can feel. We feel that we are waking up, that something is becoming clear. *But where does it come from?* If we hadn't been asleep, that energy could not have come through. And, furthermore, whatever it is that comes through, however great and wonderful it is—whatever it is, it's much less than whatever is still in the concealment.

---

6. Psalm 126:1.

1.15 There Is Always More God in Concealment Than Is Revealed

It's a crazy thing to say, but if we could add up amounts of God, the amount of the divine totality which is in concealment is infinite, and actually the amount revealed (and available to our conscious minds) is finite. We are really all messed up, me included. We are nuts, because when we have a revelation we think we've really got it, and we are so sure we know what God is, whatever was revealed. We get excited about that, and we want to hold onto it. And sometimes, God forbid, we get into arguments about whatever it is we want to hold onto. But the truth is what was revealed to me was revealed to you. We love what was revealed to us. The energy of revelation is wonderful.

But watch out for Amalek that can sneak up behind us, and give us a poke in the back—get ahold of us. Because the amount of God that's in the concealment is greater than the amount of God you could have in the revelation. That's the crazy part of it.

There's another scriptural verse that says: "You make darkness your hiding place."[7] God is hiding in the darkness. In the darkness is where God is to be found. At the places in which we find God, we are necessarily getting a partial revelation. *Any revelation is a partial revelation. It's appropriate to the time and place where it comes through.* We love the revelation! I'm not saying we shouldn't like it; *I'm not saying it isn't good. I'm just saying that as good as we think it is, there's more God in the darkness than there is in the light.* And that's why there's more and more revelation. *That's why there's continuous Torah.*

1.16 Closing Intention

Probably all of us have gotten into Zen at one time or another, and when you heard about satori, or experiencing a flash of enlightenment, for the first time, you probably thought, "Well, if only I could get my satori that would be it!" And then all of a sudden one day you meet some Roshi, and he tells you, "I've had satori already some sixteen times—some big ones, some little ones." Who knows how many times there's going to be revelation, and what revelation you're going to get, what enlightenment. And every time it breaks through, we think: "That's it." And it is. *It is it.* But at the same time, there's more of it where we can't see—because there's always more God in the concealment. And Purim is the time where we most clearly see that. So may we be blessed this Purim to use the deep power of the story to wake up from the concealment of concealment, and realize the presence of God permeating the darkness, and blessing us with continual revelation, continual new Torah.

---

7. Psalm 18:12.

Chapter 2
Rebirthing Beginnings on Pesach

2.0 What's in a Name?

"Rose is a rose is a rose is a rose / Loveliness extreme."[1] What the poet captures here is the perennial journey to understand and to experience the power that resides in a name, like the rose—but what's in a name anyway? Just as the rose remains the symbol of secrecy in literature, so too does the Name of names itself. There are many names for the divine, but during Pesach none is more powerful than the Tetragrammaton, the *Shem Hameforash*, the most explicit and unutterable name, the way that we name that which everything is resting on and drawing from is the name *yud-heh-vav-heh* (the "Name").

According to the foundational Jewish mystical text we call Zohar, everything is somehow expressed by this name, *yud-heh-vav-heh*. *It is everything* and *everything is in it*. And every secret is somehow related to these letters. It is the hermeneutical-spiritual DNA underlying all of creation: it represents the basic structure of divine energy which results in manifestation in the world, which results in time, which results in the human body.

2.1 Secret of the Seasons

Time matters. Every moment has imbedded within it a texture of divine dynamism. And so every month of the year has a special verse from the Hebrew Bible that goes with it, according to the mystical tradition. And these verses, and their excerpts, always have the four Hebrew letters of the Name, in some particular order that corresponds to the energy of the month. Usually, this means that there is a verse with a sequence of at least four words, and one will begin with a *Yud*, one will begin with a *Heh*, one will begin with a *Vav*, and another will begin with a *Heh*—*spelling out the divine dance of the month as a dynamic permutation of YHVH.*

So the mystics over the centuries studied the Bible very carefully in Hebrew, looking for hints where these letters come together; because the Name is so powerful, there's so much energy in that Name that if you can

---

1. Gertrude Stein, "Sacred Emily" (1913), in Geography and Plays (New York, 1922).

find a place where those four letters come together, it could give you a clue to some deep significance. As in the alchemical, scientific, or raja-yoga tradition, seekers within the Jewish mystical tradition applied their insight and mind power toward looking for hints. These are hints that help us learn more about who we really are and what the world really is and how everything works. A lot of the mystical tradition, you could say, is basically that. It is *gilui sodot* or "revealing of secrets"—secrets of heaven, secrets of the earth, and secrets of our souls. And these secrets are windows into reality that we must find and open. It is an invitation to experiment with the new view to see what it can do for us. People have been guided in their search to certain powerful sources and places, and because of their motivation they have put themselves deeply into the investigation of what could be found by opening that particular window. Often, if they discovered something, they wrote a *sefer*, or holy book, about it. Or, if unsafe to publicize, they shared it with someone trustworthy, hence our oral traditions.

What they were doing was studying the flow of time and seeing what they could learn about the energy of different *tekufot*—different seasons or periods of the year. Like the Julian calendar, the Hebrew calendar has four seasons. Each season has three months: in spring, the months each have a biblical verse beginning with *Yud*; in summer, *Vav*; in fall and winter, with *Heh*. As one season ends and another begins, there is a tremendous release of energy, like a power surge.

2.2 Alignment, Flow, and Joy: Together Heavens and Earth Rejoice

And so when they were studying how the energies implied by the Name relate to the year, they came to the conclusion that *Nissan*, which is one of the two most powerful months of the year, is a month that is related to the power of the name *yud-heh-vav-heh* in the *natural order of its letters*. It's the only month of the whole year for which the energy of the divine name is expressed in perfect order. So the name for *Nissan* is the Name, *yud-heh-vav-heh*.

And the scriptural verse that is connected to those *roshei tevot*, or acronyms, is: *Yismechu Hashamayim, V'tagel Ha'aretz*, "The heavens are rejoicing and the earth is in great joy."[2] *Nissan* is a time of tremendous joy. It is the only month of the whole year when heaven and earth are rejoicing *together*.

Even though the letters of the Name are the infrastructure of every person and everything and every interaction, *at most times of the year there is a disconnect, something is hidden or out of order. And when the letters are out of order, we are out of order; we are confused and unhappy. But when all the energy of the letters is in the right order and they are revealed and*

---

2. Psalm 96:11.

we are in alignment with those letters, then heaven is happy and we are happy. That is the potential of the month of *Nissan. Yismechu Hashamayim, V'tagel Ha'aretz.* It's a beautiful image: heaven is having a fabulous celebration, and we are at the party.

2.3 *Nissan:* New Year of the Goddess

It is a happy new year. The Jewish tradition actually has two months that mark the beginning of a new year. In the collection of rabbinic teachings called the Gemara, one of the most famous disputes is whether the world was created in *Nissan*, or whether the world was created in *Tishrei*. And generally we think that the world was created in *Tishrei* (or maybe a few days before, actually, if you really study the texts carefully), and we celebrate Rosh Hashanah on Rosh Chodesh, or the new moon, on the first of *Tishrei.* But the Torah calls the month of *Nissan* "the first of the months—*Hachodesh hazeh lachem rosh chodashim.*"[3] This is the *rosh* (or head) of all the months, and that's why the rabbis have this *machloket* (or dispute) about it: How could this month be the head, the *rosh* of all the months, if the month *Tishrei* is the beginning of the year?

*Time matters. Accordingly, when the mystics look at the year, they divide it into two halves, an upper half and a lower half—*the light months and the dark months. The months from spring to fall, and the months from fall to spring. *The months from fall to spring are considered male months; the months that are provided for by the male aspect of divinity,* which is usually called the Holy Blessed One, *kadosh baruch hu.* And the months *from the month of* Nissan *until the beginning of* Tishrei, *those six months are the feminine months or female months*; those six months are provided for by the feminine aspect of divinity, which is known as the Shekinah.

If we look deeper into the mystical secrets of the months written by the sixteenth-century Safed mystic Rabbi Isaac Luria, we see that he teaches that this month of *Nissan* is the month of the *gulgolta d'nuqbah.*[4] This arcane mystical term of *gulgolta d'nuqbah* is akin to the *sahasrara chakra* of the Goddess. In other words, what *gulgota d'nuqbah* literally means is the crown of the head of the *Shekinah.* In terms of the texture of divine time, what is revealed in this month is the crown of the head of the Shekinah. *All winter, the Shekinah, the goddess energy is hidden.* This is obvious in most places in the world where during the winter months you do not see much new growth; all evidence of the goddess is below the ground. And when you look at the way the calendar works, it makes sense that we celebrate *Tu B'Shevat* on the fifteenth of the month of Shevat because that is when the sap is supposed to start rising in the trees, but it is not revealed yet: you do

---

3. Exodus 12:2.
4. Sha'ar haPesukim, Sefer Tehilim.

not see the fruit yet.

But the month of *Nissan*, which is the month of spring, the month of *Aviv*, this the month when the top of the Shekinah's head crowns, like a fetus emerging in her rebirthing and starting to be revealed. It is like the Shekinah is poking her head out. You see signs of divine energy, you see signs of growth; you see fruit and leaves starting to appear. It is one of the two most powerful months.

There is a scriptural verse that states: "the wise person keeps their eyes in their head [*b' rosho*]."[5] The Zohar then questions this verse— well, where else would their eyes be? And the answer is that *rosh* doesn't just mean the head; it means the source, it means the beginning. *A wise person keeps her awareness on (or at) the source. In* Nissan, *that source is revealed in a very powerful, special way so that we can better pay attention to it.*

The whole point of the month of Nissan then is contained in its letters: *nun, samech, yud, nun.* The *"yud nun"* at the end is like a plural form, so you can read it *nissin*, or, in other words, *nissim*—this month is the month of miracles. The month of *not* understanding and of seeing everything as miraculous: *of realizing the miraculous nature of existence.* Of experiencing a taste of the crown *chakra* of the Shekinah, pushing her top higher. An energetic display that completely overwhelms any capacity to rationalize or analyze the way things are, but puts us into the state of radical amazement—an amazement that is overwhelmingly thrilling.

So we have the verse *Yismechu Hashamayim V'tagel Ha'aretz*: when the Shekinah pops her head out, you can actually see the energy of all those lotus petals unfolding. Heaven and earth are filled with joy at the miracle of the single bloom opening up to reveal its scent. *To embody this teaching through meditation, follow the Crowning Exercise for Nissan below.*

2.4 Crowning Closing Exercise for *Nissan*

In this exercise, we will attempt to embody the teachings we have just learned. We will be moving through the four mystical worlds of divine consciousness known as *ABY"A: Atzilut* (Emanation), *Beriyah* (Creation), *Yetzirah* (Formation), and *Assiyah* (Doing).

For those of you familiar with Yoga, we will start in *Bala-asana*, or Child Pose, and move through modified versions of *Vajra-asana*, or Thunderbolt Pose, and *Tadasana*, or Mountain Pose.

1. Sit on your knees, feet together with your buttocks on your heels. Close your eyes. *He'chacham einav b'rosho.* The Zohar teaches us that a wise person keeps her awareness on (or at) the source.

---

5. Ecclesiastes 2:14.

2. Take a deep breath and as you exhale let your body fall forward, resting your forehead on the floor (or, if not possible, on your knees), reaching your arms above your head along the floor.
3. Bring your arms to your sides, palms up to receive. You are now in a fetal position.
4. Relax. Breathe gently as you imagine yourself curled up like a fetus in the womb. You are now in the realm of *Atzilut*, where everything is present but unexpressed. You are pure *Hokhmah*, the seed from which all your potential can grow.
5. Inhale as you sit up on your heels, placing the palms of your hands on your thighs and keeping your back straight. As your head rises, imagine the seed within you beginning to sprout green shoots as you move into the realm of *Beriyah*, creation. Now imagine that green force of life coursing through your body, awakening your internal organs, tingling in your fingers and toes.
6. Continue to rise up to a standing position slowly, pushing down with your legs into *Malchut* and feeling the energy of the Shekinah as the green shoots at your crown break through the surface of the earth. You are in the process of formation, in the world of *Yetzirah*, in the season of spring. You are the bridge between earth and sky, so feel yourself pushing down through your legs and feet to secure your roots firmly in the ground while your upper torso and head grow away from your roots toward the sky. Take a moment to feel the point of balance within that connects what is above with what is below. Is it in the heart? *Yismechu hashamayim v'tagel ha'aretz*, heaven and earth are together in this joyful state.
7. Continue to breathe as you stretch your arms up above your head, palms facing your ears, stretching your fingertips as far as they can. You are entering the world of action, of *Assiyah*. In your stretch, you bring all your inner potential into the outer world. Feel how the heart and the mouth are aligned within you, on the bridge connecting the world of *Assiyah*, the earth, with the world of *Atzilut*, the heavens. You are full of potential ready to be expressed. In a moment you will open your eyes, and then your mouth, as you reenter the seeing, speaking world. Remember this channel of divine grace that exists right now in your body. You have created the energy of joy. Remember to keep the mouth speaking from this dimension in your heart so that you may spread the energy of Pesach, the energy of *Nissan*, throughout the whole year. Open your eyes.[6]

---

6. Based on Kabbalah and Yoga and adapted from "The Seed Exercise," Paolo Coelho, The Pilgrimage, trans. A. C. Clarke (New York: HarperCollins, 1992), 30.

2.5 Truly Tasting Matzah During Pesach[7]

Most of us don't really like matzah. We love our chametz (leavening). Matzah is just flour and water baked no more than eighteen minutes. Eighteen is the gematria of *chay*, which is the Hebrew for "life itself." So, matzah is pure life as it is, unadorned, unenhanced—the taste of pure life itself without embellishments.

Generally, to deal with our lives, we need chametz. We need something to make life interesting and tasty. We become so attached to our craving for chametz that we lose the taste for pure life itself. But our tradition teaches that the essence of Life, the *Chey ha-Chayyim*, is what we mean by the divine totality. So, in losing our taste for pure life itself during the course of the year, we become more and more estranged from the source of ourselves and all that exists. To get that taste back, we need to be reminded that God is there in the essence of pure life itself. In eating matzah, we can rediscover what we really crave, the Taste of Tastes, so that in tasting it again, we can find it in everything just as it is.

2.6 Tasting Matzah

But how can we really taste matzah? In life, many of the things that are most refined and ultimately most pleasing are often things that are classified as "an acquired taste." We don't necessarily like them the first time we try them. But connoisseurs tell us that if we keep trying something really good, eventually we'll get it. The hidden charm, beauty, and delight are revealed only to one who believes it is there and who is willing to devote herself to the quest. And yet, sometimes the things we develop a taste for are themselves only another form of chametz. So, we have to be very careful if we want "the real thing," because the Taste of Tastes can only be tasted when one is *beli mashehu chametz*, when all chametz has been eliminated. To taste the best of the best we have to eliminate the things that coarsen our palates.

2.7 Attachment as Chametz

Before we can even taste matzah, we have to know our chametz. What are the attachments, distractions, and habits that block us from tasting the taste of pure life itself? According to the Oral Law of the Mishnah, we are to search for chametz—"*'or le-arba'ah asar.*"[8] Conventionally, that means the search for chametz is usually done at dusk on the fourteenth of *Nissan*. But if we look more closely at the precise language of the early rabbis and

---

7. Dedicated to the blessed memories of Yehudah Yosef ben Shoshana, beloved son of Dr. Arnold and Sue Feldman and Alison Louise Johnson, beloved daughter of Bob and Rabbi Naomi Hyman. Sponsored by Dr. Dena Drasin, Eryn Kalish, and Josh Jacobs-Veld.
8. mPesachim 1:1.

read it literally as "light for four ten," we can find in these words the spiritual advice to shine light on our chametz in all the ten *sefirot* or spheres of all the four worlds of divine consciousness. As the scriptural verse says, *"Ner YHVH nishmat adam*—a person's soul is a divine light."[9] In checking ourselves for chametz, we need to focus our inner divine light of awareness on the *chametzdik* aspects of ourselves in all four worlds: in action, feeling, concepts, and, yes, *even in our spiritual life. Where are we stuck? Where are we relying on something other than the Source of Life itself to make our lives palatable?*

2.8 Burning vs. Seeking Chametz

This is, of course, not a process in which we can be completely successful. Nevertheless, in order to truly taste the matzah, we have to make the sincere effort to first locate (and intend to eliminate) our chametz. When we look for our chametz (*bediqat chametz*), the Tcheriner Rebbe points out that we say a blessing over "burning chametz" and not "seeking chametz," even though the act of burning (eliminating the chametz that remains after the process of seeking it) doesn't take place until the following morning. The reason is because the power of shining the conscious light of our souls on our chametz already begins the process of its elimination.[10]

2.9 Seeing What Is Clearly

To succeed in this practice, we have to make sure to look very carefully in those places where our chametz is likely to be found, where we can clearly see what it is. In this way, we prepare ourselves to taste the matzah. We don't have to and, in fact, can't find everything. The rest we can renounce and disown. In sincerely examining the chametz that we can find, we are able to strengthen the divine light of our souls. As a result, we nullify every tendency to identify with chametz, conscious or unconscious. In that sense, we can then be *"beli mashehu chametz*—without any chametz at all."

2.10 Reb Natan's Prayer

There is a profound prayer by Reb Natan of Nemirov that captures this ethos, in which he prays to be granted the power to really taste matzah on Pesach and to be able to be *beli mashehu chametz* all eight days, so that after Pesach, when we begin eating chametz again, he can still taste the matzah.[11]

May the *Chey ha-Chayyim*, Source of Life and Taste of Tastes, bless all

---

9. Proverbs 20:27.

10. Tcheriner Rebbe, Sefer Nachat ha-Shulchan (Bene Beraḳ: Neḳudah tovah, 2017).

11. Reb Noson of Nemirov, Liqqutei Halakhot, Orakh Hayyim, vol. 7, Hilkhot Pesach (Jerusalem, Hasidai Bratzlav, n.d., #8), 526.

of us with the power to fulfill the prayer of Reb Natan. This Pesach, may we all really taste the matzah! A joyful and *"matzahdik"* Pesach to one and all.

2.11 Leaping Beyond to Unconditional Love

Can we ever really leap beyond our conventional views of existence?

The spiritual level of Pesach involves many things: leaping beyond our conventional view to reach the clarity of pure *Chesed* (understanding that everything that exists and happens is an expression of divine love and grace); disclosing the hidden, secret Shabbat that is always present within the ever-changing flow of time; and empowering the heart's true desire to praise its Source. But how do we get ourselves into a condition in which such lofty goals may be attained—through the mitzvah of *bediqat chametz* (finding our "leavening agent")?

2.12 Looking for Chametz

The question really is, "What does looking for chametz mean?" There is a great prayer from Reb Natan of Nemirov that can help us in this. As brilliant as Reb Nachman's teachings are, for me, it is his prayers that are often most instructive. Rebbe Nachman gave his disciple and scribe, Reb Natan, the practice of transforming all teachings into prayers in order to move the teaching from the mind that hears, records, and classifies to the mind of the heart: to the intelligence of the heart that is in direct relationship with the Source. Reb Natan's prayers speak directly in the language of the heart that relates to Source as "You," as something that is present, as Presence and Being. So Reb Natan has a special prayer for the month of *Nissan*, preceding Pesach. Reb Natan says something like this: "Please let me eat this matzah, let me taste and eat this matzah all the days of Pesach and let me not have even *mashehu chametz* . . . not even the least bit of chametz during the days of Pesach so that I'll be able to eat chametz the rest of the year." That's his prayer and focus—the secret of really doing Pesach: "Let me eat matzah for eight days and not have the least bit of chametz so that the rest of the year at least I will be able to eat chametz."

2.13 External vs. Internal Cleansing

So, you have to ask yourself, "What's he talking about?" Everybody knows that before Pesach, Jews do an external cleaning. Some people go to all kinds of extremes to make sure that there's not a crumb of chametz (anything with leavening) in their house. We have the spiritual instructions called *bediqat chametz*, namely, that you should look for chametz and you should burn the chametz if you find it; you have to find it and get rid of it.

But the funny thing is that when you do the practice of looking for the chametz, you say the blessing, *al bi'or chametz* (for burning leaven), even though you didn't actually burn it yet! So, why are you saying the blessing over burning the chametz when you're just looking for the chametz? That's the secret! Because when we are looking, doing the *bediqat chametz*, we are bringing our awareness to recognition of the leavening agent in our experience of chametz. Doing the mitzvah of *bediqat chametz* means that you are using awareness to find chametz in yourself. You can learn from the fact that the blessing that we say when we do this search is not *al bediqat chametz* but *al bi'or chametz* that the looking itself is already part of burning the chametz. When you shine the light of awareness on the places in yourself where this chametz appears, there's already a process of eliminating it.

2.14 Bringing in the Light of Awareness

The scriptural proof text is: "*ner Hashem nishmat adam*—the light, the candle of GOD is the human soul."[12] The candle with which you look for the chametz is the awareness of the heart that you are shining on all the places in yourself, all parts of yourself. Therefore, the exoteric instructions say you should do this process during "the light of the fourteenth of the month." "Light" here means "sunset"—when the light is changing from one day to the next, meaning at dusk. But Reb Natan points out, as did others, that all the exoteric instructions have deeper meanings. Why do the instructions say precisely, "light of the fourteenth (of the month of *Nissan*)?" They say this because you have to bring the light of awareness to the "four and ten": four worlds and ten spheres or *sefirot*. You have to bring the light of awareness to the ten *sefirot* of all four worlds. It is this inner examination that can raise us to the level of Pesach so the mouth can speak from the heart and Pesach can reveal the hidden aspect of Shabbat, and we can leap beyond the rational mind and believe in all the ways we think things are working, to the place of recognition of Divine Providence, "something's happening but you don't know what it is."[13] Something IS happening but you don't know exactly what it is, and that's as close as we come to knowing.

2.15 Divine Guidance as Hide-and-go-seek

In doing this, we begin to realize that we are being pulled into Pesach. *Chesed* (the right hand of GOD) is pulling us into Pesach. There's something guiding us, and it's that *Da'at*, that consciousness that opens us to Divine Guidance that is playing hide-and-go-seek with us most of the time. Each time we have a Shabbat or a Pesach we get an opportunity to look through that window into the way things really are just at that moment—it's so precious, so priceless to have that opportunity. We should be able to look through the window that opens to where heaven and earth are rejoicing

---

12. Proverbs 20:27.
13. Bob Dylan, "Ballad of a Thin Man" (Highway 61 Revisited, 1965).

together and understand that everything that is happening is being guided by that vision which is always calling us, sometimes only in the gentlest way and sometimes in ways that aren't so gentle, but we don't realize that those ways are also expressions of grace: expressions of the Love Supreme guiding the entire universe.

2.16 Looking to Unlock Mind-blocks

So, in following the instructions of *bediqat chametz* to look for chametz, we are looking for all those places which block us in our minds from recognizing Divine Providence: seeing where we are held down, where we really don't quite believe it. We have to go through each of the four worlds, and to begin with, we have to go through our actions (World of *Assiyah*): How do we act? How's our *Malchut* doing, our sense of what we think is powerful? Do you really think that a few people in some powerful institutions are really determining everything that is going on in this world? That's chametz: the thing that's blocking us from recognizing that Life doesn't really work that way. There is something behind the scenes. There's something beyond what we can see that is really guiding the whole show. You have to take an account of your soul, of your self. When I really take a look at myself I'm looking for chametz, my chametz. What are the places where I fall into the trap of falling asleep—so I think that this is happening like this and that's happening like that and that's why I get angry about this or get angry about that or whatever it is that is blocking us, that's taking us away from Shabbat? That's chametz.

2.17 World of Action ·

This is the world of action: *How do I think it works? What do I really believe is going on here? Moreover, I have to check myself out: Where am I blocked and where am I holding on to something that is constricting me, in this case, keeping me in the narrowness of* Mitzrayyim?

2.18 World of Emotion

Then you have to look at the emotional level of *Yetzirah*, how feelings are aroused and whether we are expressing them with attachment or identifying with them. That is the realm of feeling. Then we have to go up and look at our construction of the world, or our ideas and concepts and beliefs, which are the level of *Beriyah*, to see if we have any chametz up there. Are there concepts that we really think are true that bind us and limit us because of our attachment to them?

2.19 World of Spirit

And then we have to go to our spiritual world, our spiritual life and see where we are bound there—we have to look for chametz in *Atzilut*. That's sometimes a tough one because we have to see whether we are holding on to beliefs and practices that we might think are very spiritual, but nevertheless might be blocking us from something deeper. It's very easy to get attached in that level, and that can lead to a lot of disappointment and frustration. If you have distortions in the spiritual world and the way things are, it can strengthen our sense of being separate. Our sense of knowing, which in a certain sense is something that grows, is something that we always have to be transcending. Rebbe Nachman famously said to his students that "you think my knowing is something special, but my 'not-knowing' is way higher than my knowing."[14] You want to have a lot of "not-knowing" in your spiritual world, in *Atzilut*. If you have a lot of not-knowing, there's a lot of room for more knowing and then you can feed the knowing to somebody else so you keep opening to not-knowing and that way, you can keep receiving. There really needs to be a lot of humility. Moshe Rabbeinu is called "the most humble" of all people. In the spiritual world, it is always good to have the sense of not so much attainment, that you have not attained so much. A lot of the Hasidim, Rebbe Nachman especially, always emphasized you should always see yourself as a beginner, like the "Beginner's Mind" espoused by Suzuki Roshi.[15] It is better to be able to begin anew and never think that you did anything yet—that's a Hasidic principle.

So *bediqat chametz* is the meaning of Reb Natan's prayer, "Please let me taste this matzah for eight days." There shouldn't even be ANY chametz at all during Pesach. In general, a dish doesn't have to be 100 percent in order to be kosher. Sixty parts kosher can cancel one part not kosher. But when it comes to Pesach, Reb Natan wants no chametz at all. You can't fix chametz by sixty times more matzah. So you want to have NO chametz, no chametz at all!

So, while you do the search, how can you succeed in this? How would you even know that there isn't still more chametz? Even so, that's the mitzvah—that I'm going to look and going to take the time and reflect and see if I can find my chametz. But I don't assume even then that I managed to find everything. So I burn the rest and do a ritual where I say, "If I missed something, it's not mine. If I missed it, it's not mine." After the search, you have to make the radical move of dis-identifying with any chametz that you couldn't find for the sake of Pesach. We've just disowned any chametz that you couldn't find. Do your best and after you do it you just deny that any of the chametz that might remain is yours.

---

14. Reb Noson of Nemirov Letter #17 (1926), Sefer 'Alim l'Terufah (New York: Hasidai Batzlav, 1976), 20–21.

15. Shunryu Suzuki, Zen Mind, Beginner's Mind (Boulder, CO: Shambhala Publications, 2010).

2.20 Pure Consciousness as Matzah

So, matzah represents pure consciousness we call *Da'at*. Ordinarily, "consciousness" doesn't come without chametz. Chametz represents all of the extensions—all appearances within pure consciousness itself. All of the garments are our chametz; all the levels of concealment (of the underlying reality that can't ever be seen) are chametz. On Purim, we learned how the Divine Presence of Shekinah is dressed up in all the garments of the world and that's basically the way the world is all the year—except for the week of Pesach. The week of Pesach we want to reach the level of the divine totality without garments, or *Shekinah beli levushim*. This is *Da'at shlemah*, the pure consciousness of *Da'at*: the pure *Da'at* of no chametz. We want to be there!

We want to be there for that week. We want to dedicate ourselves for a week, and especially on the Seder nights, that not even the least bit of chametz should even be there, not even the least. Not even in the least veil should separate us from the level of recognizing Divine Providence or *hashgachah*. The whole week of Pesach we want to jump up beyond the level of the rest of the year. The rest of the year, to some extent, to live in the world you're going to have chametz. We live in the world of chametz— what other world is there?

2.21 In the World but Not of It

But how are you going to live in the world of chametz without getting lost in it? The miracle of Pesach enables you to realize that state of "not even the least chametz." So we need to make that leap to the place where your heart can open up and speaking comes from the hidden place in the heart, that place of just pure, pure, pure, pure, pure Shabbat energy, the pure energy of the world-that-is-coming, the place where everyone will know and see that All is One and One is All. Everything is interconnected and that Intelligence that unites everything, that creates everything, that transforms everything, that enlivens everything, that revives and refreshes, that is present should be revealed and known to all of us.

This energy should really, really, really be felt in all its good fortune in the month of *Nissan*, the month of miracles, the month of *every* miracle— the miracle that once was and the miracle that can be and that will be. *Nissan* is the month of the miracle of the first mitzvah, and we should run with a whole heart, full of love to do that which can connect us most deeply to the One concealed in our actions. We should examine ourselves carefully on all levels and all worlds, and we should be able to find our chametz. Through the power of looking at it with a clear mind and with goodwill and good intention, the removal of (seeing through) that chametz should already be effective. May we have the merit to be able to renounce all chametz, even the tiniest bit, for the period of Pesach.

2.22 Closing Intention

May we really taste the matzah of Divine Providence, the matzah that needs no embellishment or concealment. Taste being for what it is. May we get such a taste that the rest of the year we will be able to eat chametz because even when we are eating chametz after Pesach we'll still have that taste of matzah.

Chapter 3
Making the Inner Journey Count:
From Pesach to Shavuot via Lag b'Omer[1]

3.0 Inner Journeying as Torah

To receive Torah there needs to be an inner qualification. It is an inner process in which we try to prepare ourselves to be prophets, to speak words of Torah, and to know what it means to live lives of Torah. Remember, there two kinds of Torah. Written Torah is already there. But there are two different types of Torah. There is no fixed meaning to what it means to be Jewish in an essential way. If there is an internal meaning to Torah, then it is not manifest in Time and Space. Not only in every generation do we have to receive the Torah, but also we need a new Torah for every year. Because the Torah we had for last year is already gone, already in the past, and since in Time and Space everything continues to change, there has to be a continuous process of renewing Torah. That's not an easy thing to do. We had to get to Passover to become receivers, to align ourselves to that Torah, known as the Torah that preexisted Time and Space, known as *Torah Kedumah*, for the people that are tuned into it. You get a lot of preparation in showing up for Passover, eating matzah, and eliminating all the barriers in your mind that separate us from the transmission source. Then you can get this blast of being freed from all the stuff that has bound us, known as *Mitzrayyim* or Egypt. Getting released from being stuck is the liberation from Egypt, or *Yetziat Mitzrayyim*. Our minds are so blotted with so many beliefs and thoughts. But it is what is beyond the mind that allows us to receive the Torah. Getting relieved of leaven allows you to get out of the constricted mind level that is our default mode. From there the problem is that we are not used to it. We are constructed in such a way that, after a very high experience, you return and your mind begins closing up the space. The next seven weeks are meant for opening. Pesach is that opening, where God opens the space and lets the transmission go into you. Just be there. But we need more than an occasional high experience; we need transformation by processing and integrating the light that comes to us on Pesach. It's

---

1. Shave l'kol Nefesh (Nahalat Shalom, May 3, 2015).

one thing to eat matzah, but it's another thing to digest it, as Reb Zalman would say. You have to be able to digest to something that is completely pure. So, we have to build a system that can handle a higher caliber of light. The counting of the Omer is a process qualifying us to receive Torah for ourselves. The Haggadah says that each person has to see herself as having gone out of Egypt. The same thing is true with receiving Torah—you have to receive it. So, we have forty-nine days to create vessels to receive the Torah we need now—that is, the Torah-of-the-world-that-is-coming, the Torah that we are moving into. Getting to number fifty, we are beyond Time and Space—for seven and seven stands for the fullness of Time and Space, and fifty stands on the other side, the fiftieth gate, the gateless gate you cannot find within Time and Space. But it is via the gateless gate that the Torah came down to Moses and through which he disappeared. So we need to reach that gateless gate. That is where we need to get there.

3.1 Barrier Point as Event Horizon

So, if we are talking about forty-nine and fifty, then why should we separate out the thirty-third day in this process? The hint to the thirty-third day in the Omer is not explicit, but if you look with a deeper eye, there is a verse (Genesis 31:47) from a later perspective that was discovered by the high people who contributed to the Oral Torah. It is *Gal Ed*, "the barrier point" that separates Jacob and Laban. *Gal Ed*, "the barrier point," contains the same letters as Lag b'Omer; it is an event horizon, a crossover point where the light gathers. What kind of a crossover point is it, then? All kinds of hints exist in rabbinic literature. For example, in the Talmud the story is told about Rabbi Akivah, who embodies the source of the entire Oral Torah. During the period of the Omer counting, Rabbi Akivah had 24,000 students who died due to a plague. Why did they die? It was because they did not respect each other.

3.2 Gateless Gate of *Lag B'Omer*

On Lag b'Omer, it was the end of the plague and his students stopped dying, but it was also the same day that Rabbi Akivah ordained his five top students, among them Rabbi Shimeon bar Yohai, or Rashbi. These vessels for bringing the Oral Torah were not able to do it; they were lost. The reason they were lost is that they did not respect each other. But the same day of loss is the day when he ordained the channel for the entire mystical tradition of the Zohar. Rashbi symbolizes the entire Oral Torah that came through Rabbi Akivah, especially its deeper layers. There are sources that say that Rashbi died on *Lag b'Omer*. In the *Idra Zutah* of the Zohar, before he dies on that day, he transmits the final teachings of Rashbi on his last days of the world, because there is something special about such a high person teaching at that moment. The strictures become so transparent, so that even in the case of Rashbi all this great gnosis was already coming through him, but the Torah he gave over on this last day was the highest. At the end of *Idrah Zutah*, we are invited to celebrate the *hillula* or "wedding celebration" of Rashbi, but this wedding is really a euphemism for the passing of a tzaddik. There is a certain mythic equation between Moses and Rashbi as tzaddikim, that is, that Rashbi was on the same level of Moses, but what is intriguing here is that the very source of the Oral Torah itself was with Rashbi and not with Moses on Sinai. The intimacy of Moses's passing was through a kiss, vanishing through the gateless gate, so that it is impossible then to find his grave within Time and Space.

3.3 Mythic Equations, Auspicious Time

There is a certain mythic equation between Moses and Rashbi, from which we can derive tremendous lessons. One of the things being implied is the parallel of giving over the Written Torah and the *Idra Zutah*. According to the tradition, Moses, our Teacher, passed on mincha of Shabbat, known as an "auspicious time," or *et ratzon*. This time of divine favor, mincha of Shabbat, defines its most favorable time as *rava d'ravin*. This special moment is when heaven and earth are so interconnected, in which heaven is about to take something back. So if you have a deep prayer, then that is the time to share it. Lag b'Omer is an "auspicious time" (*et ratzon*)—that's the bottom line.

What does that mean specifically? All of Rabbi Akivah's students are dying, until Lag b'Omer. Rabbi Meir, Yehudah, Yossi, Elazar ben Shamua, and Rashbi are the most important—so that Lag b'Omer means the continuation of Oral Torah. Death means there is no transmission. Opening up the channels for Torah of the world-that-is-coming is a remarkable thing. Why do we need an "auspicious time" (*et ratzon*)? Counting the Omer is a preparation for receiving Torah, but it has a problem of *Din*, or discipline. Whether you deserve it or not, you receive the light on Pesach. It's a failsafe without carrying the burden of your balance sheet. Through the accounting of our lives, judgment is how we evolve.

3.4 Problematic Judgment

But *Din* is problematic. We all fall prey to judging ourselves and others. Rabbi Akivah's students did not respect each other, and that is what happens when you have so much judgment for yourself and others. The tighter I'm holding myself to judgment, then all I see are the flaws in others. The fact that these students are trying so hard, with so much judgment, ruins the whole transmission. The effect of judgment is shattering, not unification. When it comes to receiving the Torah, "[the Israelites] encamped at Sinai" where the Torah could be received and had to be in a state of togetherness, as Rashi teaches. We know that numerology of "one" (*echad*) is equivalent to "love" (*ahavah*) as thirteen, equivalent to the thirteen qualia of divine compassion. So you see the problem—we need to have a gap, the marker that bears witness to the boundary where judgment ceases. The customs reflect this, insofar as we practice mourning rituals until the thirty-third day, and then it abates, because on Lag b'Omer, harsh judgment ceases and it is sweetened. In the *Idra Zutah* in the Zohar, Rasbhi teaches that in "the past the standards were based on judgment, but for us, our thing is about love." We hang on love for putting it all together—that is the level of *Lag b'Omer*.

3.5 Boundary Point Between Akivah and Moses

Let's now move this up a little deeper. From Oral and Written Torah, between Akivah and Moses, there is another related issue of the boundary point. There are two new years' days, one in *Tishrei* and one in *Nissan*. The difference between marking the beginning at two times of year—one is a beginning of the cosmos (*Tishrei*), and in fact, every moment is a new beginning, now is a new beginning; the other, the beginning of (*Nissan*).[2] Ervin Laszlo fascinates me here on this point. Insofar as the nature of the cosmos is as it is, it would have been impossible to have happened completely by accident, and yet he does not believe in intelligent design.[3] This all fits into an emerging cosmology, and the update which Kabbalah requires in order to be more in accordance with contemporary science. The world is the way it is, not by design, nor by accident. Rather, he proposes a theory of inheritance. This means that evolution precedes this particular iteration of the cosmos. This reminds us of the rabbinic tradition that there were many cosmoses before this one that were created, destroyed, and created again. The cosmos is breathed in and out of existence, according to the Vedic tradition, getting absorbed and breathed out again, in different ages. This can also be reconciled with the quantum idea of multiverse, many iterations of the universe. If in fact evolution is not limited to merely this iteration, then

---

2. Recall that Judaism has several new years: (1) Nissan is the new year for counting the reign of kings and months on the calendar; (2) Elul is the new year for the tithing of animals; (3) 15th of Shevat is the new year for trees and first fruits; (4) Tishrei is the new year for counting years, leading to the Sabbatical and Jubilee years. See mRosh haShannah 1:1: "The four new years are: On the first of Nisan, the new year for the kings and for the festivals; On the first of Elul, the new year for the tithing of animals; Rabbi Eliezer and Rabbi Shimon say, on the first of Tishrei. On the first of Tishrei, the new year for years, for the Sabbatical years and for the Jubilee years and for the planting and for the vegetables. On the first of Shevat, the new year for the trees according to the words of the House of Sha mai; The House of Hillel says, on the fifteenth thereof."

3. Ervin Laszlo, The Akasha Revolution in Science and Human Consciousness (Rochester, VT: Inner Traditions, 2014).

if it happens naturally, it could be that we inherited the evolutionary process of a prior world! Then we come to this world, but it is not by accident this world has all these qualia; rather, it took many previous iterations. This iteration of the cosmos may only be here for a while, then its purpose and energy will be exhausted and absorbed, and what comes after will build on what we are doing in this particular iteration of the cosmos.

3.6 Implicate Order, Explicate Order, and *Hitlabshut*

Rashbi is meant to be archetype of the "boundary crosser." There is an *implicate order* and *explicate order*, as theoretical physicist David Bohm referred to.[4] The implicate order is where is the cosmos comes from and points to. *Hitlabshut* in Kabbalah is not so much about clothing itself.

A better way of understanding it may be as something more implicate informing something more explicate. The world is receiving form from that which is beyond. That is exactly analogous to the process of Oral Torah, so we are being informed by that from which everything comes. We are deforming it, by making it become what we are becoming. So Rashbi represents that boundary point, the thirty-third day of the Omer, so that in the myth he was both born and died with the same time-space. So, if it was not for the spiritual power of Rashbi, we would not have the Torah of the future, because it takes so much collective power to carry it forward. You need 600,000 people to bring the Torah of the future now—it cannot be just people. It has to be 600,000 people, then. The way the world is now, we need six billion people to get to the level of unified consciousness and love that supersedes the quality of *Din*.

Rashbi is the lineage holder. In the secret tradition of *gilgulim*, or reincarnation, Rashbi is the reincarnation of Moses—the same soul! The higher the light you want to bring down, the more people you need. You need a people who are capable of bonding together, as opposed to the 24,000 students of Akivah, who were so fixated on their own spiritual attainment that it kept them from transcending it. Akivah was one of the ten martyrs killed for teaching Torah by the Romans. He died reciting the Shema, completing the last letter of the word *echad* (or one), attuned to the tittle of the letter *dalet*, joining together implicate and the explicate world orders with complete transparency. None of Akivah's students could do this until Rashbi. "What we are doing depends upon love"; otherwise, you will be dominated by judgment. We basically cannot do it on our own—none of us! We might have the aspiration, but it is too much for an individual person.

3.7 Becoming Coherent Within Oneself

Ervin Laszlo points out that the entire cosmos is a system of systems, a

---

4. See David Bohm, Science, Order and Creativity (New York: Routledge, 2016).

supersystem made up of many systems. The system symbolized here is the Tree of Life. This tree is a universal symbol in many traditions that understand what unification means on the cosmic level. It is only because we have become such creatures of judgment that we have forgotten how interdependent we are. We have to begin by reorienting ourselves to inter-connectivity, and that goes back to the issue of Rabbi Akivah's students—the first thing, then, is to have respect for each other. Now you may find it surprising that, as far the Breslov tradition is concerned, Reb Nachman is the reincarnation of Moses and Rashbi. You have to know that the only way we can do anything is to do it together, so we have to treat each other with a tremendous amount of respect. For a system to be healthy, accord-ing to Laszlo, it needs coherence, which means all the parts fit together. Reb Nachman teaches that there are three main points for coherency, where good is defined by the coherence of the system. First, for inner coherence, one must be a coherent being. To be *minei u'vei*, to be coherent in yourself, then one needs to be a *mityarei*—to integrate *chesed* and *Din*—a balance between being soft and loving, and being critical and judgmental. We have to then get into the integrative sphere of *Tiferet*, as the Vitebsker teaches.[5] Jacob was one of the exemplars of being a *mityarei*. After Jacob became capable of dealing with Laban, he went through training to deal with the prepackaged persona until he could reach the level of meta-programming to reach his brother Esau. Why did Jacob go out of his way to meet up with his brother Esau? The Zohar teaches that the most ingenious thing Jacob did was the way he handled Esau. It was because Jacob was one of the few *mityarein*, because he could sweeten the judgment. We run away from the difficult places. Who wants to deal with it? We just want to be happy. But it just doesn't work, and then you lack inner coherence. We have to all learn to sweeten the judgment, not running away but integrating the judgment within something that is higher and sweeter. You need *'emunah*, a higher vision, to sweeten the judgment. If you cannot even see your own judg-ments, then you cannot have coherence.

3.8 Seeing and Hearing Good Within Others

Secondly, you have to have to see the goodness in others. Reb Nachman teaches that the little good I have left, I'll make into music by looking for good in myself and others.[6] You have to have a *hevrayya*, or people to do this work with. Akivah found the sweetening point through his five students. That coherence depends on seeing and finding that good point in other people. The totality needs every single being, and every single being

---

5. Rabbi Menachem Mendel of Vitebsk, Peri haAretz, Parshat Vayishlakh (Jerusa-lem: Mechon Peri haAretz, 2011), 84–90; ibid., Parshat Acharai Mot, 298.

6. Liqqutei Moharan, no. 282.

has a "special point," or *nekuda tova*, the *Gal Ed*, the Lag b'Omer in every person, where divine love comes through that person. It is not possible that there is not some place where the divine love is not manifest in some unique way! What flows out of that oneness into multiplicity is the unique holiness of each and every being. Whatever my "special point," there is something so special in the other person that I will never be. So try to see in every person what is special about him or her. Then, you need to be bound together, what the Vitebsker calls *dibbuk haverim*, to be able to interconnect to the "special point" of others in the group. Look at each person in such a way for that unique expression of godliness. Then the Oral Torah has to come through every person in order for it to be complete as *Torah Shleima*. You could learn every holy book in the world, but you remain incomplete and lacking coherence unless you listen to the Torah of your friends.

3.9 Coherence of the Group

Third, you need coherence with a teaching. Each of us has to have *dibbuk haverim*, to be able to be interconnected to the "special point" of others in the group, but then you have to have someone above that draws the teaching down, an archetype like a Moses, Rashbi, or Reb Nachman. We have Torah because someone wrote it for us, but you have the Torah of each and every one of us and the Torah of each other. But for it to cohere, there has to be that archetype of the tzaddik.

3.10 Beyond Judgment

So on Lag b'Omer, we celebrate that point that takes us beyond the level of judgment, and makes it possible for the Torah of the future to come down through us and for us to participate in it. The articulation and reception of the Torah of the world-that-is-coming, requires realizing on Lag b'Omer the debt that we owe to the whole lineage of the transmission of the Torah that precedes us. We are not just preservers but future-oriented. We are on a journey to the archetypal Promised Land, where God and evolution are leading us. It is important to understand how the future is leading us, but we should never forget that something is pushing us. The tzaddikim in the Garden of Eden are pushing us into the world-that-is-coming. Rashbi and Reb Nachman are pushing us to get there. The power of the teachers of the Oral Torah, those who brought through the evolving Torah, are pushing us forward. We are dependent on their prayers. Let's face it, Reb Zalman, *o.b.m.*, is a *Melitz yosher* for us, a tzaddik who is praying for us. Like in a marathon, suppose a runner crosses over. Instead of taking the reward, he is cheering us on! Once a person like that is no longer in this world, he no longer has his constriction, but is praying purely for us. So Lag b'Omer is about the recognition that we are part of a lineage; we are not sui generis, and we did not just invent ourselves. The good things that put us here are really praying for us.

3.11 Closing Intention

In my early days when I was getting loaded up with provisions for the day, I had a vision of the messianic day. I had a vision where I could see the world-that-is-coming. The Sufis, the Buddhists, the Hindus. But where are the Jews? And I see four people running by with Torah; this is the world-that-is-coming. It's like a relay race, Rashbi took it to where he could take it, so don't judge him for what he could not do—you must take it where it now has to go! Lag b'Omer is not all about judgment; it's about love. When we dig into that love, the twenty-fifth level of tribunal, the cosmic tribunal, because of the coherence principle, it is rooted in the cosmos itself. If you want to sweeten the judgment, know the twenty-four levels of the tribunals, or *batei din*, and unless you know all twenty-four levels, then you cannot help others. Even if you have someone who knows the twenty-fifth level, the twenty-five letters of the Shema, like Akivah who was hovering on the tittle of the twenty-fifth letter of unity. Even when you have someone like Akivah in the world, the energy they generate is used for other things. That energy creates Jews by choice, or *geirim*. We do not need a biological Judaism—we need to all see ourselves as *geirim*. We are all Jews by choice because the power that sweetens all judgments is expressed through our intentionality and volition—not just following rules. Akivah descends from *geirim*, not by virtue of biology, but because he was tuned into the tittle of the twenty-fifth letter of unity. Lag b'Omer is a time to let go of all judgments needed to do the counting, but once you reach the horizon event, then the fire of Torah comes out to illumine and warm our hearts. There is nothing deeper that we need to learn than this Torah. None of us can do it by ourselves. I cannot do it without Rashbi, without my friends. You have to have a strong enough base, if you want to bring down *anything high and good, it is the coherence factor. This should be a coherent teaching, within ourselves, with each other and with those that are pushing us ahead.*

Chapter 4
Heroes Making Real the Hidden Torah of the Future for Shavuot[1]

4.0 Truly Getting Together

What does it mean to truly get together? Although commonly called "Festival of Weeks" or Shavuot, because it occurs seven weeks after Pesach, the early rabbis called this festival a "getting it together" or *Atzeret*. We "get ourselves together" through the process of consciously counting the forty-nine days between Pesach and Shavuot. Reb Natan teaches that this process is alluded to in the scriptural verse: "I took my bitterness [literally, myrrh] along with my spice."[2] In other words, to "get ourselves together," which is the only way we can receive the Torah on Shavuot, we need to go through a seven-week process of consciously witnessing both the positive and negative parts of ourselves. We have to become whole through recognizing and owning our "shadow" as well as our "spice." Without this wholeness, we cannot receive new Torah, because the holy sparks of the potential for new Torah are buried in the very shells or *qelippot* of the shadow. However, if we are brave enough to bring the light of consciousness to the shadow, we can not only release the extremely contracted holy energy that sustains the *qelippot*, but also significantly expand that energy when it is released. So, during this seven-week experience of Counting the Omer, known as the *sefirah*, I took my bitterness along with my spice, which is the very way we get to Shavuot.

4.1 Without Wholeness, No Peace

"Her pathways, those of Torah are ways of calmness and all Her pathways are Peace."[3] In Hebrew the word for "being whole" (*SHaLeM*) and the word for "peace" (*SHaLoM*) have the same root (*SHLM*). This teaches us that receiving Torah—the Ways of Peace— and achieving wholeness is basically the same thing. Indeed, the mystery here is expressed in the Zohar's teaching: "*Orai- ta kudsha berich hu ve-yisrael chad hu*—Torah,

1. Shavuot, 5770.
2. Song of Songs 5:5.
3. Proverbs 3:17.

the Blessed Holy One, and a whole person are essentially one."[4] So if we want Torah which guides us in the Ways of Peace and we want to know the Blessed Holy One whose name is Peace, then we ourselves must seek peace through a total integration of all our parts, bitter and spicy. That isn't easy, but it becomes easier when we take to heart another secret, namely that Peace and Love are also inseparable. This is indicated by the well-known numerology or gematria: *echad* (one) and *ahavah* (love), which both equal thirteen, teaching us that the key to wholeness and peace (which have the same root) is the power of Love. Generally, the dark places within us are refugees from Love, qualities that we hide because they are so "unlovable." But the more they remain concealed and unloved, the more they appropriate precious energy that we need to be whole. And without wholeness, there is no peace.

4.2 Suffering Fragments of a Reckless Dictator

We may try to complete ourselves in myriad ways, often in the form of various cravings, but ultimately the only effective remedy is Love itself, because Love is the divine power that unites everything always. Unfortunately, the Love actually present and revealed in the world of time and space is always limited due to our current state of consciousness, which is a result of divine contraction called *tzimtzum*. We therefore suffer from the libidinal impulse known as *yetzer hara* that undermines our higher aspirations. The impulse that produces such suffering fragments us, separates us from others, and is driven by insatiable cravings that conceal the very element that could satisfy us. This condition our sages called being under the control of our hearts. For our purposes, it would probably be better to understand this as tyranny of the lower mind, in which the *yetzer hara* is like a reckless dictator.

4.3 Actual Love and Power of Love

However, while the amount and *quality of Love* actually present in the world of time and space is always contracted, the *power of Love* itself is unlimited. It is only that in our current state we can't yet hold the full *power of Love*. The contracted state of *actual Love* is itself an expression of the unlimited *power of Love* that enables us to maintain our precious existence with the potential of expanding our *capacity for Love* through aspiration. In coming to terms with this paradox, we can find the holy sparks in the Shadow, which contains just enough Love to exist (unless we contribute more energy to it through failing in our aspirations).

---

4. Zohar III:73a.

4.4 Expanding Capacity to Love

What is aspiration? Desire for the guidance of Torah and knowledge of the Holy Blessed One. But this aspiration can never succeed without expanding our capacity to Love, because Love is the very nature of Torah and Divinity Itself. For Rebbe Nachman, those who are successful in their aspiration are called:[5] "Heroes of Divine Power, Makers of the Divine Word."[6] One can become such a hero only through integration of the *yetzer hara* and releasing its sparks. That is to say, such a person, who is also likened to an angel, gains extraordinary power through finding the Divine Power of Love present in the shadow and not just in the "spice." Such a person is called a "Maker of the Divine Word" because through integrating the shadow, Torah is then revealed in the very place where it was hidden. The Hero of Divine Power makes Torah emerge in the world of appearances.

4.5 Revealing Concealed Torah of the Future

This conscious effort to expand the Power of Love and bring it to places of concealment is the secret of drawing new Torah into this contracted world of time and space. In our tradition, we generally divide Torah into two categories, the revealed, exoteric, or *nigleh* as opposed to the concealed, esoteric, or *nistar*. Conventionally, people often think this division distinguishes the exoteric biblical and rabbinic teachings from the esoteric mystical teachings of Kabbalah. But Rebbe Nachman's understanding is far deeper. *Nigleh* refers to all Torah, exoteric and esoteric alike, that we presently have. But *nistar* doesn't mean already existing esoterism—it refers to the Torah of the future. It is Torah that hasn't entered time and space yet, because the consciousness here is not yet high enough to "make" it. This is the limitless Torah of the Divine Mind Itself or *Torah sheveDa'ato*, which is expressed as the unlimited Power of Divine Love. Through our aspiration to achieve integration by finding and releasing the greatly contracted energy of Divine Love concealed in the shadow, we can draw more of the unlimited Torah and unlimited Power of Divine Love into our expanding and evolving world of time and space. In doing so, we may be liberated from the oppressive and depressing influence of the *yetzer hara*. As the rabbinic exegesis makes clear, don't read *charut* or "engraved into the Tablets," but read *cherut* or "freedom from the libidinal impulse" that comes through released and enhanced sparks that "make" Torah.

4.6 Closing Intention

The conclusion of Rebbe Nachman here is that while few of us may have

---

5. Liqqutei Moharan, no. 33.
6. Psalm 103:20.

direct access to the ultimately hidden Torah of the Divine Mind Itself, everyone has access to some level of "higher mind" or *Da'at*, a level of consciousness that reflects the Divine Mind Itself. Within that higher consciousness, whatever its present level, is the source of our aspiration. Through joining our hearts to that higher consciousness, we can gain greater access to the Power of Love that can free us from the tyranny of the *yetzer* and make us whole. The more of us that can thus aspire to become "Heroes of Divine Power," *the more of the Hidden Torah of the Future we can bring down now and "make" real in our world of time and space.*

Chapter 5
Seeing Clearer Through the Luminal Darkness of *Tisha B'Av*[1]

5.0 Difference of Darkness

One of the darkest days of the Jewish calendar is the 9th of Av, also known as *Tisha B'Av*. According to our tradition, *Tisha B'Av* was the date of the destruction of both the first temple in 586 BCE, and the second in 70 CE. But the first temple and the second temple were very different entities, and, according to our tradition, their destruction hints at very different things.

5.1 Torah of the First Temple

The first temple was the temple envisioned by David and built through his son Solomon. It was a temple that existed before Torah in the way that we understand it, the way we have it now, because at that time they only had the Written Torah. They didn't have the Oral Torah. When we think of Torah today, we are basically thinking of the Oral Torah. Talmud, midrash, the commentators—everything that we have is the Torah of human interpretation, the whole process of the human effort to mediate and apply divine guidance.

But in the first temple they didn't have that kind of Torah. What they had in those days were prophets. On the other hand, in the first temple they had all kinds of things that we later lost. For example, by the time of the second temple they didn't have the Holy Ark, which contained the tablets of the covenant. Some people think it's in Ethiopia—you might have seen Indiana Jones, for instance. The ark was in the first temple, but lost thereafter. In the first temple, there were all sorts of incredible things, because the period of the first temple was the period of miracles. In the first temple, the Shekinah was said to be actually present in the temple. The divine presence was in the temple—literally right in the temple. The Holy Ark was in the temple. The tablets were in the temple. The heavenly flame was in

---

1. Tisha B'Av, 5771. In memory of Miles's mother, Miryam bat Mikhel ve-Leyka, who passed away on the 21st of Tammuz.

the temple. The oracular dice known as Urim and Thummim were in the temple—the High Priest had this breastplate with these stones, and they could receive prophecy by looking at these stones. All of these things were in the first temple. Divine inspiration known as *ruach ha'kodesh* was in the first temple—already for the early rabbis, all this inspiration dwelt there.

5.2 But the First Temple Was Destroyed. Why Was It Lost?

The first temple was lost, according to rabbinic tradition, because of three things: because of *avodah zarah*, *gilui arayot*, and *shfichat damim*. The three worst things you can do are the three cardinal sins in Judaism. Let's explain each one of the three now.

First, not worshipping God—literally, *avodah zarah* means "foreign worship"—can be understood in all sorts of ways. I like to understand *avodah zarah* the way the Baal Shem Tov understood it: he equated it with any form of "self-worship." It is then connected with the quality of *gaavah*, of seriously taking yourself as something that exists independently of the Totality (YHVH). You know the self-made man who worships himself—that's *avodah zarah*! If you're worshipping anything but the One power itself, which is all that exists, in its myriad forms, it is idolatry of the first order. If you think you're something else: that's *avodah zarah*! If you're turned toward anything else besides that One: that's *avodah zarah*!

It's one of the cardinal acts that, according to the rabbis, if someone coerces you to do, on pain of your life, you should allow yourself to be martyred instead. You simply can't do it. And so, it's associated, in a way, with a quality of "sacrifice" known as *korbanot*. A person who refuses to commit *avodah zarah* makes himself or herself a *korban*—that is, I make myself an offering to God. If I'm not a sacrifice to God, then that's *avodah zarah*!

It's as simple as that! If I really have deep conviction in the teachings of our tradition, that there's really only One, and nothing is outside of that, and certainly there's no way that I could be; if that's the case, I'm not outside of it either—so really there's nothing else for me to worship, except the divine totality itself: only that One which is creating and sustaining and destroying and changing and empowering everything. You can think of it in different ways, but the more I think about it, the more awesome and amazing and inspiring it seems to me. The very recognition of this is its worship.

When it comes to the "service of the divine" that we call *avodah*, there are different ways of doing it. But the original meaning had to do with the way it was enacted in the first temple, because they had the sense that the indwelling presence of the Shekinah was right there with them.

That temple was constructed as a microcosm of the totality itself. The ancient Israelites had knowledge of a sacred geometry, and they knew how to make a building—and remember, the temple has very specific plans, how many boards here, how wide, how high—and people have studied it, just like they study the Egyptian temples. So, the ancient Israelites understood sacred geometry, and because of sacred geometry, the temple was built in such a way that it was a microcosm of the totality itself, and since the totality is filled with the divine presence, the scale model, as it were, is filled with it, too. And because it was built that way and the Shekinah was in it, it was filled with wonders.

The first temple was a temple of seeing—*imago templi*. Everything was visible. You could see the Holy Ark known as the *aron ha'kodesh*. You could see the divine presence right there, you could see the fire—you could see all these awesome things.

That temple was destroyed, according to rabbinic tradition, because of these three things, as mentioned earlier. The first, as we now know, is *avodah zarah*, worshipping something other than the One, other than the totality. The second is *gilui arayot*, which means sexual behavior that is not wholesome. And the third, *shfichat damim* means, basically, murder. People were murdering each other, they were not honoring sacred relationships, and they weren't living as sacrifices to the One, the Totality. They weren't living in service to God. This energy was very undermining, to such an extent that together unwholesome sexual relationships, people killing each other, and people not surrendering to the power of the Shekinah, not offering themselves to the Shekinah undermined the stability of the entire community and the entire culture, and as a result the temple was destroyed.

5.3 Torah of the Second Temple

But the second temple was completely different. The second temple didn't have any of these wonders, and the rabbis didn't say that the Shekinah was really present in the same palpable way in the second temple. Rather, what came in in the second temple period was Torah.

You might wonder, as did the rabbis: *Why didn't the second temple last?* The second temple was destroyed because people hated each other or what is known as *sinat chinam*. The second temple was destroyed because of senseless hatred.

Notice the tremendous difference between these temples. With the first temple, it's very grave, heavy, overt things that brought it down. You can see very easily how with things like that it's very difficult for a religious culture to cohere. The implication is that with the second temple, people weren't doing all these terrible things. They weren't murdering and doing obviously evil deeds. But it was brought down because there was division—*inner division*. Looking down on others, hatred of others, not honoring others—*that's all it took*.

There's something very paradoxical about this spiritual history. On the one hand, it seems that with the first temple they had all the wonders, all the marvels, and it was very magical. They had prophets, and prophets had these incredible experiences—visions of God and all kinds of powers. And all of this was openly revealed, on the level of seeing. But the things people did wrong were also very overt; you could see them.

The second temple doesn't seem to be so fantastic, but it's really deeper, because it's connected to what's inside people. And what's inside people is powerful enough to bring down the whole temple. When it gets that deep, you don't need such overtly terrible things to upset the equilibrium, to upset the balance. The equilibrium of the second temple was undermined just because people had bad opinions of other people—that's *sinat chinam*.

Just as the first temple was connected to the quality of *seeing*, the second temple was connected to the quality of *hearing*—because the second temple wasn't governed by prophets; it was the beginning of the period of Oral Torah. It was built by Ezra and Nehemiah, and what did they do? They went around and they read Torah to people—they had public readings of Torah. Before that, in the first temple, they weren't reading Torah to people; people weren't hearing Torah—it was all about prophets. You had some incredibly inspired people that stood out, and divine inspiration came through them, and you could see it.

But when it came to the second temple, you had somebody reading Torah and explaining it, and people were listening. It's not as amazing, it's not as fantastic, but it's really deeper. And it's more democratic. The responsibility has come down to every person. From the perspective of spiritual history, it wasn't quite there yet—but it was moving in a democratic direction. The second temple is the beginning of collective responsibility. It's a temple that was built on hearing Torah, and the Shekinah in that period was the community of Israel known as *Knesset Yisrael*. It wasn't that the Shekinah was in the temple and you would go and worship there, but there was Shekinah consciousness in every individual soul. The collective, all the souls put together, then becomes the place where the Shekinah hovers during the time of the second temple.

5.4 *Sinat Chinam*. People Were Against Each Other.

For the second temple to exist, you had to have a community of mutual respect that we call *Knesset Yisrael*. You had to have a community in which every person would see the divine presence in every other person. The fact that people were divided: that's what destroyed it.

There were no rabbis in the first temple, and there were no rabbis in the second temple, either! Rabbis came along after the second temple was destroyed. They came in the wake of the destruction of the second temple, when Yochanan ben Zakkai escaped from the Romans, and he got permission to create the first yeshiva in Yavneh. That was in 70 CE, and after that some of the surviving Pharisees gathered in the town of Yavneh, in the Galilee, and they began to create rabbinic Judaism—*something from nothing* because we don't have the temple any more. We haven't had a temple since then; we have what the rabbis created out of what was left when the temples were destroyed.

The rabbis said a couple of very interesting things in this regard. One is that *anybody who has deep knowledge of God or* Da'at—*it's as if the temple was rebuilt during their life. Anybody who has an enlightened mind, anybody who has direct knowledge of God: if that person is in the world, it's as if the temple is in the world.*

Another thing that the rabbis said was that when it comes to the first temple, because the problematic behavior was obvious, you could also see when this behavior ceased. It was all on the level of *seeing*, on the level of the overt. But when it comes to the second temple, everything was more *hidden*. You couldn't really see *sinat chinam*, because it was *inside people*. You can't necessarily see hatred or lack of respect. Sometimes you can, but sometimes it's hidden so deep in people's hearts and because you can't *see* it, you can't *see* the end of it. And that hatred is in fact why we still don't have a temple two thousand years later. Not only did it bring down the second temple, but it's made it virtually impossible for the third temple to be rebuilt—unless through what Rav Kook called "senseless love" or *ahavat chinam.*[2]

5.5 Responsibility of Interpreting Torah

In the wake of the loss of the second temple, however, the rabbis brought Torah to the world in the sense that we understand it—Oral Torah. Written Torah just means the letters and the words as they are arranged in the Torah scroll, but what we really mean by Torah is everything that students of the Torah have learned and taught over the past two thousand years. That's Oral Torah—all our rabbinic literature. That's the way that Judaism works—you don't even imagine that you could understand Written Torah without Oral Torah—Written Torah does not stand alone. The rabbis introduced a very sophisticated, deep hermeneutic, and it's up to us to figure out what exactly God wants from us. And *that's what Torah really is—assuming the responsibility of interpreting and mediating what we've received.*

5.6 Freedom of Torah

That's really Torah of freedom, of *cherut*. It's not Torah written in stone, that Moses wrote with his finger. It's the rabbinic effort to reclaim the origi-

2. R. A. I. Kook, "Ahavat Chinam v'Sinat Chinam," in 'Orot haQodesh, vol. 3 (Jerusalem: Mossad HaRav Kook, 1996, #10), 323–24.

nal tablets that Moses broke, that were written with the finger of God. Torah written by the finger of God is Torah of freedom or *cherut*, not of *charut*, graven-ness; it's Torah of infinite possibilities.

5.7 Thinking Through the Third Temple

When we think about the third temple, we have to continue the work of the rabbis of Yavneh. Their third temple is the temple of *Da'at*, the temple of direct knowledge of God. The rabbis were working on the temple of the human heart, the temple that would be built through the fixing of our nature, through our evolving, through our each becoming a miniature temple. We ourselves have to become the microcosm.

The second temple necessitated a bonding together of all Israel in order to maintain it, but they couldn't do that because they didn't have enough Torah yet. After that temple was destroyed, Oral Torah really began to evolve, and the emphasis of Oral Torah is that every person really needs to become a temple of his or her own—consider how deep that is! That means I don't have to go anywhere else to experience the divine presence. Shekinah is right where I am, if I'm a temple. The divine presence is everywhere I go.

5.8 Third Temple as the Earth

It seems to me that this is where we are now, except that now I would say that we have to move beyond even that. The second temple was based on a conception of *Knesset Yisrael*—that all the Jews have to love each other. The third temple requires that we go way beyond that—it has to be a one-world temple. The prophets talk about the third temple being a house for all people. What house is big enough for all people? It has to be the *world itself.* Only the world itself is big enough for God to say, "This is my house for all people."[3] *The earth itself is the third temple. This is the temple that we have to dedicate ourselves to.*

In the mystical tradition of the Kabbalah, every month is associated with a particular flaw or place which is ripe for rectification. The months of Tammuz and Av, where the three weeks fall, are associated with a flaw in *hearing*, and a flaw in *seeing*. The truth is that we are impoverished in terms of *seeing* and of *hearing*—how we *see* ourselves, and how we *see* the world.

5.9 Seeing the Whole World as Third Temple

The correction comes through hearing words of Torah, hearing true words, the words that have the power to fix the way we *hear* and *see*. If we look at our spiritual history, we surely want to fix the hatred and disrespect of *sinat chinam* that brought down the second temple.

---

3. Isaiah 56:7.

But now we are trying to fix the entire way we see on the level of the third temple: *we need to see the whole world as the temple of God*. If we are not seeing that, something's wrong with our *seeing*. Hearing the Shema, that *haShem* is One, can fix the way we *see*. Because however it might appear, the truth is that all is really One. The whole world is nothing but the temple of God.

5.10 Shedding Tears for Jerusalem

Whoever sheds tears for Jerusalem will also get to experience its joy. To experience the joy of the third temple, you have to experience grief at its absence. The three weeks are the time for that—the three weeks are the time to really grieve for the brokenness of the world. We are so jaded, so conditioned to accept the tragedies of the world that we hear about daily everywhere. But now is the time to allow that in, to understand how we are connected to it, how it's all taking place in the temple of God. If you can't shed tears for the brokenness, you're not going to get to the place of the third temple.

Tammuz and Av are both like the eyes in the face, in part because, for mystics in the Lurianic school of Safed, this is the time for a correction of seeing.[4] And the verse in Lamentations that we read on *Tisha B'Av* captures it succinctly: "*Al eleh ani bochiya; eini, eini yordah mayim / Ki rachok mimeni menachem, meishiv nafshi*—Because of all these things I'm crying; my eye, my eye is dripping with water / Because the comforter who can restore my soul is far from me."[5] When we say soul there, what that means is the "world-soul" or *neshamah klalit*. There are various ways the individual can feel OK, and, thank God, we are in a time and place where we personally are more or less safe. But really, for as long as it's all one world, we are deluded if we are not feeling the suffering of others.

Currently, we are between the second and the third temples, though many sources say we are getting close to the end, that we are a lot closer to the *end* than we are to the *beginning*. Every generation contributes to the building of the third temple; according to the rabbis, it all adds up.[6] It's the work of all generations. We've invested at least two thousand years in this third temple, and now we are getting very close to the end of this period. If only we should see it in our own time, we should see the fixing of the third temple, the rebuilding of the world.

---

4. R. Hayyim Vital, Derushai Tiqqun Haztot, in Sha'ar haKavvanot, Derush #1.

5. Lamentations 1:16.

6. R. Yosef Hayyim of Bagdhad, Sefer Benayhu, vol. 1, on bBerachot 3a (Jerusalem: n.p., 1898), 3a–b.

5.11 Third Temple as Microcosmic Orbit

There's a practice that can help us a great deal in transforming ourselves into microcosmic temples: you can circulate your breath around what the Taoists call "the microcosmic orbit"[7]—inhaling from the base of your spine up to the pineal gland in the middle of your skull, and then exhaling through your third eye down to your heart. As you do this, you visualize the path of the breath, and inwardly sound the letters of the divine four-letter name which is associated with the month of Av. As you inhale you sound *ha–va* and as you exhale sound *ya–ha*.

When you circulate energy like this, you may see a lot of light. Don't do this practice for so long that you obliterate yourself; when the light has built up a bit, switch to the mantra "*ozer dalim*"—God helps the downtrodden"[8]—and stay with that for a while.

5.12 Closing Intention

May the merit of this practice and of the Oral Torah help us all transform into completed pieces of the third temple, speedily and in our days. And may we all be blessed to feel what we need to feel during the three weeks, during Tisha B'Av; may the world be safe; may the fixing of hearing and seeing take place and be whole and complete, and lead us in the direction of the other side, the side of the birth of messiah, that's also related to Tisha B'Av; and may the mayim that runs from our eyes when we feel the pain of the downtrodden that runs through this world be transformed, through our devotion, to "the life-giving waters that flow down from the transcendent source of pure compassion"—mayim chayim nozlim m'levanon. Amen.

---

7. Michael Winn, Qi Field, and Shamans Alchemists, "Daoist Internal Alchemy: A Deep Language for Communicating with Nature's Intelligence," Conference on Daoist Cultivation: Traditional Models and Contemporary Practice (Vashon Island, WA: May 2001).

8. Numbers 19:2.

Chapter 6
Why *Tu B'Av* Is as Great as Yom Kippurim[1]

6.0 Time to Lament and Mourn

Amid the three weeks of lament and mourning that began on the 17th of Tammuz, many questions arise. Beyond the three weeks, we like to be looking ahead rather than back, to be aware of where we are, and when we look forward to the Torah of the future, on the sacred calendar, the next big sign we see is *Tu B'Av*, or the 15th day of Av. What is the meaning of this day? To understand this, we have to consider it in relation to the three weeks of lament and mourning that began on the 17th of Tammuz.

6.1 Spiritual Power of Weeping

Let's start with the verse from *Eikha*, or Lamentations, "For these things I weep; mine eye, mine eye runs down with water; because the comforter is far from me, even he that should refresh my soul; my children are desolate, because the enemy has prevailed."[2] We have been talking about the spiritual importance of being able to cry. Crying is related to the purification of the eyes. The spiritual power of weeping is related to two levels of weeping. The first level is the weeping of a child and the next level of weeping is that of an adult.

6.2 Dialectic of Cosmos

The grandfather archetype in *Saba d'Mishpatim* is hyper-literally about the exercise of justice or *mishpat* (which is not the same thing as inauspicious judgment known as *Din*). Justice or *mishpat* is about the way things are supposed to be and how to deal with and sweeten inauspicious judgment known as *Din*. So, judgments are unavoidable, especially concerning the three weeks with demons, oppositional forces, and the dialectical construction of the cosmos itself—which means there are forces of judgment that are inherent to the nature of existence. This is why contraction or *tzimtzum* is necessary. Without contraction, we would have no world at all. We

---

1. Shave l'kol Nefesh (Nahalat Shalom, July 19, 2015), dedicated to the memory of Carole Kessler, o.b.m.
2. Lamentations 1:16.

would have nothing but pure god-ness (*Elohut*), what Vedanta calls pure consciousness. It is the purity of that which does not change, but in its infinite nature, it manifests reflections of itself. Out of its nature, it can spontaneously manifest reflections of itself which are nothing but refractions. It cannot be nothing but itself; otherwise, nothing could appear. The fact that we exist within sensible experience means that what ultimately exists is still there, but it has become hidden and concealed from our perspective. All the ephemeral forms that we do see are there in some kind of contracted, reduced form.

6.3 Sweetening Judgment

We are experiencing its reduction in every moment and every experience that we have. Contraction or *tzimtzum* is necessary, without which there is no world at all, but with contraction or *tzimtzum* there will be judgment. But we talk about *Torat Chesed*; it is a divine mercy that enables us to sweeten the judgments, even though we cannot eliminate them altogether. But we can have a process of sweetening through wisdom, so the more we are invested in Torah, the more we are invested in sweetening the judgments.

And so the old master of judgment in *Saba d'Mishpatim*, who can sweeten judgment, finds himself weeping. But he fears that if people see him weeping, they would think he is weeping like a child. So, one form of weeping is the cleansing of the energy of judgment. It is a purgation that eliminates judgment. But do not think I am weeping as a child; rather, I am weeping to draw down mercy. It is a weeping that results from the connection to the thirteen channels of mercy, which we have the power to draw down into this world to sweeten judgment. So, then the world can exist, even though we cannot eliminate judgment entirely.

6.4 Time to Confront Judgment

We don't just have one Rosh Hashanah, the Day of Judgment. Rather, every year we have to confront and fix it, given that every world we create will have judgment. But *Rachamim* is the purest form of divine love. And so *Rachamim* is what we are after, with the preparations that begin in the month of Elul. But first we have to get through the three weeks, and then the 15th of Av. *Tu B'Av* is the key to bring us into Elul.

I do not stipulate what we should be crying about. Every one of us is deployed to weep about something unique in the world. Rather, each of us has a unique inner point of goodness and each of us has a distorted way of looking at the world because of our limitations. We give the world an evil eye.

6.5 Weeping and Messianic Consciousness

The power of messianic consciousness is associated with smell, so we do not want the world to stink. The fragrance of each and every soul can be smelt in its purity, but when you give someone the evil eye, it makes things worse. We all have our own eyes for weeping, and each of us has our unique way of seeing goodness, so it is up to each of us to identity through introspection what are the things we are crying for. Whenever I see that someone is oppressed or someone is abusing power, those things add up. But it's for you to ask yourself: What are those things I'm weeping about? That is what these three weeks are about—to give us the space and time to recognize that we all have things to weep about.

In all my seven decades of embodiment, I have never seen a perfect person who has not been prone to anger, jealousy, and other such emotions. How is it that an enlightened person can feel angry or feel lust? It does not mean that you are a vegetable. The main thing that one actually does have responsibility for is the way we relate to the experience, but you cannot eliminate or avoid the experience.

6.6 Preserved Tablets, Known but Not Determined

Al-Ghazzali speaks of the "preserved tablets," which are a symbol of the place where everything is known, the source of all knowledge. In other words, it is the divine mind, beyond the contraction of the world. It is beyond human comprehension, because our minds cannot grasp that which is beyond time and space. It is a knowledge that is not sequential. Remember Maimonides teaches in the *Guide* that God is the Knower, Knowing, and the Knowledge—which is incomprehensible to us.[3] We think the process of knowing is a third thing, but from the divine mind it is all at once, and for Al-Ghazzali[4] it is called the "Preserved Tablet" (*al-lawh al-Mahfudh*), *known* already but not *determined*.

6.7 All Depends on Attitude

Everything feels like it is taking so long, but billions of years are nothing compared to the timeless eternity. Nevertheless, we have a modicum of freedom or *behira*, to do something, to act as if we can make choices, because we do not know what is in the "Preserved Tablet" and what will

---

3. This refers to the scholastic dictum: intellect, intelligens, intellectum, whose Hebrew equivalent is: sekhel, maskil, muskal. Another formulation renders it in Hebrew as hadeah, ha-yodeah, v'ha-yaduah; see Maimonides, Sefer ha-Mada, Hilkot Yesodei ha-Torah, 2:10.

4. "Preserved Tablet" Al-Ghazzali on Koran 85:22, see Ghazzālī, Kitāb sharḥ 'ajā'ib al-qalb [The marvels of the heart: Book 21 of the Iḥyā' 'ulūm al-dīn, The revival of the religious sciences], trans. Walter J. Skellie (Louisville, KY: Fons Vitae, 2010), 27, 58.

happen henceforth, as we experience these events through sequential time. Therefore, the rabbis teach: "Everything is under heaven's control [as it is all written in the "Preserved Tablet"], except the fear of heaven." The only thing we can do depends on the attitude we take.

You can think you are the doer here, as the separate ego, or you can have the conviction of *'emunah*, putting your trust in what is beyond your capacity to know. You should believe there is something like the "Preserved Tablet," that there is a field of knowledge that is too vast for our minds to grasp, because you can only see through your eyes. Nevertheless, your eyes are part of the Divine vision; your eyes are one of the ways that God sees what's going on here. That's why it's so important to be able to cry. You have to be able to see and to ask, "What are the things in the world I need to cry about?"

6.8 Types of Weeping

The tradition is that there are two different types of weeping, one for one eye, and another for the other eye. Recall that the first level is for the child in you that has never been able to grow, to get over what it needs to get over, and the other eye of weeping is for the sage, for the wisdom part of yourself, to draw down compassion into the world. With your other eye, you are saying to God: "Look, I'm your other eye here, and this is what I see—there is too much judgment in this world; you need to draw down more grace and mercy and sweetness!" If you cannot weep on *Tisha B'Av*, then you cannot really be in the space of the *Tisha B'Av*. As the Sages teach: "Everyone who mourns for Jerusalem will have the merit to share in her joy. And anyone who does not mourn for her will not share in her joy."[5]

6.9 Temple as Human Heart

The temple is a symbol for the heart itself, the place in the human heart, which can feel the divine pathos. The prophets, for Heschel, are those who have that sensitivity to feel the divine pathos.[6] If God were in this world, how would God be feeling? Seeing certain things here would make God weep. But we are God in this world; we are the eyes of God in this world, so we have to weep. Crying on the 9th of Av will paradoxically lead you to tremendous joy. The paradox is that the one who knows what to really cry about, is the same one who can really experience the divine joy. But you have to cry first—so that's the 9th of Av! "For these things I weep; mine eye, mine eye runs down with water; because the comforter is far from me, even he that should refresh my soul; my children are desolate, because the

---

5. bTa'anit 30b.

6. Abraham J. Heschel, The Prophets, vol. 2 (New York: Harper & Row, 1962), 4, 6, 7.

enemy has prevailed."[7]

6.10 Intensity of Wrath Cooling

You lose your soul when you give the world an evil eye, and so in making the world a little bit worse, you lose a little bit more of your soul. If you want to get your soul back, then you need the comforter, that is, the comfort of the messiah: the consciousness of the messiah. Despite the fact that *Tisha B'Av* is the highest point of divine wrath, as the culmination of the three weeks and part of the middle forty days, it is the peak of wrath. Following the afternoon service of mincha on *Tisha B'Av*, the divine mood shifts. During the first part of *Tisha B'Av*, you hit the most intense peak of divine judgment, and, once you hit midday, things start to cool down. The momentum here starts to shift in the other direction, and that's where messianic consciousness is born for the Talmud.[8] For when that divine judgment subsides, the soulful conscience of messianic consciousness begins to be revealed. That's where it begins, but where you can really begin to understand what this messianic consciousness really is about has to do with the *Tu B'Av*, the 15th of Av, which comes six days later.

6.11 Texture of Forty Days

To really understand this, we really have to understand the significance of the one hundred and twenty days from Shavuot to *Yom HaKippurim*, which is divided further into three periods of forty days. That's the process we have to understand.

As we approach *Tisha B'Av*, we need to have space for crying. The myth behind it concerns the power of the sixth or seventh of the month of Sivan. There is some uncertainty concerning which day is Shavuot. But Torah tells us to count from the day after Shabbat, which means Pesach. That is when we begin counting the Omer for forty-nine days. You get to the fiftieth day, which is Shavuot, meaning weeks. So, we count seven weeks, but the Torah does not specify exactly which day of the month it begins, whether it is the sixth or seventh of the month of Sivan, that leads to the event of *Matan Torah*.

6.12 Bringing Down Primordial Torah

What does *Matan Torah* really mean? According to our story, that is when Moses our teacher ascended into the cloud to receive Torah. It does not mean that Torah came down. It means that was when it was possible to receive Torah. Moses ascends and disappears—what does that mean? It is something like going to, what the Sufis call the "Preserved Tablet" (*al-lawh*

---

7. Lamentations 1:16.
8. bTa'anit 30b.

al-Mahfudh)—going to the cloud of unknowing. It is completely beyond the range of human knowledge. Now, what the Sufis call the "Preserved Tablet" (*al-lawh al-Mahfudh*) is what the Kabbalah refers to as *Torah ha-Kedumah* or "Primordial Torah." This "Primordial Torah" is not the Torah we can see in this world; the Torah we can see in this world is what it looks like when it has been reduced to a level that human beings are capable of experiencing. But what Torah is in essence is beyond the level of human minds. So, in order for this Torah to come down, it takes a very exalted soul, which is what Moses our teacher represents—the prophetic capacity for a human being to transcend the human mind and to be able to, through divine blessing, grace, and love, receive an imprint of the *Torah ha-Kedumah* or "Primordial Torah" and bring it down. That basically is what Moses our teacher did, but it took forty days for that process to occur.

Moses our teacher disappears for forty days. And what happens? We experience the mistake of the Golden Calf known as *Cheyt haEgel*. The people cannot deal with the disappearance of Moses our teacher, and the people cannot see the source of this *Torah ha-Kedumah* or "Primordial Torah." So, they need this Golden Calf, some kind of thing they can see and then say: "This is your god!" This is what you can see, and they go for that. So, the very nature of this Torah myth is an image of "not seeing clearly," or *ra ayin*—not being able to see what really cannot be seen.

So having a "good eye" or *tov ayin* is actually not seeing with my eye of judgment. But I have *'emunah*, trust in the imageless image, in what I cannot see. That is what I trust on being real, in my *'emunah*, and that is that everything is for good. While Moses our teacher is disappearing, and God cannot be seen, the people simply cannot deal with it. So they make a mistake by not seeing clearly—in making this mistake, they need to see something and call it "god." So, the rabbis teach that this episode leads to divine weeping, one of the "For these things I weep; mine eye."[9] Putting my *'emunah* in something that I can see, in something that does not deserve my *'emunah*—*that* is a false god. That is what an idol is—anything that you worship that you can see, rather than understanding that everything that you can see is coming from something that you *cannot see.*

6.13 Misusing the Eye

If everything you can see is coming from something that you *cannot see,* then you should put your *'emunah* in what you cannot see; that is where it is all coming from. If you need to see something, that is a misuse of the eye, not seeing rightly. That is what leads to divine wrath—whenever we are investing our *'emunah* in something that does not deserve it, then God weeps, as it were. It is not going to work out for you. You are going to get a

---

9. Lamentations 1:16.

bad *gilgul*. Maybe there is something in the short run, but in the long term it does not work out because you are not trusting in the things that have real value.

Torah says that "Moses was in the mount forty days and forty nights"[10]—what happened at the end of forty days? If you count from the seventh of Sivan forty days then you get to what? You reach the 17th of Tammuz, which is the beginning of the three weeks of lament, leading to total catastrophe on the 9th of Av. This is really an essential association, insofar as the 17th of Tammuz is supposed to be the day when Moses our teacher came down from Mount Sinai with the tablets of the covenant. And what does he do when he comes down the mountain? He smashes them to pieces, because he sees that the Israelites are going around with the Golden Calf—they did not have the *'emunah* to wait until he came down with the tablets!

6.14 Sweetening by Breaking

This in itself is an amazing thing because the Talmud teaches that this was one of the three things that God allowed Moses to get away with. You did the right thing, Moses, by smashing the tablets! *Yshar koah asher shibarta!* The Talmud says that you eliminated the contract, for if you would not have done so, the level of judgment would have been overwhelming. But you tore up the contract, so the Israelites were only guilty of being stupid; whereas if you would have held them responsible for the contract, it would have really been terrible! Moses our teacher was a great intercessor for the people, sweetening the judgment by breaking the tablets.

But there is another piece of this story we do not always remember. That is, the story tells us that the tablets were inside the Holy Ark in the Temple. When does Moses our teacher come down with the second tablets? Yom Kippurim! So on the 17th of Tammuz, Moses our teacher comes down Mount Sinai with the first tablets and breaks them. But the rabbis teach that within the ark, both tablets were present—the broken and the whole. What did Moses our teacher do after he had smashed the first tablets? He went and collected every shard, and preserved all those sacred fragments.

6.15 Dealing with Being Human

So there is no tzaddik, there is no saint so great in our tradition that makes no mistake, experiences no temptation. The greater the saint, the greater the temptation is. As long as you live in this world, you are going to be facing challenges, and none of us are really ever going to be so good. The

---

10. "And Moses entered into the midst of the cloud, and went up into the mount; and Moses was in the mount forty days and forty nights" (Exodus 24:18).

real issue is how we deal with being human. So in that regard, having *yirat shamayim* or a deep sense of awe is to know that "everything is under heaven's control [as it is all written in the "Preserved Tablet"], except the fear of the heavens,"[11] keeping in mind that there is a power running the whole show.

6.16 Closing Intention

It does not mean there is someone actually *there*, like in the *Wizard of Oz* dictating what this one is going to do and what that one is going to do. It means that underlying this world of appearances there is some deeper substrate without which nothing else would exist. So, every moment is being spontaneously manifested. Although we are independent characters in this movie, we don't realize we are playing these roles. But if you are a really good actor, you know you are playing a role—that is the level you can get to! You can wake up and know that you are playing the role. You can play it with awareness that you're playing the role, or you can play it with attachment and think that you really are the roles that are given to you. If you do, then you fall into the suffering and causing of suffering for yourself and others. But it's not really true!

---

11. bMegilla 25a.

Chapter 7
Carve New Tablets for Yourselves—Along the Journey of Elul

7.0 Points of Supernal Heart as Collective

Why is Moses, our teacher, not able to enter the Land of Israel? Reb Nachman has a teaching in which he explains.[1] He explains that the rock (*tzelah*), according to the Zohar, is associated with the higher heart (*lev elyon*). It is associated with the central point of transmission (*nekuda p'nimit*) that is a certain kind of soul. Peace in the world depends on the presence of this transmission point, the collective soul which is like a "supernal heart" (*neshamah kelalit*). Recall that the three main centers which G. I. Gurdjieff focuses on include the heart and the ganglia where the nerves converge, where all the sensing of the body depends on a central point. But the spiritual heart of all existence from which Torah is transmitted, the "supernal heart," is not always there.

7.1 Individual Souls vs. Collective

When Miriam the prophetess died, the well of Torah dried up. That is what happens when this "supernal heart" is not present. By Torah in the world, Nachman means the flow of impressions that can reach every mind, and by virtue of reaching every mind, each one is satisfied and soothed and guided for each level of being present in the world. The problem is that this "supernal heart" is not always there; and, when absent, there is a lot of discord in the world, because the impressions that need to be absorbed and digested by each particular mind are not going to be received from that "supernal heart," which is essential for the flow of Torah to descend. In his terms, when the "supernal heart" is not present, then there is controversy (*machloket*), instead of guidance to provide the source of orientation from the "supernal heart" for each and every soul. So, when individual minds are thrown to their own devices then controversy reigns.

---

1. Liqqutei Moharan, no. 20.

7.2 Distribution Point of Creative Energy

What Nachman is saying is that when this "supernal heart" is present, divine guidance can manifest from the supernal source called *Arikh Anpin* (Beyond Disturbance) and the flow is mediated by the hypostasis called *Zeir Anpin* (dialectical mediating station) to *Nuqbah* (receiving/birthing station). For our purposes, *Nuqbah* is the heart of the world, the distribution point from which all flows of *ruchaniut elohut* (creative energy) branch out.

Nuqbah is in a precarious situation. When it is not a good time, there is opposition from the exterior forces, and this is what happens when Miriam's well is not there. The point here is that when Moses our teacher finds himself in inauspicious times, when the "supernal heart" cannot transmit what needs to be transmitted, Moses receives the message to speak to the rock. But instead he gets angry at the people and hits the rock. Sparks do come out, but God says that because you acted in a way that did not increase my holiness, you cannot get to the Land of Israel.

7.3 Automatic Transmission of Supernal Heart

The heart transmits psychic impressions so that the teachings of Torah can be manifested in a receptive way. This is what Gurdjieff would call automatic transmission, that is, that everyone would be receiving good impressions for good living. But when that source is not there, then something needs to be done to restore it. Moses screws up. Why? His mistake is that he does not speak to the rock or the "supernal heart." As Isaiah says: "Speak words of comfort to Jerusalem," which is exactly what Moses did not do. Instead, he went forward with anger. Usually, this moment when Moses and Aaron fell down on their faces is understood as an expression of humility, but here Reb Nachman reads it in a deeper way: that they fell down on the job from their higher level, because the "supernal heart" was not present!

7.4 Pouring Out Supernal Heart

What does this speaking to the rock really mean? Speaking means *shofekh sikhato*, that is, "pouring out your heart" like water, which is a way of defining prayer. It is prayer without which it is very difficult to restore the "supernal heart." There needs to be an intervention if the "supernal heart" is not present. Then something has to be done in order to restore the order of Torah in the world. So, there has to be a prior prayer (speaking to the rock) before the Torah can come down again. When we get into the month of Elul, the task is to restore the "supernal heart," because this "supernal heart" was present on Shavuot and then lost.

7.5 Coming to Terms with Suffering of Contraction

For, on Shavuot, the "supernal heart" was present because of the presence of the first tablets received. But as we know there was a massive screw-up: the mistake of the Golden Calf, and, as a result, everything that was favorable turned into judgment. Through various responses, including the contrition of the three weeks during which we can come to terms with the suffering nature of our contracted state, we finally get to what is called an "auspicious time" (*et ratzon*). Not only this new month but also the entire forty days up to Yom Kippur is called an "auspicious time."

7.6 Directing Supernal Heart Energy

Let us learn how to direct our energy to the "supernal heart." There is a way of elevating yourself in meditation, by seven steps, until you expand through the seven steps, from the astral to the solar to the galactic to the all-worlds body until we get to the highest, deepest place we can go. We are begging that the flow can be restored that will grace all of us with the form of Torah that can satisfy our hearts and our souls—and not only our hearts and souls, but the hearts and souls of all beings, everything that receives its meaning from that "supernal heart" (*lev elyon*).

Rabbi Gedalyahu Shor has a wonderful teaching on the month of Elul that I find very meaningful. Rabbi Shor explains the difference between Shavuot and the forty-day period that culminates in Yom Kippur: "This month of Elul is called 'auspicious time.'" Just as in the archetype of this period, that is an "auspicious time," so it is an "auspicious time" to all who attune themselves to the meaning and purpose of what can be realized at this time: the secret of the archetype of the giving of Torah. Recall that the second tablets come down on Yom Kippur, just as on Shavuot, but there are key differences.

7.7 Holding Torah in This World

This whole forty-day period of return is a process of cultivating the possibility of holding the Torah in this world. The first tablets were broken into fragments. So, what is the relation between the first and second tablets? In order to get the first tablets, those who received it had to be on the highest level. The verse teaches something remarkable: "I told you: that you are Gods, and that you are formed on the highest level."[2] The first tablets were a transmission from the god-source to the god-receivers—from god to god. The first tablets were a non-dual Torah, for it exists between the One and One, so that even when it appears there is more than One, there is only One.

---

2. Literally, "I said: You are godlike beings, and all of you children of the Most High" (Psalm 82:6).

From the One that is Only One, to the One that is All in Everything.

7.8 Divine Body

To have the desire you have to go higher to fuel this period of Elul. There is a crucial difference, as the archetypal condition of the singular god transmitting Torah, like a "supernal heart" stimulating one cosmic divine body, and every part of that body is as divine as the heart. But you started out as gods, so if we only remember where we started from, this verse would resonate. Most of the time, we do not even think where we came from. If so, we are programmed to think about the grossly material to the mind that is full of complexes and complaints about the world, but when do we really remember where we came from?

7.9 Retracing Our Steps Through a Thread

There is a fantastic teaching I've seen about mitzvoth. People have the wrong idea, that because you have a house, you need to affix a mezuzah. But if we were in our right minds, we would understand that a house exists so that the mitzvah of mezuzah to be affixed on the lintel could be realized. It is like a thread that connects you back to where you came from, when you were in the condition of coarse body. In the Chabad teaching, Rabbi Shneur Zalman explains that the condition of being embodied entails not being cognizant of the chain of being that connects us to the source, to the "supernal heart." It means retracing our steps, expanding to our bigger bodies which we don't know any longer, which are ultimately contiguous, so that we recognize ourselves as the All in Everything. We think we are a Being from Nought (*Yesh m'Ayin*), but we don't see it, as it's not readily available to our senses. The point of mitzvoth then is to enable us to hold onto a thread that connects us back to where we came from. The principle is that mitzvoth are everywhere, so that everywhere you go, there is a mitzvah. We can make lists, but how many mitzvoth are there really? Who knows? To think that there is a finite number is a very one-sided brain way of reducing things. There must be mitzvoth for everything, everywhere you go, for every circumstance, for every condition. There are certain acts that are tried and true, having served the purpose of hidden gnosis. To be a thread, it has to connect us to the concealed *Hokhmah*.

7.10 Multi-perspectival Guide of *Middot*

There are so many languages here, so it is worthwhile to open ourselves to a multi-perspectival way of approaching some kind of objective space. To connect us to the concealed *Hokhmah* means to link us up with that element in our being, that focal point within consciousness that is beyond time and space.

One way of putting it is through the *middot* or qualia. The whole world is a matter of six infinite depths or extensions. That is a way of constituting the field of objective reality. But that field of objective reality is appearing to an awareness that knows it, and that was there before that field, as in the liturgy: "Before this field even appeared, there was something already there, and that something is still there" (*"ad she-lo nevra ha-olam"*). The field and its various veils come between us, and that which precedes all things is still there. What a mitzvah has to be is that which gives us a handle on where we are coming from, who we are in the archetypal sense. The highest level is what we are being reminded of. We are these gods, the plural of the singular. Collectively, we are the plural version, the original level, which is the level upon which the Torah is transmitted from the singular god to the collective gods. In that condition, there is nothing you have to do; it is spontaneously given to you. The Vedantans are referring to this as the original undistorted state of pure being, in which there are no separate doers. There is nothing that anyone has to do to change things. There are not going to be disagreements, for god is giving to gods, and the god that gets it does not need to ask for it. God is giver and god is receiver, taking the light and giving the light—all as a gift. What comes in is the notion of testing (i.e., reflection).

This is really interesting insofar as it is likened to a tiny little interruption. What caused this interruption between god giving to god? In that interruption came the sense of that worthiness. The question or doubt arises whether this is deserved or not. What comes is this interruption in the timeless, pure state, so that we have to assume that there is something not totally satisfying with static perfection: even though it sounds great in describing it. It would be even more satisfying to god if there were also justice, and some way of deserving this gift, not only getting it for free.

7.11 Beyond Qualia of *Middot*

What would it be like if the gift had to be earned? This is what ushered in the conditions of time and space, for at the highest level, there is just endlessness, as described by Gurdjieff,[3] so that it becomes tiresome and lonely. It becomes unbearable. With the unbearable loneliness, there arises the desire for something different, and here emerges the test, so that there would be value in the process of creation. If you remain in the highest level beyond the qualia, then there is nothing more than god giving to god, for no good reason. The lower worlds are not there at all.

---

3. G. I. Gurdjieff was born circa 1866 in Alexandropol (present-day Armenia). In 1922, after settling in France, he reopened his Institute for the Harmonious Development of Man. He died in Neuilly, France (near Paris) in 1949. For a reading guide on Gurdjieff, see http://www.gurdjieff-bibliography.com/Current/index.html, accessed June 14, 2017.

7.12 Reciprocity of Lower Worlds

But the lower worlds are reciprocal. For Gurdjieff, that is, you have to do something to earn your existence here, and beyond that, these concepts do not exist. You can see the sorry state we have gotten ourselves into. We no longer look for the way to repay our debt to god in our relationship to everyone and everything. So, the test is given to see if we are worthy to receive the gift of the flow of Torah, which contains the unification of all conditions, adjusted to their source. But the test puts that all in jeopardy.

God tried the Israelites with the temptation of the Golden Calf. Following this erring, failing the test, we have to ask ourselves deeply, how did we get here? And archetypally, in the state of embodiment you can be tested, but in the angelic state you cannot be tested as to whether you are deserving of the gift that comes from the divine source. We only have a choice, because we think we have a choice. But we don't understand how we are hooked up to the source. The Golden Calf is the story that leads to the 9th of Av, during which, if we do not wake up to the terror of the situation, to the condition we are in, we will have no way of regaining that "auspicious time" (*et ratzon*).

7.13 Regaining Second Tablets

But we can regain that "auspicious time" (*et ratzon*); we can get back to that level of being worthy of receiving the Torah in the form of the second tablets. You can be given Torah at the highest level of the first tablets, but they are going to shatter because they are too pure for us to receive at our present levels. What we have to understand is that the 9th of Av embodies our abject hopelessness. If it is conscious suffering in the right way, then it leads directly to messianic consciousness. You have to hit rock bottom to become the state of re-creation and return that we call *teshuvah*. What you can get are the second tablets, never the first ones. What's the difference between the two?

7.14 Divine Hardware and Software

The first tablets, according to Exodus 32:16, are formed and written by God. Another way of saying that god gave to god, forming the revelation and the form that receives. It is all a god-to-god transmission: "Do not read chiseled into the tablets, but freedom through the tablet."[4] What does freedom mean, from the impulse for evil and death (something like Vedantan *moksha*, the restoration of a consciousness that knew that everything is god)? Bondage comes from the state of consciousness in which you are confused, having lost that thread that connects you back to Nothing of *Ayin*. It is in

---

4. bEruvin 54a.

that place that you have no freedom, finding yourself to be preprogrammed, all coming from a state of confusion, not from the "supernal heart" that is the source of Torah. There is no death, thus it is the freedom of eternity, for there is nothing there that can die. There is an analogy between the outside and the inside, between the planetary body and the more interior bodies, the exterior body and what vivifies it, so the body is like the tablet while the soul is like the letters. The hardware and software are divinely made.

But concerning the second tablets, according to Exodus 34:1, "God said to Moses: Chisel out for yourself two tablets of stone, just like the original ones, and I'll write upon them the same words that were upon the first ones, the ones you shattered." The first tablets are all on the divine level, while the second tablets are brought down to earth. The second tablets are proportionate to our embodied state. Yet what is written in them is exactly the same words. That is because of failing the test of the Golden Calf—that you want to have a God that you can see in this state—projecting a false god. In the meantime, Moses is receiving from god to god. That inability to ascend to that level of being gods seals the fate of the need to receive the Torah in a way that could be held. It has to be adjusted to a form that we can receive.

7.15 Eternal Inscription of Divine Letters

So how did the letters get into the second tablets? When the first tablets were shattered, they flew up into the air, into the collective consciousness. The letters are always there. But we have to make ourselves into a tablet, to be worthy of having the divine words inscribed within us.

7.16 Non-dual Tablets

The question is if the first tablets were on the highest level, of god giving to god, so then how did the Israelites on such a level happen to slip up? Taking this further, we go back to the perplexity and an answer found within our tradition. Rashi[5] explains that the Golden Calf episode proves that the Israelites were never worthy of such a reception. The mystical tradition, however, teaches that on the highest level the source and its reflection of the divine are one. So that helps us to understand that it is all non-dual. But the reflection is after all only the reflection, not the source itself. Knowing that we are all created in the divine imprint (*tzelem Elohim*) prevents us from hating another. But on the highest level, who is this other? There is only god and god reflecting god back to itself!

---

5. Rashi is an acronym for the medieval biblical exegete from Troyes known as Rabbi Shlomo Yitzhaki (1040–1105); see Elie Wiesel, Rashi: A Portrait (New York: Nextbook, 2009).

7.17 Source and Reflection

The subtle distinction between the source and its reflection, between the first and second tablets, is that even on the highest level, in order for that level to continue to exist, the source is doing something to maintain the level because what is being received is totally and automatically coming from the source itself (*siyyua d'shmaya*). As long as this aid is coming from the source, all is well, but as soon as this transmission is taken away, even though "The Everything" that exists within the reflection is still perfect, nevertheless, it slips down into a lower level of being. Why? Because the reflection is no longer being maintained as peer to peer, god to god.

7.18 Giver and Receiver

Now there is a distinction between the giver and the receiver. The receiver has slipped and is no longer a perfect reflection. *Why did it happen then?* Not because they were not on the highest level nor because their merit was deficient, but it occurred in order to teach them the lesson of return (*teshu-vah*).

What does it mean? This means that only beings on that highest level have the capacity to exist in that perfect form without doing anything about it. But if there are going to be beings like us, who exist in the lower worlds, who have the potentiality to realize the kingdom of heaven, then there has to be a kind of spiritual work to regain the "lost" reality of the highest state. The highest state itself is a reflection of the unmediated reality itself. But the fallen state is a distorted reflection of the reflection, a reflection further removed. In that state, you have to do something, in order to transform it into something that truly reflects its source. Otherwise it devolves into being nothing more than coarseness.

So, traditionally, the devotional practice for these days of Elul, known as "auspicious times" (*yemei ratzon*), is working on the prayer practice. It is that longing to reconnect and restore the "supernal heart" into the space of all existence. To be able to care whether that center is present—this is the work!

7.19 What Prayer Is All About

Nachman talks about prayer as words of fire, which is what it really takes to make this happen. It is easy to be misled by the passionate self when you see words of fire—but too much passion is destructive. If there is not an integrated balance of all three centers, then the imbalance of excessive emotionalism will generally lead to something stupid. When you can warm up your heart so your prayer flows from a state of inspiration, the words that come in that condition can carve into the stony heart a reflection of what god is writing. That is what prayer is really about—after having lost the first tablets on which God did the writing; I'm inscribing the second tablets.

But the shards of the first tablets were housed with the second tablets. Maybe we don't have those sacred fragments any longer, perhaps they are in Ethiopia. Be that as it may, we don't have to worry, because the ark is the collective consciousness and can never be lost. The letters that can form the divine gift to enable us to be normal people, as Gurdjieff teaches, knowing who we are and where we are, only requiring us to carve a space in our own hearts where those letters can be housed. When the need for return emerged in the archetypal myth, just as now, those letters can be rewritten into our hearts with the hand of god, but only if we make the spaces available for them inside our hearts.

7.20 Carving Your Second Tablets

So, returning in *teshuvah* is taking forty days from the beginning of the month of Elul, and making an effort to pray as often as you can with the greatest sincerity. Whatever form it takes, all prayer has to come from the personal accounting. Suppose you did *selichot* every day as is the Sephardic practice—it's not necessary or even most effective to do it exactly like them. But think of the structure of your prayer (whatever its content) as a perfect service of the heart—so make your own order of *selichot* service. It is not a matter of quantity but a matter of quality: so that there will be a carving in the heart that frees us from our personal *Mitzrayyim*. When it comes to the return of *teshuvah*, it really requires an inner process of "carving" the second tablets that we make ourselves, rendering ourselves as open and prepared as we can so that god can write the letters in our hearts.

While we need to apply ourselves to this process, we must add to it, as the Kotzker rebbe teaches about revelation, something powerful. "When you go out to war," [6] going out to develop the consciousness of prayer can be construed as a Jewish mindfulness practice. But the work is that in my awakened state, I want to be praying. Every time I awaken, I look to see where I find myself, and then I turn that into a prayer to be sustained, to be held, to be enabled to receive Torah wherever I find myself. To make that a practice over the course of every day of Elul is highly desirable.

Scripture states in Numbers 10:9 that when you have a war in your own land, there are many reactive efforts required. You have to make an effort, i.e., inner adjustments, in order to be victorious in this world. Yet the Kotzker is teaching that in this other case, you do not need prayer. *What is the difference?* When you are doing the inner practice, and you are afflicted, your work is clear. But when you go out, when you are looking outside yourself, then you are looking from god's eyes, you are looking from the

---

6. Deuteronomy 21:10.

other side, and there is no struggle. But within yourself, you do have to do the work on yourself to stay awake.

7.21 Inner vs. Outer Consideration

There is a parallel in Gurdjieff, to *inner* and *outer consideration*. You don't want to be reacting to other people. In your own land: there is where you need to be in constant prayer and *teshuvah*. But when it then comes to the outer consideration that is when god gives you everything—there is no battle there. So god gives you power over the enemy. What the Kotzker rebbe teaches here is that when you invoke your personal god and a true god: when god becomes your personal god, the god within you, this is the reflection of the highest level.

Recall that the first words on the first tablets were "I the Lord Am Your God"—when god is actually your god, when you are the reflection of god. If you want to get to that place of the personal god, that is Torah. When you say that, you are receiving Torah. You have to beg for it, according to Reb Nachman. Prayer and Torah are two sides of the same coin.[7] Try to be only one and not the other, and you are incomplete.

How important is the prayer that cost Moses the opportunity to enter into the Land of Israel!?! I'm too lax when it comes to this stuff, but, as the rabbis suggest, we should be praying constantly. We should be praying more, at least make it a conscious aspiration that everything is a prayer for the month of Elul into the ten days of *teshuvah*. Before you do anything, make it a prayer, so that you make it a mitzvah. If you make everything a prayer, then it is a mitzvah, which is a thread that reconnects you to the source, from which we are all hanging by an invisible thread.

7.22 Closing Intention

May we all be successful in this work, to make this effort in becoming and getting back to the level, the reflection of the reflection, god giving to god, that as many of us as possible should have blessing in this.

---

7. Liqqutei Moharan, no. 20.

Chapter 8
Correcting Our Corrections on Rosh Hashanah[1]

8.0 Change as Self-transformation of *Teshuvah*

Can people really change? The great mystic and visionary, Reb Nachman of Breslov, emphasizes the importance of doing self-transforming practices known as *teshuvah* in order to complete and enhance our preliminary attempts at *teshuvah*. In doing so, according to a Talmudic teaching, we can reap the benefits of two worlds, "this world," known as *olam hazeh*, as well as the world-that-is-coming, or *olam ha-ba*. This can be understood in several ways. First, is the foundational teaching that whatever we do to reflect on our deficiencies and to correct them always arises from the specific perspective of our current level of development. Since every perspective is itself relative and provisional in regard to yet higher possibilities, we need to see beyond any sense of present attainment and begin to envision what still lies ahead: the world-that-is-coming. In this way, we can transform our self-transforming into something even more evolved. The old-paradigm approach to *teshuvah* places particular emphasis on refinement and improvement of the "individual self" and its relationship to other "individual selves." That is the *teshuvah* of this world or *olam hazeh* and has served us well within the parameters of previously established levels of consciousness. But what of the *teshuvah* of the world-that-is-coming or *olam ha-ba*? To begin to attract the future, we need to turn ourselves in the direction of a more evolved self-model. We can think of this turning as a shift in awareness from thinking of ourselves as separate, rigidly defined, particulate selves with distinct borders to bringing into greater clarity a sense of ourselves as interactive, inter-dependent, co-creating waves equally participating in the Ocean of Totality (YHVH).

8.1 Beyond Self-criticism: Correcting Our Correction

"Correcting our correction" or *teshuvah al ha'teshuvah* is not another level of the *teshuvah* of self-criticism and seeking forgiveness for the uncomfortable and regrettable effects of our apparent and isolated particularity (which remains nevertheless a necessary precondition for most of us). Rather, it

---

1. Rosh Hashanah 5770.

is an unfolding, embracing, turning beyond mere particularity toward recognition of the way(s) that we are already present within the Great Ocean within which we are all inter-participatory waves.

8.2 Refining High-command Consciousness

In the month of Elul, the focus is on preliminary, particulate *teshuvah*, ridding ourselves of the tired, old, and outmoded selves of *olam hazeh*. To enter the new paradigm of the New Year, we need to turn ourselves toward the higher *teshuvah* of the world-that-is-coming, or *olam ha-ba*. This means deeply focusing on a vision of a future in which our wavelike selves will literally be our second nature. In this way, as we turn toward the "Head" of the New Year known as Rosh Hashanah, we can refine our "high-command consciousness," or *mochin*, toward greater awareness of the world-that-is-coming.

8.3 Closing Intention

May we all merit great success in the practice of recognizing and releasing into the most positive future form of the Divine Dreaming that is already present within our presence. May we have greater success in this coming New Year in cooperatively creating greater awareness of the ever-changing harmonies and melodies of all dancing wave-selves that collectively contribute to the incomparable beauty of the Ocean of Being. May we be written and sealed immediately in the Book of Life for the good that is coming.

Chapter 9
At-onement as the Secret of Divine Pardon on Yom Kippurim[1]

9.0 Stripping Overlays as *Teshuvah*

Life feels like it's just smoke and mirrors. Ordinarily, we experience a world that we consider overwhelmingly real. But the ephemeral world of our ordinary experience can be better understood as "smoke and mirrors" known by the acronym of *ASHa"N*.[2] This smokiness doesn't mean that the world and everything in it is not real. It's just that its true reality is concealed from us and manifests as "space, time, and the perspective of an individual, ego-centered mind and consciousness" known as *Olam, Shanah, Nefesh (ASHa"N)*. We find life problematic, due to the lack of clarity inherent in our ordinary existence, and so we blame ourselves, others, and what we think of as "God" as responsible for our dissatisfactions. But Torah—which comes to reveal what is deeper and truer, beyond the smoke of our limited and conditional understanding—offers us an "answer" we call *teshuvah*, by means of which we can break through the karmic barrier that crystallizes during the course of each yearly cycle and forgive ourselves and everything else. This "answer," the practice of *teshuvah*, implies returning to our source, through stripping off the smoky overlays of all the levels of who we think we are and what we think the world is.

9.1 The Day of At-onement Itself At-ones

Teshuvah is something that can be practiced at any time. For some highly evolved people, it is a constant practice of readjusting, remembering, and retuning oneself to the very source of manifest consciousness, "Guardian of Israel" or *Shomer Yisrael*, the ever-awake divine consciousness that watches over and witnesses all that manifests. But even the most commendable and diligent practice of *teshuvah* cannot match the power of "The Day of

1. Erev Yom HaKippurim 5771. In appreciation of all your support and gratitude for all those who generously donated in memory of my father, Itzhaq Aizik Dov Ber ben Shimon ha-Kohen, z"l.
2. Sefer Yetzirah, 3:4.

At-onement" known as *Yom HaKippurim*, which in rabbinic speech is simply known as *Yomah* or "The Day" with a capital T. The efficacy of "The Day" is one of the greatest secrets of Torah and defies comprehension by our uni-perspectival, egocentric minds. Generally, when we practice some form of *teshuvah*, the results are proportionate to our efforts, and despite even our very best efforts to "do *teshuvah*," a piece of independent existence remains operative.

9.2 Day as *Devekut*

But Maimonides teaches that "the very power of The Day itself At-ones."[3] As human beings who are the smoky expressions of the underlying divine fire, we have to feel regret for all of the shortcomings that we associate with ourselves, the actions of others that sadden us, and basically everything we feel that is related to a sense of not having fully succeeded in playing our divinely deployed roles and the world not having yet achieved its full potential. But that regret and remorse most commonly associated with "repentance" is only the most external aspect of *teshuvah*. The heart's remorse is itself a sign of the inner divine presence, since conscience is itself a divine quality and its inner expression is an intimation of divine love and non-separation from the divine source known as *devekut*. But the power of the unique Light that is disclosed only on "The Day" is so great that such a superficial awareness of *devekut* is only a mere awakening and this Light has the power to attract us beyond all our manifest forms until we reach the level of transparency alluded to in scripture: "For on This Day, at-onement occurs beyond all manifest forms of individuated self, to purify you of the weight of remorse for all you think of as your misdoings. In the very consciousness of the Totality, you will be purified."[4]

9.3 Day Returning to Light Itself

What then is the "secret" of this amazing teaching? In general, all our experience can be understood as "actively striving to progress toward the *omega point* of evolution's *telos* and re-centering ourselves again and again in the very source from which the evolving manifestations of *ASHa"N* emerge," known in Hebrew prophetic language as *ratzo ve-shov*.[5] Before "the smoke" even appears, on "The Day," however, everything is *shov* returning to the Light itself. That all-attracting Light is the secret of the Thirteen Qualities of Divine Compassion. The unveiling of this Light ultimately elevates consciousness beyond our individuated, self-centered perspective that is called "free will," known as *bechirah*, to the level in which there is

---

3. Maimonides, Hilkhot Teshuvah, 1:3.
4. Leviticus 16:30.
5. Ezekiel 1:14.

a merging with the higher consciousness and Divine Mind of the Totality, known as *Yedi'ah*.

From this perspective, it is clear that everything all-together is always already integrally moving according to the Will of the Totality and the very nature of existence itself *IS* the "evolutionary process" known as *Tiqqun Olam*. And this is the very heart of conviction or *'emunah* and Love Supreme or *Ahavat Olam*. From the perspective of the "higher consciousness" or *Yedi'ah* of the Great Light of the Thirteen Qualities of Divine Compassion, the very basis of all existence, it is clear that "you" as a manifestation of the totality cannot possibly have done anything wrong (even though there are karmic consequences). Or more correctly, you could not have done anything other than what the "Will of the Totality" or *Retzon HaShem* required of "you." So, this At-onement and its realization is in itself the secret of divine pardon. The Great Mind within which "you" are a dream and a thought loves its creation and covers over what on the "ordinary level of consciousness" (or *bechirah*) we consider our faults and shortcomings. From this higher perspective, we recognize that even our intentional misdeeds are considered as merits. *YHVH* loves and blesses every one of us for the mere fact of our existing!

9.4 Closing Intention

May we all have the merit to realize this on The Day of the great pardoning, of At-onement. May we all have the merit to bask in the purification of the Thirteen Qualities of Divine Compassion.

Chapter 10
Acting Out of Love from the Shade of Sukkot

10.0 Interconnective Pathways of Peace

Everything is interconnected, so we have to find our way to Sukkot. We have to understand what the way to Sukkot is, because if we know, the Torah is the pathway of peace. It's the way to peace. It's a path, a pathway that wends its way through the changes of the year. Recall how Elul is preparation for Rosh Hashanah.

And in that process, we actually passed through Rosh Hashanah, and we are kind of on our way to Yom Kippur. We are midway between Rosh Hashanah and Yom Kippur, which we call *Aseret Yemei Teshuvah*, the ten days of turning, the ten days of *returning*. There is an important kabbalistic image that goes with those ten days that can be a bit technical, but it's a powerful symbol that is associated with these ten days. During these ten days between Rosh Hashanah and Yom Kippur, a kind of spiritual surgery is performed on the body of the cosmos and the body of who we are, the integral whole that makes us who we are, the way we are constructed. That means on all levels—body, mind, and spirit and beyond—every aspect and level undergoes a *tiqqun*.

10.1 Cycle of Sacred Loop

A *tiqqun* means that it goes through a correction. It goes through a process of correction, and in the process of this correction, it gets to start anew. It's restored, because we are dealing with a cycle, with something like a sacred loop. We understand the course of the year to be a repeating cycle, and, at this stage, we have the opportunity to get back on track and on course. That's one of the meanings to *teshuvah*, to get back on track, to return to a more pure condition. One of the verses that's associated with this time is Leviticus 16:30—"Before YHVH" or "in the presence of YHVH," or even "prior to YHVH," at the level before what YHVH symbolizes or means, even before that appears, there is a dimension of reality which has no name, but which is the source, the root source from which YHVH itself manifests.[1]

---

1. Literally, "on this day shall atonement be made for you, to cleanse you; from all

10.2 Day of the Name

Let me explain—there is a core principle in Hasidism and in Kabbalah which talks about the *Yom HaShem*, "the day of the Name." The day of the Name actually is the day that follows Yom Kippur. The day that follows Yom Kippur is not just any day, but it's a day that's called "the day of the Name." Recall that there's a four-day period between Yom Kippur and Sukkot, and that four-day period is associated with the process of the manifestation of a new name. What name? The name YHVH, which has four letters. The name is called the *shem hameforash*, the name that refers directly to the *Anokhi*, to the "I Am," which is the basis of everything that exists, according to this unified field theory, that the whole cosmos is an expression of a field of divine power. That field is called YHVH. That name itself is a symbol and represents through the forms of the four various letters the display of all the phenomenality in the whole existent world. It means there's a way you can identify or recognize every single thing that exists as somehow located on one of the letters of YHVH.

10.3 Giving Form Through the Name

So, after Yom Kippur comes the day that the new Name comes into the world for this year, the name that will hold the divine powers that will run and determine the nature of this New Year. Of course, there is the assumption here that we have something to do with that name, just as it has something to do with us, but we are not talking about where that name comes from, which we can't have anything to do with, because it's always the same. That doesn't change. There's a verse that the Hasidim like to quote, "For I YHVH change not,"[2] in which they're not talking about the YHVH, which is the basis of all of existence and which is constantly involved in an evolving process, but there is a substrata which we cannot name, which is why to the extent that we refer to it, we call it *Ein Sof*, that which has no limitation. When you say something has a name, you're giving it a form.

This name YHVH, for those who are familiar with Indian thought and Vedanta is like *Brahman Saguna*. In Vedanta, there's *Brahman Nirguna* and *Brahman Saguna*. Brahman with attributes, that's YHVH, and then there is *Brahman Nirguna* that has no attributes, that's *Ein Sof*, or, more precisely, *atzmut Ein Sof*. The most essential nature of *Ein Sof* is pretty much what the Hindus call *Brahman Nirguna*, that is, *Brahman* without any *gunas*, without any qualities.

---

your sins shall ye be clean before YHVH" (Leviticus 16:30).

2. "For I YHVH change not; and you, O sons of Jacob, are not consumed" (Malakhi 3:6).

10.4 Nothingness Always There in the Name

Just as they have this sense that there is a source from which everything comes, and to which everything returns, some of the Vedanta teachers would say those who practice meditation with this kind of view may be able to recognize that there's this space between thoughts. When the mind becomes completely empty, it's possible to have a glimpse in a reverse direction, to see into the *Ayin*, into the no-thingness that is always there, and that is like a pause between each moment of pulsation, each moment of manifestation.

The moments of manifestation of the empowered form, the form that will be the underlying structure for the entire year that is coming, is like the *Brahman Saguna*, which will be the name for that year. When I say "name," it is not like as if it has a *different name* each year, but that the name YHVH is different in its qualities and strength each year. It isn't always empowered in exactly the same way. The only thing that's constant is the code. The code of those four letters represents this substratum that all forms of manifestation depend on, the basis of existence, which is equated with the "I Am," with *Anokhi*. YHVH *Eloheikha*, "I Am is the YHVH," is both the source of everything that exists, and it is also the source of liberation. "I liberated you from *Mitzrayyim*," which is also the source of release from the smoky, confused condition or state of contraction.

10.5 Extending the Channels of Compassion

This period from Rosh Hashanah to Yom Kippur is essential for our contribution to pulling down the new Name, what's called in Hasidic language, *hamshakha*. It means drawing forth or pulling down a new name that will enable all of life that is manifest to have the energy, the qualities, that it will have for the next year. That's really the work that we are doing, or one way to understand the *avodah*. So, the work that we are doing from Rosh Hashanah to Yom Kippur is to bring down the healthiest, most light-bearing source of compassion that we possibly can. The name itself YHVH is a name of love. It's the thirteen channels of compassion known as *middot ha-Rachamim*, or the attributes of YHVH.

We are working to facilitate the return of YHVH, which in itself, you could say, is the guarantee of another year. You're asking for another year. That's the guarantee of another year, that there's a new YHVH that comes after Yom Kippur. That's what we are really praying for, so that we'd have another year, and all of life should have a source of existence and maintenance for another year. Basically, it's good to think in terms of years. I think it's very good to think in terms of years. So, I would like to share some thoughts that we don't always present or think about which have to do with time and space.

As Reb Zalman translated so beautifully: "Through time and space, Your glory shines." Through time and space, Your glory shines. YHVH is the glory that shines through time and space.

10.6 Yearning for Eternity

For some reason, if you'll permit me to say so, we are not happy with time and space—we want eternity. In a sense, we will have eternity. We have eternity, and because we want eternity, we often talk about *the eternal*, to the extent that we can, because the glory in time and space is difficult. It's painful for us to deal with mortality, to face it, to face the fact that we are mortal beings, and, yet, I think that's precisely what we are. What I'm saying is that I think that somewhere along the line, we went off track. Where did we go off track? We went off track in what is called the *chet Adam haRishon*, the mistake of the first Adam, or I should say, the *story* of the mistake of the first Adam, because it is a *story*, but I'm not sure that we get the story. If we looked at that story, and of course, we would recall that the mistake of *Adam haRishon* is eating from the tree, *Etz haDa'at Tov v'Ra*, eating from the Tree of Good and Evil.

10.7 Getting to the Land of Israel

I think it seems to be like a normal reaction. It certainly has been my reaction many times when I have gone over that story. I think it's fairly typical that people say, "What's wrong with that?!? What's wrong with eating from the Tree of Knowledge? That sounds like a pretty good thing!?!" Yet it seems like Torah is actually saying it's not. It is the cause of *losing* the Edenic existence, of being thrust from the Garden of Eden. Really, if you take a panoramic view of the entire Torah, you could say, perhaps, that it begins with the expulsion from the Garden of Eden with a story about a catastrophic mistake, and then it offers a way to get to the Land of Israel. When I say "getting to the Land of Israel," first of all, I'm talking about this as a spiritual story. I'm not talking about somebody's political ideas. Really, I think of it as a universal story, not one about any period in time or particular political events, but the perennial story.

10.8 Never Lost Forever

The perennial story, then, would be re-cognizing, getting a chance each year when you get the Torah anew; you get another chance to see, "Well, what was the *chet Adam haRishon*? What is it that gets us thrown out of Eden?" Conversely, as a result, because of divine compassion, even though we make a catastrophic mistake, nevertheless, we are offered a way—the way of the Torah to get to the Land of Israel. There is a kind of communication, a voice of divine grace that says *even though you make a mistake, a fundamental mistake, nevertheless, you're not lost forever.* You can still get back. Once the mistake has already been made, then the story is about how we get to the Land of Israel, which requires a long journey.

10.9 Eden as Another Chance

We are getting another chance, and in order to get another chance, we have to, as the Torah says, "make this purification before YHVH." The purification, in a way, is a return to the Edenic state. Exactly what would be the Edenic state and what is it that causes us to lose that Edenic state and the need to find our way again would be questions worth thinking about.

I want to get to this story of Sukkot, but I'll just inject this little reflection, which I think is worth some consideration, and that is what the mistake revolves around. I'm just repeating what is literally the case. It revolves around eating from the tree, eating from the knowledge. There's one commandment in Eden. There's only one commandment: *just don't eat from the Tree of Knowledge of Good and Evil.* In a way, that's the whole thing. If you want to stay in Eden, just don't eat from the Tree of Knowledge of Good and Evil, because once you eat from the Tree of the Knowledge of Good and Evil, *you will be like gods.*[3]

Now, actually, *we are not like gods.* That's the problem, but if you eat from the knowledge of the Tree of Good and Evil, *you will think that you are gods.* You will think that you are like gods, and as soon as you think that you are like gods, you're out of Eden.

From there begins the story of civilization that is repeating, that is repeating and repeating and repeating, and now we are coming to, perhaps, a critical stage. What happens? If we repeatedly do the one thing that will cause us to lose the Edenic state, it seems that eventually we will run the risk of destroying ourselves altogether.

10.10 Eden as Beyond Yourself

You have to ask, what is an *Edenic state*? It's a state in which you don't think that you're God, but it isn't a state in which *there isn't God,* just you *don't think you are God.*[4] You know better than that when you are in the Edenic state. In the Edenic state, you have a relationship to spiritual beings, to something beyond yourself, and there is a sense of appreciation, and a lot of other things that go with it, but because the very immediate result of eating from the Tree of Knowledge of Good and Evil is thinking that you

---

3. "For God does know that in the day you eat thereof, then your eyes shall be opened, and you shall be as God, knowing good and evil'" (Genesis 3:5).

4. "I said: You are godlike beings, and all of you children of the Most High" (Psalm 82:6).

are god or even godlike, which is also, I think, a stretch. And that's part of the problem, that I think we want to support our sense of being gods by noticing how we are godlike. That may be the secret of the entire problem that we have, basically.

What I want to connect this to is one of the better signs. One of the things that make me more hopeful is when I meet especially younger people who are into Judaism, and I see what they are into—one of the things that seems to be the strongest is what they call "earth-based Judaism." It seems to me what is emerging is something like what I will call a "neo-tribalism." It's not the tribalism of the past. I think it is a different form, not the tribalism as it has survived within the world that is outside of Eden, within the non-Edenic state in which tribalism takes forms of ultra-nationalism and things like: "I identify with this, and you're not me, and therefore I don't like you, and you're my enemy," and all of that.

10.11 Eden as All Stages of Life

In the Edenic state, there aren't any enemies, basically, but there might be different tribes running around. Tribes are like supportive affinity groups. They're groups that have a kind of collective identity and a cooperative nature, something like guilds. That means they support each other in order to be able to maintain their existence. In the course of this existence is mortality itself. In the Edenic state, you don't really have eternity. You have all the stages of life. You have birth and death, you have entrance and exit. You have sickness and health—all of these things are there, but they're not a problem because *you don't think that you're God*, and *you don't think that you are eternal* or that you should be eternal, but you *recognize the place of the world in which you are.*

10.12 Planetary Gnostic *Tiqqun*

It seems to me there is a *tiqqun* that is occurring, and I feel it's a *tiqqun* that we very much need. This is part of the integration of what I call the *gnostic* and the *planetary*, where we have to put a much greater emphasis on the *planetary* than on the *gnostic*. Let me explain. What I mean by that is that, within the non-Edenic state, all of these mysticisms develop. Most mystical paths are basically about a way to get out of here, not to be an embodied being, to have some doubt about the reality of the world because it's too difficult, it's too painful, it involves mortality, and we want to be gods. To be gods, you have to be beyond coming and going, you want to have some kind of eternal state.

Even the quest for what is beyond, to a certain extent, it's a result of eating the truth of the Tree of the Knowledge of Good and Evil. It makes us want to have something to aspire to. In the Edenic state, you really don't aspire to anything. You just live your life, just like all the other animals. In the Edenic state, all the animals are present. Yes, it's the case that there's a food chain, and some of them rely on others, one relies on this one, one relies on that one. It's all supportive, but, basically, the idea of the Edenic state seems to be nobody takes what they don't need, because they're not there to try to get more and better than things actually are in their native state. They just want to basically enjoy it. *What is wrong with that?*

10.13 Eden as Part of the Meal

Once you eat of the tree, the fruit of the Tree of Knowledge of Good and Evil, you want something better. It's not enough. I have a favorite restaurant in Albuquerque. I try to go there once a week, and I always sit, basically, in the same table, which is next to the window that's facing the foothills, and I always sit in that table because I just want to look at the mountains. I don't even think about anything; I just look at the mountains, and that's what I want. Behind me, because this is an Indian restaurant, they're blasting away these *Bollywood* movies. Now they know, because I go there all the time, they know where I want to sit, but usually, for a long time, I'd come in there, and they'd always seat me so that I could see the screen, because they thought, "Oh, you want to watch . . . here comes someone, he wants to watch the Bollywood." Then you can listen because they've got music and dancing and all this stuff. I'm not saying there's anything wrong with it, but I don't go there for that. I don't want to see the *Bollywood.* I want to just look at the mountains and eat. When I look at the mountains, I feel that it's part of the meal. I'm eating the food and my eyes are taking in the mountains, and I'm just really happy to be there. I'm not trying to get anywhere. It's natural. It's all natural. I'm just doing and being—that Edenic state.

Why would I be talking about something like this? Well, it has something to do with Sukkot if you look at it in a certain way. What are we doing on Sukkot? Now, Sukkot, according to the system of the Torah, which is this path that goes in a certain order, progresses from one thing to another, where what you do before is what prepares you for what comes next. We are saying that in order to get to Sukkot, basically it's a good idea and maybe the best way to get there via Rosh Hashanah and Yom Kippur. But, don't worry, the medieval French commentator, Rashi, already claimed that there is no chronology in Torah, that there's no beginning. There's no before or after in Torah. There is a certain kind of principle that since everything is cyclic, you can start anywhere, so don't get scared if you didn't do everything perfect according to somebody's idea of perfection for Rosh Hashanah.

10.14 Eden as Starting Where You Are

You can start where you are. You can always start where you are. You come into the circle where you are, and then you go from there to the next thing. Once you get in the circle, basically, you want to stick with the circle, and then you'll stick with the circle, and you'll eventually come around to the same point. When you come around to the same point next year, you will understand how the circle got you to Sukkot and how helpful it was to go through Rosh Hashanah and Yom Kippur, and how that enhanced the experience that you could have on Sukkot. From that perspective, when we recall that—from Rosh Hashanah to Yom Kippur—we are doing this spiritual surgery that is the purification to restore ourselves to a kind of Edenic state. The Edenic state is a state in which *we don't think we are gods*.[5] We get over the poison, what Torah calls the poison that, in the story, the snake has snuck into us, has injected into us, through the mistake of eating from that tree, which seemed very desirable. That is what Adam says: "It's very desirable." So, we have to watch out for it.

Actually, a lot of people are confused, and, in our tradition, we have gotten confused, because we've generated teachings that are non-Edenic teachings. They're teachings that are expressing the poison of the fruit of the Tree of Knowledge of Good and Evil. For example, the idea that physical pleasure is a harmful or evil thing, that's a big mistake, in my opinion. In my humble opinion, that is a big mistake. There's nothing in the Edenic condition that would be threatened by the enjoyment that a mortal being can get from being in this world.

10.15 Threats to Eden

What is it, then, that threatens the Edenic state? We already said that it's the glamor; it's the allure of being like gods, which is precisely the thing that gets us out of Eden. I think this is what Torah's teaching us, that we could recognize that there's something that has tempted us that tempts us so strongly out of the Edenic state, and we can call it by various names. You can call it the egocentric mind, if you like. You can call it the *yetzer ha'ra* or the libidinal impulse. It's been called by many things, but what it comes down to, fundamentally, is the eating of the fruit of the Tree of the Knowledge of Good and Evil, with the result being that somehow, from a being that was able to appreciate its existence in an Edenic state, one became a threatened, defensive, aggressive, fearful strategist in a non-Edenic state, who, instead of recognizing the great blessing of existence itself, becomes caught up in the quest to *eternalize* itself and to *maximize* its power—to be God, to become like God or be God, and all that goes with that.

---

5. Psalm 82:6.

We have to rethink this verse in Psalm 82:6 and what it really means when it suggests we are "being gods." I think this is a very important issue, that a lot of our spirituality needs to be refined, and some of these ideas about "we are gods" are very dangerous. We are not separate from God, and that is a very important thing. It is not only possible, but probably very important, to identify and be able to hear the voice for God in ourselves. In the deepest depths that we can realize, if we look into ourselves, we can find a source of unity, a source that is loving and directly connected to the source of all life. Even if we have the clearest recognition of that, it won't make us less mortal. It won't be like Mira Alfassi's interpretation of Sri Aurobindo,[6] which seems to be a very dangerous distortion, namely, that we can become immortal human beings and live forever. That's to say we are going to become immortal human beings and be able to live together, live forever. Let's try to live together first.

10.16 Living the Edenic Way

The aspiration to live forever makes it very hard for us to live together, because the earth is limited, it has limited resources, and this is the way it goes. One generation comes and another leaves. That's part of the poignancy of the whole trip. That's what we are part of. We are not going to be God and live forever, but we could, if we live in an Edenic way, in an inspired way, and if that's what it means to be enlightened, then we can contribute to the ongoing process to the circle of existence. We can contribute to the annual re-enlivening of the earth. We can play a role in making sure that it continues that there is *kiyyum*, a ground of being to exist. Otherwise, there probably won't be, or let's say there very likely won't be. That's the way it looks to me, that if we go on with the way of life that is based on what I call eating the fruit of the Tree of the Knowledge of Good and Evil, then we are at risk of destroying the possibility for an Edenic experience on this earth, not only for ourselves, but also for the creatures in the sea, the creatures in the air, and the larger ecospheres.

The Tree of Life is already in the center of the Garden of Eden. The danger is trying to get it, is to appropriate it if you have eaten of the fruit of the Tree of Knowledge of Good and Evil. That's what gets us. You have people that are trying to figure out how you can live forever. They're going to freeze your body until we can revive your brain, you're going to have a bionic, an artificial, post-human, living on Mars, in the wake of having destroyed one planet first. That's the danger of eating of the Tree of Life, which is eternal, when a person is polluted by the eating of the Tree of the

---

6. Sri Aurobindo (August 15, 1872, Calcutta—December 5, 1950) began his Integral practice of Yoga in 1904. See: http://www.sriaurobin-doashram.org/ashram/sriauro/life_sketch.php (accessed June 14, 2017).

Knowledge of Good and Evil.

10.17 Edenic Purification as Forgiveness

How do we do the purification? Purification, which is the spiritual surgery, has to do with forgiving—forgiving ourselves for having eaten the fruit of the Tree of Knowledge of Good and Evil, and not blaming ourselves and others. The way to get back into the Edenic state is precisely by not blaming ourselves. It's by forgiving ourselves, because the very tendency to blame is an expression of what is called judgment. That is what these *dinim*, the word for "judgments" in Hebrew, means: looking to see what is wrong with something. What is wrong means, *"How is it not to my advantage, how am I endangered by something, how am I threatened by something?"*—all of these sort of things, rather than, *"How do I live with the way things are?"*—which is the Edenic state.

10.18 Edenic Purification as the Voice for God

The kabbalistic answer is how to do the purification. We do the purification by isolating the *dinim* (judgments) from the *hasadim* (compassion). The Kabbalists and Hasidim developed a psychology based on the rabbinic idea that the internal state of the human being is basically a kind of conflict between different forces, generally called the *yetzer tov*, the good urge and the evil urge, *yetzer ha'ra*. Adopting language from the *Course in Miracles*, I like to say that the good urge is the internal "Voice for God" that we have. There's a voice in each and every one of us that is actually telling us how to be in the Edenic state, but generally, it's drowned out by other voices, which are the voices that are nurtured and nursed by the fruit of the Tree of Knowledge of Good and Evil, and that drowns out the voice for God. The voice for God is a very simple voice, and it is a voice that loves, not condemning, and not really judgmental.

According to one Hasidic system, we do the purification for ten days. We concentrate for this ten-day period, the ten days of *teshuvah*, on isolating the *dinim* in ourselves. That's to say, we have to be watching for any judgmental thought that comes into the mind-stream. Every time you see yourself judging yourself or somebody else, you forgive yourself for that. You say, *"Oh, there I am, that's the judgment, that's arising. There it is."* So we are leaving the *hasadim* free of the judgments.

10.19 Fixing Vessels to Hold Light

There's a principle in the Hasidic psychology that you have to fix the *keilim* (vessels), before they will be capable of holding light, otherwise, you get what's called *Shevirat haKeilim*—that's what we learn from the Lurianic system, the *keli* is the vessel. The understanding is that there is what the

Hindus call *Brahman Nirguna*, or we call the *Ein Sof*. There is the limitless, formless, beyond phenomenal source of everything, and that is represented as pure light as it was called, *Or Ein Sof* or "unlimited pure light." When we call it unlimited pure light, we are saying that it's too much. We and it cannot exist at the same time. If you have nothing but pure light, there can be nothing else. It is ultimate brightness, it's the light that blinds; it is not the light that one can see by.

My friend David Cooper, the meditation master, once gave this example. I heard him teaching one time in Florida, it's like when you go into a movie theater. I remember having had the experience many times, especially, when I was a kid, we would go to the matinees. When you would come out, one of the effects was that your eyes had gotten used to the darkness. So, the light would be blinding, and you couldn't see anything. This is blinding light. There's blinding light, and there's illuminating light. The pure light of *Or Ein Sof* is blinding light, but for us to see this world, the light has to be limited. It has to be lowered, and when it is reduced, then you can make out a world.

10.20 Restarting in the Right Direction

My hope is somewhat raised when I see that the young people, who are creating a kind earth-based neo-tribalism. I include myself in this; we have too much of a tendency to start from what may be the wrong direction. I think that, even for the kabbalistic system, although it still has something very profound to teach us. I'm not saying to throw the whole thing out. When I look at all of these systems of Kabbalah or Vedanta or even Buddhist cosmogony, it seems to me they all want to start with nonexistence, and then sort of say how something comes out of it, and then they prove to you that what comes out of it doesn't really exist.

10.21 Remnants of Edenic States

Now, I want to say, even though I have been strongly attracted to that and I have studied such things for many, many decades and resisted and even looked down upon another way of looking at Reality—for which I'll forgive myself, because that's a judgment. I forgive myself for this thought—I remember when I used to hear, for example, about Native American spirituality, I was hearing a different story. I'd read Ken Wilbur, and Ken Wilbur would tell me, "Oh, well, they just never evolved beyond a certain point." *Maybe it's the reverse. Did you ever think of this?* Maybe they have remnants of the Edenic state, even though, unfortunately, they've had to live with us, so they've lost and been corrupted and poisoned, just as we have. *Maybe we are the ones who have lost something rather than they're the ones who have not evolved.*

Of course, from our point of view, which is so smart, being based on eating the fruit of the Tree of the Knowledge of Good and Evil, we think: "*Hey! They didn't get all this stuff that we managed to do.*" Well, who's destroying the world, the smart ones who evolved or the ones who actually know how to live in it and on it? I'm not saying the "noble savage" thing, either. It's nothing to do with being perfect or knowing everything, just saying there's something that may be a little bit mixed up, even in our spirituality. It may be upside down. If it's starting from spirit, as Ken Wilbur would like to say, why don't we just start with the earth, and why do we think that this isn't real? Because we want to be gods?

10.22 If Only in Eden

What if it is real, and we are just flesh and blood, mortal beings who are on this earth? What is wrong? What's so terrible about that? I mean, couldn't it be that's the way it is? If it is, what is wrong with it? Why does it have to be something else? Maybe this is the way it is!?! Maybe it's also true that it comes from something that is formless and indescribable, which you could call the "Great Spirit" or call it whatever you like. Maybe it is that that formless, incomprehensible basis of all that exists is present within this manifest world as well, and one can have a relationship with it, and maybe you can speak to it, and maybe it speaks to you, and maybe there's communications?!? What is wrong with that? Why do we think there's something wrong with that? Maybe we've got it all wrong and maybe the Torah, even though we are not getting the message, maybe the Torah's reminding us of that every year—that you could be in Eden.

You could be in Eden is not some other place. It is not some other world. It isn't like some other planet. It is not some other dimension. There are these discussions—Maimonides has discussions, these kind of scholastic discussions—about whether the Garden of Eden is actually a place in this world.

Maybe Garden of Eden *is this world*, which would be something like, perhaps not exactly, something like what the Buddhists came to—not in the earliest stages, but in the development of Buddhism when they came to the *Madhyamaka*, and some of the enlightened Buddhists were starting to say—there is no difference between samsara and nirvana. Samsara is nirvana. This world is the Garden of Eden, if you know how to be in the Edenic state. If you think that you are God or like God or need to be God or in order to be able to have a good life, you have to be more than you actually are, you have to get better than you actually are, you have to stop somebody else from holding you back, then you won't be in Eden. You'll be in samsara; you won't be in nirvana. Is nirvana somewhere else? Is the Garden of Eden somewhere else? Or is it just a possibility that we are losing because we make a colossal mistake?

10.23 Getting Back to the Garden of Eden

Suppose that's the way it is, then we wouldn't need to have a *tiqqun* because "we've got to get back to the garden," as Joni Mitchell[7] sang. All this stuff, it's amazing. It's floating around, but we don't put it together or take it seriously enough to actually live by it. I think that the Torah's saying, OK, last year you got a new Torah, you brought it down, there was a new name, the YHVH that came down the day after Yom Kippur last year. And let's face it, what does Yom Kippur stand for? In the cycle, in the mythic cycle, it represents the dispensation of the *luchot*, of the second tablets of the law. The second tablets. They say there was two times, and Moshe, our teacher, first went up on Shavuot, for forty days to bring down the *luchot*, and Moses himself made a mistake, basically by getting angry and trying to force the issue.

10.24 Asking for What You Need with Grace

Let me just slip in here a little piece from Rebbe Nachman who says, "for these reasons a person should never be a *schvitzer*, never try too hard. You should pray, ask for what you need, basically in a nice way, *b'tahanunim*. You ask with *chen*. The word *tachanunim*, it has root in the *chen*, which means grace. You should grace and charm a person. That is *chen*. In a gracious way, you ask the source of life in a gracious way for what you need. You don't make demands. In a gracious way, you ask for what you need. You ask for your needs. Don't force the issue."[8]

Last year, through the merits and the efforts and the contribution that some folks made through the process of the ten days of return, they contributed to the manifestation of a new form of YHVH, a new basis for energy for that year. *What are we talking about? We said, who will live, who will die?* It's all dispensed. It's a dispensation for a year. It's not eternity. It's not as if the message was, *Here's the secret that you can get out of being a mortal being here, and you'll be a god and live forever. Here's something to want to aspire to, that you want the best for yourself and for your family and for everyone else; that they should all get another good year.* We are asking for that in the form of *tachanunim*—not demanding, we are just asking in a very general way, because that would be the human thing to do. That's what an Edenic being would do. It's not a cutthroat operation, *Oh, give it to my family, don't give it to them, because we are the gods, and they're just who-knows-what. They don't even amount to chopped liver!* We recognize what we are and what everybody else is, also.

---

7. Joni Mitchell, "Woodstock" (Ladies of the Canyon, 1970).
8. Liqqutei Moharan, no. 20.

10.25 Peril of Human Beings Becoming Gods

And not just human beings! One of the great fallacies, one of the great consequences, of eating from the fruit of the knowledge of the Tree of Good and Evil is *anthropocentricity*. Once we start thinking we are gods, we mean, by extension, human beings are gods, and everything else is chopped liver. It doesn't matter that if we eat and extend our population even more, that we destroy who knows how many species of other beings, because they don't count for anything. Then, after we've destroyed all of them, because we are so smart, we'll have some kind of artificial food. Then, we'll decide who will get that, because we'll be the gods and the other ones won't be good enough for us. We don't want somebody else to have it, because if they all have it, then we won't be the gods. Then, after we've destroyed this planet, we can be the gods on some other planet and so on and so forth.

10.26 Luck of Another Year

We are all lucky to be here because YHVH gave us another year, and there are all kinds of tzaddikim, or devoted ones, that prayed for us and that because of their presence on the earth, they drew down a divine response. They elicited a divine response because they had *chen*. The principle is that we are not separate from the source of all life. If it didn't want us to be here, we wouldn't be here in the first place. Simple as that. It must want us to be here. Therefore, it loves us, because otherwise we wouldn't be here. That being the case, then we can be very grateful and, in a gracious way, we can ask for another year. In order to have the *chen*, that Rebbe Nachman talks about, we have to fix ourselves and our vessels.

So, that's the problem. I hate to say this, but I'm saying it only because I think it's really true. You look at the whole history of the Jews, and the prophets are constantly trying to straighten them out, not saying, "*You've got it all right, everything you're doing right*," but it's exactly the opposite. The prophets are the ones that are saying, "*You're going off the* derekh *or path.*"

10.27 Praying for What You Want Versus Getting What You Need

Reb Nachman says,[9] Israel's prayers could be the most powerful thing in the world, but for a prayer to be powerful, you have to have *chen*. If you have *chen*, God can't resist you. If you are Edenic enough, the source of life will give you what you need. Not what you demand, but what you need. It will respond to you and give you what you need, and you will be very, very happy to have it. You will be happy, a person who is truly happy with his or her lot, with what he or she gets. That's the way of a true tzaddik, a truly

---

9. Liqqutei Moharan, no. 1.

righteous person, and that's what a Hasid is, and that's what it is to be truly happy in the Edenic sense: if you're happy just by the very fact that you are here. Just by the very fact of existing. I mean, that's a fantastic gift.

Some people with a lot of *chen* helped us get another year. Now we are here and maybe we can help ourselves and we can help other people, that they should also have the benefits. We can pull down a new YHVH, which will bring positive energy into the *Otzar ha-Chayyim*, the "source of life," which is the spiritual treasury that has the budget for everything that is needed for the next year, for all who are going to be here with us to receive what they need. In order to get this *chen*, if you want to get *chen*, you need to forgive yourself and forgive everyone else very radically. The effective way to do that on the ten days of return is by isolating the *dinim*. We're really looking out for all the judgments in ourselves and sweetening them. It's called "sweetening the judgments." Sweetening means I forgive it, I forgive you.

I was talking to my dear friend, Hazzan Richard Kaplan, just the other day, and we were talking about, I'm not going to mention a name, because there would not be a lot of *chen* in that, but we were talking about a certain political figure who doesn't seem to be representing an Edenic worldview. So, I mentioned and recalled the one teaching of Reb Nachman that is the most important teaching of all of his teachings, as we have said over and over, is the teaching of the *nekuda tova*, the "good points"; how important it is to locate, to remember that there is a good point in every single person. You can say, *"What about so-and-so, who is saying all these lies and vile things, and seems to be doing all these terrible things. Well, I wish they wouldn't."* Don't you think there was maybe some good point in the course of the day? Maybe that person maybe has a pet cat. Maybe there was one moment, when he looked at his cat and he said, *I can see you need a little bit of milk,* and they have some special moment, when he gave the cat a little saucer of milk. Wasn't that a good thing? That in itself is good, even if the rest of the day the person was just completely insane with the poison of eating the fruit of the Tree of the Knowledge of Good and Evil. In that moment, that one moment, the person proved that there is something good in himself. There is something inherently good, and that's what Reb Nachman is saying: *I dare you, I challenge you to find anyone, however evil, even one person, anywhere, however wicked they may appear to you, however many* dinim *there are piled on the image of that person, however many* dinim *arise within your own body, I challenge you to find one person for whom there isn't some* nekuda tova. Now, you can say, *So what if there's one* nekuda tova? *Justice is on my side! They're evil!* OK, you want to stay with that? Then you will never get back to the Edenic state.

10.28 Tearing Yourself Apart for Coherency

It imprisons you. That's the spiritual surgery we have to do during these ten days of return. We have to be willing to do this little operation on ourselves. It's basically tearing yourself apart. You simply tear out all the *dinim* and for ten days, you're going to sweeten them, by letting them go. By that point, if you did Elul, if you go through the whole thing, it doesn't seem so radical when you get to the *penimiyut*, the "inner meaning of the tradition." It can sound very challenging if you didn't do any preparation for it, but if you have been sort of adding the pieces up and you work a little on this and you go through and you add a little of that, then the whole thing starts to be more coherent and come together. You're training yourself, as a tzaddik-in-training, to make the choice for God's sake: *le'Tzorekh gavoha*, making the choice for God's sake and not for your sake or for your own self-interest, which is a mistake.

We train ourselves all year in that. Then, when you get to Rosh Hasha-nah, you're ready to have an intensive ten days. In these ten days, we are going to do the work that comes before we get to the new YHVH that will come into the world, into our world, beginning on the day after Yom Kip-pur. These are the four days that lead up to Sukkot. We are going to do this work of sweetening and forgiving, because when we do the sweetening and forgiving, then we are going to be able to draw down divine Love through the attractiveness of our own *chen*.

10.29 Making Ourselves More Beautiful

So, we are making ourselves more beautiful. We are going to draw down the thirteen channels of compassion. When you come to Yom Kippur, we can draw down the thirteen channels of compassion, the inner qualities of YHVH, so that the apparent separation between our world and the divine realm has been neutralized. That is called the *bittul* of Yom Kippur. Then, on Yom Kippur, there's no separation between the innerness of YHVH and our own interiority. If we can succeed in that, then in the four days begin-ning the day after Yom Kippur, this new YHVH manifests, and it starts to appear in the world. It sets a new budget for the needs of all existence, for the world-that-is-coming.

10.30 Edenic State of Sukkot

Finally, we get to Sukkot. You build the sukkah. Now the sukkah is called *Tzel d'mehemnuta* in the Zohar. In Aramaic, this means "the shadow of faith." Before I unpack what the Zohar means by "the shadow of faith," I have to tell you about a Hasidic master who only learned one tractate of Talmud, the tractate of *Sukkah*! Reb Zusha of Anipol is one of the highest of the early Hasidim and the brother of Reb Elimelekh. He spent all this time just learning that tractate. This was the only thing he ever learned. Sometimes, in the course of a whole year, he didn't get past the first word! He always had his Talmud, and he didn't go anywhere else. Why? Because he was in Edenic state, and he didn't need to go anywhere else. He didn't need to go anywhere else.

There was another rebbe. The mitzvah is only to build a sukkah for Sukkot. Most people take it down after the eight days. But there was a rebbe who lived in a sukkah all year. He says, *People think, "Oh, it's a mitzvah, we have to build this sukkah and then we have to spend a certain amount of time in it . . . "* Here's the mitzvah, this is the exact number of minutes that you have to be in the sukkah in order to fulfill the mitzvah of being in the sukkah. There's a Hasidic rebbe who sat in the sukkah all year long! He only wanted to be there. He didn't go anywhere; he was always in the sukkah. Just think about that. That's the highest of the high, to be in the sukkah all the time. Why? *Because he was in the Garden of Eden in this world.* Being in the Garden of Eden when you're in the sukkah in this world means you really have your head together and you're not just doing a mitzvah by rote, as the Hasidim warn us against.

The craziest thing you can do is just do a mitzvah by getting out the cookbook and saying, *This is how you do it,* and then going through the entire recipe and never tasting anything. It's as you said, *Oh wait, I made the cake, and that's all I have to do.* The Holiest of Holies, they don't take down their sukkahs. This Hasidic rebbe, he never took his sukkah down. Why should he take it down? Do you know what it's like, what it's like for a person like that to be sitting in *sukkah*? They're back in Eden, they're in Gan Eden. When you're in Gan Eden, you couldn't be happier. *What else did he need? Why do we think we need something else?* He didn't live in Minnesota. Some people live in Minnesota, and they can be in Eden, too. You have to have the right clothing. It's not worth saying that there's only one way to do it. Maybe he had a heater in his sukkah in Minnesota.

10.31 Shade of Faith

Anyway, the point is, when you're in the sukkah, wherever it is and however you need to equip yourself so that you can be in Eden when in your sukkah, because otherwise, there's no point in just doing the mitzvah and saying, *I did it all right, but I live in Minnesota and it's too freezing for me to be out here more than five minutes, so what was the point?* You figure out what is the point of being in the sukkah, and then you figure out how you make the sukkah so that you'll be able to actually be in *Tzel d'mehemnuta.* When you're in the sukkah, you want to be experiencing the shade of faith.

Let's go back to tractate *Sukkah* itself. Rabbi Elezar says, that when the Torah says that the Israelites were camped in sukkot, Rabbi Elezar says sukkot were the clouds of glory. Rabbi Akivah said, no, it was actual sukkot. They had booths. Rabbi Elezar says no, it was the clouds of glory. The sukkah is the clouds of glory. The clouds of glory are what enable the Israelites to know the way to the Land of Israel. They're led by the clouds of glory. That's how God led them in the right direction. Otherwise, they wouldn't know the right direction. That's the way: the state, the condition within which a person knows how to get to the Land of Israel, which is basically the way to get back to Eden once you have been expelled because you ate the fruit of the Tree of the Knowledge of Good and Evil.

10.32 Let the Edenic Soul Lead You

If you just look at it in the way that Reb Zusha would look at it, you're not looking at it in an oversophisticated way. Just look at it in a very simple way, the way that somebody with an Edenic soul like Reb Zusha would look at it. What does it mean that there would be clouds of glory? "Clouds of glory" means I recognize that I'm being led by God, wherever I am, right now. *I'm not god, but God is leading me.* God is showing me the way. God is always showing me the way to the Land of Israel. The Land of Israel in the spiritual iconography means a place that is always under divine providence, or *hashgachah*. It means the place that God's eye is always seeing. This Land of Israel means a state of consciousness in which you know that God is watching you. That's the Edenic state. God can't stop looking at you because you have so much *chen*.

To be clear, I'm not advocating quietism, that's to say nonrecognition of injustice, oppression. I'm not advocating inaction. I'm advocating inner purification. Inner clarity and inner purification means that if you have to act, which you always have to do, there is no alternative to acting; when you have to make an action, make the action of a person who's filled with Edenic qualities and not filled with hate, fear-driven aggression.

Being in the Edenic state doesn't mean that you don't recognize or that you lose the ability to feel compassion and even urgency to take certain courses of action that would ameliorate suffering, which would release and redeem captives. There are all kinds of positive mitzvoth that the prophets talk about, and these things are really important. The things we *actually do* may be more important than the rituals that are focused on some spiritual advantage that we may think should take priority. I think this is really being a person and an *earth person*, which is what we are—we are Adam. The very name *Adam* is from *Adamah*. We are part of the earth. We belong here.

10.33 Edenic Bliss of Being Alive

In certain ways, evolutionary biology has got a clearer view than some of the so-called spiritual understandings of what we are. We came from the earth. We evolved out of the slime. We are still part of it. We are part of this world, and part of what we are is a good heart. That, I think, is a true idea that the rabbis have always stressed, that the highest quality is *to have a good heart.* Having a good heart means that you do not like to see someone being discriminated against, harmed, and looked down upon, unappreciated, ignored, hurt in any way. Nor do you like to see the creation itself be harmed, destroyed, so that other beings—not just yourself—other beings and other species don't have what they need in order that they can share the joy and bliss of merely being alive.

Act out of deep love. That's what we are trying to do—to empower ourselves. These thirteen attributes of compassion are the essence of YHVH, and we are trying to bring this into ourselves. We are trying to create vessels. As I was trying to say before, the Hasidic principle is that you have to create the vessel before you can fill it with light. To create the vessel, we have to fix the *dinim* in ourselves. We have to sweep away our own judgments. Then we can have the capacity to hold the divine light, which is a light that radiates the energy of love. Our vision will not be obscured so much by the mind of judgment, but that doesn't mean that we don't see what needs to be fixed.

All the prophets in our tradition have often recognized that we get too hung up on getting out of here. Why? Why should we? We are here. The prophets are telling us, *Look, you're an earth being, and if you're a real mensch, then you are not going to like injustice and oppression and discrimination or any of these kinds of things, because you're going to have a human heart.* We want to get that back, because that's the true heart, the *etrog.* That's what we really are.

10.34 Eden Drawing Heaven and Earth

So, sitting in this sukkah means that you have drawn something of Heaven down to earth. Because of what you achieved, if you can do it, between Rosh Hashanah and Yom Kippur, you can bring down the name YHVH and bring YHVH down to earth. When you bring YHVH down to earth, you can sit in the sukkah, and you'll be in the *Tzel d'mehemnuta,* you'll be in the shadow, in the shade, which is the pleasantness, the shade of faith.

The shade of faith is, *I don't think I'm God, and I have to be like God, and I have to figure out my strategy, how I'll be able to get what I need and make sure that somebody else doesn't get there before me, because I'm in the shade. I'm basking in the clouds of glory. God has given me what I want, and I know that God has given me what I want and what I should get. What else do I need?* I don't want to be anywhere but in a sukkah, and if I really had that consciousness, if I really knew, if I could really bring down the name YHVH, I could really do the surgery of the ten days of return, Rosh Hashanah to Yom Kippur, I could really forgive myself. I could forgive all others. I would be able to return to an Edenic state in which I wouldn't be hiding from God. That's sitting in the sukkah. It means I'm sitting in the sukkah. God is hanging out with me. You brought God down to earth on Yom Kippur, and the tradition likes to say that God likes it so much that he'll hang out with you for another week. It's actually a little more than a week. It's even better.

10.35 Eden in Four Species

That's what Sukkot essentially is. Now, I will say just a little bit about the *arba'a minim*, although there is just infinitely more that one could say about Sukkot, but basically in Sukkot, you build the *Tzel d'mehemnuta*, you build this place, this structure that is not like the Empire State Building. It doesn't matter if it doesn't last forever. You don't last forever, and there's no reason you need to. *Why do you need to?*

There is something very beautiful in the idea and the understanding that everything that makes up who we are will be redistributed when we cease to be here. The *neshamah* or soul will return to where the *neshamah* comes from. There's nothing, really, to be afraid of, if you're in the Edenic state, if you appreciate existing from that perspective.

I want to say just a few words about the *arba'a minim* or the four species of Sukkot. The most important thing is to be in the sukkah. It's because we have to represent, you have to model things. You built the sukkah, but really, we need to understand how to be in the sukkah, as Reb Nachman realized when he made the journey to the Land of Israel during the War of 1812. He got stuck on a Turkish vessel, on a military naval vessel on the way back, trying to get back to Eastern Europe. He was caught in the middle of battle, and he didn't have his paraphernalia with him to do the mitzvoth the way one ordinarily does them with certain physical objects. Reb Nachman said it was very terrifying for him on that trip, but what he realized was that he could put on tefillin or phylacteries without putting on tefillin. He could be in the sukkah without actually building a sukkah.

I'm not saying don't build a sukkah. I mean, it's a beautiful thing, and it's helpful, especially if it's communal and especially if you're thinking in terms of what I call the neo-tribalism, the earth-based neo-tribalism. It's a great thing, actually, to build something like a kind of temporary structure that you and your tribe can hang out in, but you want to hang out in it in the Edenic state, because otherwise it's nothing. It's nothing. What's the point of it? If you can use it as a prop so that you can get together with your tribe, then it can be a very beautiful thing.

You have the sukkah, and you have the *arba'a minim*, the four species (i.e., *lulav*, the frond of a date palm tree; *aravah*, leafy willows; *hadas*, myrtle; and *etrog*, a citron). I'm going to just cut to the chase, so forgive me if I don't say all that much about the *arba'a minim*. In a very simple sense, the *lulav* is basically like a magic wand. It's an instrument. You have the *etrog* in one hand. The *etrog* is basically the representation of the heart. The *arba'a minim* are the other species. You have the palms and you have the willows and you have the myrtle, which are brought together to represent the integration of all the types of beings that there are on this planet. There's a type that smells good and tastes good (i.e., *etrog*); there's a type that smells good but doesn't taste so good (i.e., *hadas*); there's a type that tastes good that doesn't smell so good (i.e., *lulav*); and there's a type that is just bland and doesn't have either a good aroma or a good taste (i.e., *aravah*).[10]

10.36 Interconnecting Eden

Our homework is to figure out what those qualities are, but we'll say taste and aroma—those are spiritual qualities. Then, there's a type of person that doesn't seem to have either of these qualities. This is the type that is so polluted by having eaten the fruit of the knowledge of the Tree of Good and Evil that they don't know how to hear the voice for God within themselves. Nevertheless, when we are sitting in the sukkah, *we include all types*. We include everyone, and we are praying for the inclusion of everyone.

You connect all the parts, all the forms of existence with the purity of the heart. That's why the *etrog* has to be the most beautiful, it has to be the *peri 'etz hadar*—the most beautiful one that you can get, because the purity and the beauty of the *etrog* represents what you did between Rosh Hashanah and Yom Kippur: *This is what my heart looks like, that I can manifest now because of the inner work that I did from Rosh Hashanah through Yom Kippur. Now I have this beautiful fruit. I'm going to take this beautiful fruit, and I'm going to put it together, and I share it with all the types of people that there are in the world. I don't make a judgment and say, "Only these and only those." Some have this quality and not that, some have that quality and not this; some haven't developed many spiritual qualities yet. Nevertheless, it's all one. I have to put it all together.*

10.37 Putting Eden at Center of Consciousness

I put it all together (*arba'a minim*), and I shake it in each direction. I'm standing in the center—wherever I am, it's the center of the earth. I'm standing in the center, and I'm waving my *arba'a minim* up and down, front, back, right and left, in all the six cardinal directions. This shaking is meant to awaken consciousness. It's shaking up the awakening consciousness; it's shaking your brain. It's going to shake up consciousness so that

---

10. Vayikra Rabbah 30:12.

the consciousness of the *yechud* or unity of all that exists can be aroused and awake. The principle is found in a verse in Proverbs 24:16: "the tzaddik falls seven times and rises up right away seven times." Seven times means for the seven days. One of the beautiful things about Sukkot is you invite in *ushpizin*, a guest, that represents one of the seven spheres, one for each day.

10.38 Edenic State of Tzaddik

The quality of the tzaddik is that the greater the tzaddik, the lower the tzaddik can go. The tzaddik that can connect with the wickedest of the wicked is the greatest tzaddik. The one that has nothing to be afraid of is not afraid they'll be corrupted by anything or anyone because that's how clear they are. They're in a really clear Edenic state, and they are in touch with reality. They're not judging anyone. Then, they have nothing to fear. The principle is, the lower you can go, the higher you can rise.

The tzaddik who can descend through all seven rungs of the spheres, and even into the very depths of the oppositional forces, the *qelippot*, can then descend for the sake of rising. The descent of the tzaddik empowers the tzaddik to leap even higher than the place from which they started. This is what it's all about.

10.39 Shaking Up Consciousness

We want to be able to shake up our consciousness. We put together your heart, bound together with the magic wand that unites all types of being into one. Through that power of bringing down that degree of Edenic consciousness and love, the tzaddik is able to uplift more than just one's self. When you rise from that, everything rises with you. Don't stop to judge this. Take my word. I'm telling you, it's really true, and you'll see for yourself without a doubt, even though it sounds strange and crazy when you're running on the energy of the fruit of the Tree of Knowledge of Good and Evil. I guarantee that it's true that when you see the *nekuda tova*, and are willing to see the *nekuda tova* in any person, as Reb Nachman said, that any person isn't a *rasha* or evil anymore. You have actually lifted them up to a higher level.

10.40 Everyone Raises Someone

This is not saying that this is easy to do. It takes a great tzaddik to lift up a great *rasha*. Most of us are not yet great tzaddikim, we are tzaddikim-in-training. To be in the shade of faith, means to be able to believe this, to know this on your level. For each of us, there's a level where we can raise up somebody. Maybe we can't raise up the ones who need to be raised the most. For that, you need really a great tzaddik. Even what Reb Zalman used to call a *schtickle tzaddik*, a modicum of the devoted one, which is like us, there isn't one of us that can't raise up some people more than ourselves.

That is the essence of Sukkot.

It used to be that they would sacrifice seventy bulls that were supposed to represent the seventy nations. That was the symbol of how the power of the person who has done Rosh Hashanah and Yom Kippur can bring down the name YHVH, a new name YHVH for this year. They have the power to uplift all the people of the world.

10.41 Closing Intention

So I bless us that, on our level, we should be part of those who are uplifting all the people of the world, that we should have success in our own purification, that we should be able to do this purification before Sukkot so that when Sukkot comes, we will have contributed to the empowerment of a new name, YHVH, the name that will bestow energy and blessing to all that exist in the course of the next year. May we sit in the sukkah on our Sukkot together and really enjoy the Edenic condition of truly rejoicing in this moment . . .

Chapter 11
Preparing to Rejoice with the Torah Through Hoshana Rabbah

11.0 *Jewissance* of Torah

How do we really prepare for this next station in the spiritual journey of the sacred calendar? I want to suggest it is by cultivating real joy—real jouissance, what Boyarin calls *Jewissance*—for Torah through Hoshana Rabbah. Let me share a Torah from the Baal Shem Tov that's really about the end of the Torah (*parsha V'Zot HaBerachah*) because that's what you get to. We are getting to the end within the beginning: the place where the end of the Torah and the beginning of the Torah are interconnected. First, the Baal Shem Tov, then Rebbe Nachman of Breslov.

11.1 Leaving and Giving Torah

Everybody who's been through Torah knows that Moses, our teacher, dies in the last *parsha*. Yet we have the tradition that the whole Torah was written by Moses, our teacher. Let me add here that since it is Hoshana Rabbah, one of its traditions is to go through the entire book of Deuteronomy, which is called *Mishne Torah*. It's a repeat of the Torah. There's a sense that the entire Torah is recapitulated in the book of *Devarim*, the book of Deuteronomy. Basically, it's Moshe's swan song. He's basically saying, *Here's the Torah. I'm leaving, but I'm giving you the Torah. My admonition to you is—don't forget this Torah.* It goes through what's considered to be the recapitulation of the whole story, the whole Torah. And he includes his own death in this story!

Naturally, in this hermeneutic tradition, with the inquiring minds of the Jews, it goes without saying that this elicits comment. Many explanations have been offered to account for how it can be that Moses, our teacher, could have written the whole Torah, including the account of his own death. First of all, look at the medieval French commentator, Rashi. If you look at Rashi, he claims that Moses, our teacher was still alive. How could he still be alive? Rashi says he wrote it with a tear. He wrote those words with a tear. Rashi says he wrote the verse that talks about his own death with a tear. Baal Shem Tov says, *How could this be possible? Yet, he still had to be alive because he wrote it with a tear.*

11.2 Primordial Torah

The Baal Shem Tov says we have another very important tradition that the Torah existed 2,000 years before the creation of the world. It makes sense to me, and I think it should make sense to any intelligent student of Torah that we don't take these numbers and such things literally. The very idea that you've got a sufficient account of creation in the Torah legend is not something that really bears much intelligent scrutiny. It's obvious that we know that the earth and the cosmos are much older than the years that are stipulated within the Torah account. I don't think there's any reason for anyone who is familiar with thousands of years of the study of Torah to take these numbers literally or as *peshat*. The meaning is not that the Torah existed exactly 2,000 years before creation, but in some sense, the Torah is not limited by the account of creation. It's the source of that account.

The account of creation is an *account* of creation as a *mashal* or what we call a parable or a legend. It is an attempt to create a view of the nature of reality. Really, our whole tradition has been reexamining Torah all these years. *That is why we have the tradition of repeating the Torah.* It seems that Moses, our teacher, being an archetypal character within this whole tradition, was very adamant in urging us never to allow these words to depart from our mind-stream. Of course, that's part of the liturgy itself. We pray that the words of this Torah should never be forgotten by us or by our descendants—that, in a way, is the thread that connects and preserves our tradition. Maybe the most essential tradition is the handing over the Torah from one generation to another. But it doesn't mean handing over something whose meaning is fixed and unchanging.

11.3 Primordial Torah *Contra* Orthodoxy

One might even say that there really is no such thing as Jewish *orthodoxy*. There really can't be any *orthodoxy* because there is an ongoing process of handing over words of Torah and studying and interpreting Torah. There's not a tradition of pontificating or presenting *dogma* of what Torah means. Rather, there is this sense that we have a lineage; the lineage that according to our mythic history goes back to Moses, our teacher. So, Torah includes this story, the account of creation, *ma'ase bereshith* and the account of how to embody what is not limited by time and space through practicing a spiritual technology called *ma'ase merkavah* (the account of the Chariot). From this perspective, the Baal Shem Tov cites Rashi, who already about 1,000 years ago was saying that the Torah preexisted creation itself, meaning the Torah essentially preexists any form in which it may appear to us. It preexists any account that we may give. The way the Baal Shem Tov explains this is through referring to earlier kabbalistic and mystical sources in which there's a concept called *Torah Kedumah*: "Primordial Torah." Another way to understand it is as the raw source of information from which Torah is constructed. It's a really deep thing to contemplate what that source might be.

I'm just speculating here. This is a deep thought and to even imagine what it is that the forms of Torah that we have knowledge of derive from requires an imaginal account. When we look at what the Kabbalists have already said about the "raw material" of Torah, we find that they were inclined to focus on the obvious: Torah is made up of its letters. We have all kinds of ways of understanding letters and interpreting letters. The whole tradition is based on the letters of Torah and what they mean—even the shape of the letters, the spaces between letters, the absence of letters or the sometimes surprising appearance of letters that don't seem to be required or necessarily fit in a certain word of Torah. In a hyper-literal sense, we could say that the raw material of Torah is the letters of the Torah itself. And as such, the Torah that we have is only one possible arrangement of the letters that it contains!

11.4 Letters of Primordial Torah Without Order

The Baal Shem Tov teaches that one of the traditions that seems to be shared by mystical commentators and students of Torah is that there's no particular order to the letters of Torah. Again, it's a very deep thought, one that can be liberating. I like this idea of liberating thoughts because if you look at the letters of the name of this day, Hoshana Rabbah, one way to translate Hoshana is "liberate us." Hoshana means "please let us be free." *What do we have to be free of?* Well, one of the main things we have to be free of is bondage to some particular limiting view of the past.

11.5 Letting Go of the Past

There's a tradition where Rebbe Nachman says that the main thing we have to do is to be able to let go of the past. Letting go of the past in the way he puts it means we have to zero in on this concept that says: "the source, the reality from which everything emerges, called 'the Creator,' is constantly renewing creation."[1] *Constantly renewing.* There is no stuck-ness. Reality is dynamic.

This is one basis for saying in a somewhat irreverent sense, a somewhat humorous sense, that there is no real orthodoxy in Judaism. Actually, Judaism cannot *really* have *orthodoxy*. One of the keys for liberating ourselves from delusion of "orthodoxy" (fixed views) is to follow Rebbe Nachman's

---

1. Shabbat Shakharit morning liturgy.

pointer. He advises us that we have to remind ourselves every day of what is stated in the Siddur, *Mehadesh b'khol yom tamid ma'ase bereshith*. This literally means "every single day creation is being renewed." But some who have thought more deeply about what these words mean have said it's not just that creation is renewed every day—it's a process in which the entire creation is renewed at every moment!

11.6 Each Day as a Cycle of Creation

Nevertheless, it is a very helpful thing to treat each day as separate creation and to understand our traveling through time and space as a cycle of days. We divide our lives into a series of days, and each day consists of part of the day that is graced by the sun and another part of the day that draws its energy from the moon. Then we can speak of a Torah of the light and a Torah of the shadow. From that perspective, it's not only important but also it's absolutely crucial that we understand that every day is completely unique and new.

11.7 Re-cycling Torah

So not only is every day new, but following the cycle of the moon, we recognize a certain cycle that we call *Shanah* (year) from the word "repeat," implying "recycle." *Shanah* has the same root as the word *Mishne* in *Mishne Torah*. It's a "cycle or repetition of the Torah." *Not a second Torah*. Some people think *Mishne* means the second Torah. But it may be more helpful to understand it as meaning repeating, re-cycling of the Torah. That's what *Shanah* means. We relate to time as a cycle that repeats. That means that we have a concept of time that's *cyclical* rather than *linear*. Every day is different, but time doesn't go on forever with no end in sight. Within the cycle there's not one day that is the same as any other day. And on a more macro level in which each *shanah* is like a day, there's really not one year that's the same as any other year.

The problem is that our minds don't allow us to see clearly. We suffer from what the Buddhists like to call, very wisely, "obscurations"—reality is concealed from us. The illusion that every day is the same or that every year is the same is a habit that prevents us from recognizing the newness of each year, each day, even each moment. Let's look at it in another sense: we are stuck because of what we think the past implies. This is one of the greatest obscurations that we have to deal with. It's really like the *klal* or "principal" or "core principal" of obscurations.

If only one could free oneself.

11.8 Freedom from Thinking Traps

So, we are talking about Hoshana Rabbah, the great aspiration to be free.

What would free us would be a way out of the trap of thinking that we are stuck and that we have been determined by the past. In fact, there is something fresh about every single moment. Of course, there are things within time that come and go. We don't want to make the mistake of falling into either eternalism or nihilism. There isn't anything within creation that never changes, but there are things that really do exist, even if their existence is a pulsation and not constant.

Of course, one of the reasons why we have the obscuration is because we are so *attached* to this identification with our bodies. We see how they change. Every cell in your body is completely different than it was only a short time ago. There are things that are changing. They're coming into existence and going through different processes. They are aging and are passing away. They're things that are going to come and go. *Is the condition of being itself something that comes and goes? That's what one has to reflect on. What is it that is experiencing these changes? Are we identified with the changes or are we identified with the source of the changes, the witness or the awareness within which knowledge of the changes occurs?*

Back to the Baal Shem Tov, who is saying there's something like a Primordial Torah. Within time and space, we have years, we have days. We cycle through the Torah, and we connect the beginning and the end. There's no end that is not a new beginning. There's no beginning that isn't a continuation in some sense. The raw materials of this Torah, the Baal Shem Tov says, are the letters of the Primordial Torah. And these letters have no fixed order. They are not necessarily in the order of Torah that we have now. The letters that we have now start with the letter *Bet*. The first word of the Torah is *BeReSHiTH*. It's the letters: *Bet-Resh-Aleph-Shin-Yud-Tav*. Those letters were already in the Primordial Torah, *but not necessarily in that order*. When they're in that order, then something happens within the phenomenal realm, the realm of experience that corresponds to that arrangement of letters. The Baal Shem Tov says in regard to Moses, our teacher, that all of the letters of the Torah existed before there was any Torah. So, there could be any number of Torahs.

11.9 Torah of Obscuration vs. Primordial Clarity

I like to think that what we tend to call *prehistory* may be just the result of an *obscuration*. If there was an evolutionary stage for human beings that preceded the present epoch—which may only be about 10,000 years and before that there were millions of years when human beings were on this planet— then it is quite possible that there were *other Torahs* before the present one. The Torah with the letters in the order we now have expresses what made sense to the prophetic minds that drew down that Torah, that established this particular lineage, the lineage of Moses, our teacher. But the raw material of the Torah is much older than that.

Actually, there are a lot of sources that talk about this. There were *other Torahs* before the one that we have, made of the same raw material, but with the letters in different orders. This is discussed by Kabbalists in the thirteenth century. For example, in the Spanish Kabbalah there are mystics who talk about other Torahs, other arrangements of these letters, which means it would still be the same Torah in terms of its source. It would be the same material, but the formulation would be different. That's the picture.

11.10 Death and Remaining Letters of Torah

The Baal Shem Tov says in the case of Moses our teacher that when he got to the last moment of his life, all the letters of the Torah that he left us had been arranged in the order that we have them in, *except for the letters that refer to his death.* Those letters, which were not in the order that we have them, were channeled by Moses, our teacher. The Baal Shem Tov teaches that God told Moses what all the remaining letters were. With a tear Moses, our teacher, inscribed those letters. At the very moment that he heard those letters and this tear came out, he died. When Moses died, the letters spontaneously arranged themselves in the order that gives the account of his death. In other words, the letters were there, but they didn't actually spell his death *until he actually died.* That's the way the Baal Shem Tov tells the story.

11.11 Take This Torah of Pardon

It's very important to notice that the Torah that one reads to do Hoshana Rabbah is the epitaph of Moses, our teacher. It's his admonition, his last behest of the Torah. He's begging us basically to take this Torah. As we know, the Torah that he's giving us is the second tablets, the Torah of *Mechilah,* the Torah of pardon. It's the Torah that means that we have put ourselves in a position to receive it.

11.12 Seal Within the Seal

Keep in mind what is in the story. The image is that Moses, our teacher, is the teacher of teachers. He's the tzaddik of tzaddikim. He's the founder of the entire lineage which is called *Torat Moshe,* the Torah of Moses. Really, the one who gives the Torah, the giver of the Torah, is departing and basically begging us to keep this Torah, to never forget this Torah. He's basically leaving it to us. This leaving it to us is represented in the entire process that goes from Rosh Hashanah to Yom Kippur, which is the process of *teshuvah,* or of returning, which basically finished Yom Kippur. Yom Kippur is called the "seal." As we say, *hatima tova!* It means we wish to have a good seal. The seal means that the energy of divine pardon has been sealed. It's basically been granted, but it hasn't been worked through. It's like it's there but there's one more thing that still has to happen. The thing that has to happen is what Rebbe Nachman calls *teshuvah al teshuvah* or *hotam b'hotam*, the "seal within a seal."

What is transmitted, which is the whole basis of our tradition, which is the Torah of pardon, is so precious that it has to be "sealed within a seal." It has to be preserved. It has to be safeguarded. It has to be safeguarded in two places. The first place is in the intelligence, in the mind. That's where it reaches on Yom Kippur. If you can get to Yom Kippur in that sense, the second Torah comes down. It comes down on Yom Kippur as the mind opens up. The mind opens up to the recognition of the reality, of the truth of reality. That's the source of Torah, but it only gets into the mind. That's the first seal. It's sealed within the mind.

11.13 Sealed Energies Within a Sealed Form

"Sealed" means that its energies are held within a certain form. In other words, it's the form of the Torah that can be fully realized, fully embodied on Simchat Torah. The full embodiment can't occur until you go to Sukkot. You have to go through the process of Sukkot. Between Yom Kippur and Sukkot comes the new name of God. The day of after Yom Kippur is called *Yom HaShem*, the "day of the name." In the four intervening days between Yom Kippur and Sukkot, one *Yud* comes down, *Hey* comes down, *Vav* comes down. Four days, you have a new *Yud-Hey-Vav-Hey*. The YHVH, which spells out the budget of the spiritual energy that we have for the entire year, has already been brought down. In that sense, it's *sealed. Signed, sealed*, but not exactly *delivered*.

11.14 Sealed Energies of the Heart

In order to get *delivered*, you have to do Sukkot. I want to go a little bit more deeply into it, but the salient point is that the second seal is *gmar*, which you say after Yom Kippur is completed. You still say *gmar* ("finish it"), but *finish what?* The process of sealing of the seal: the seal within the seal. It's the final sealing, which is the actual completion of the process of *teshuvah*, as the verse states: "Set me as a seal in your heart."[2] The mind seal is not enough. This is fantastic! I know that sounds almost trite and obvious. But this is so fantastically deep; we don't actually realize how deep that is.

It's one thing to get something *into your mind*. It's another thing to actually get it *into your heart*. There's so many things that we can take into

---

2. "Set me as a seal upon your heart, as a seal upon your arm; for love is strong as death, jealousy is cruel as the grave; the flashes thereof are flashes of fire, a very flame of YHVH" (Song of Songs 8:6).

our mind. We think we understand and think we have mastered something or we think we've got the lesson. One of the things that Rebbe Zalman, and Rebbe Nachman taught, and that anyone who is vibrating to the frequencies of our lineage knows, is that it's crucial to make prayers or *Tefillah* out of every Torah. Make a prayer out of every Torah. It's great to learn a Torah. If you hear a good Torah, you get what are called *Meymei haDa'at*; you're getting the "waters of consciousness." Your consciousness is being irrigated. Your mind-stream is being refreshed. There's a tremendous delight in the reception of those waters.

11.15 New Name, New Torah

On Sukkot they used to have this water-drawing ceremony, *Simchat Beit HaSho'eivah*. The celebration of the water has to do with the final stage, with the culmination of the process of the sealing of the new Torah. The reason I mentioned the new name of God and the new Torah, is, as they say in the Talmudic language, *haynu hakh*—they're the same thing. The new name and the new Torah is the same thing, because the new Torah means the new Torah that your mind is going to be exploring during the course of the New Year. If you haven't fallen asleep, it is going to be a different Torah than your mind was contemplating the previous year.

This is why Rebbe Nachman emphases that you have do *teshuvah* on your *teshuvah*. There is no single, right way that is orthodox. There is no right way of doing something. There's the best you can do: the best, most meaningful way that you can do something with the deepest intention. That's only something that happens in one specific time and place. In another time and place, the way you did something the previous year won't look right to you the next year. You can't just repeat the same thing.

11.16 God Beyond Phenomenality

Theologically, speaking of a new name of God requires skirting a very fine line here. Invoking the great rabbi Immanuel Kant, if there's a god beyond phenomenality, we don't know anything about it. There's no possibility of knowing anything about anything that's not phenomenal. All we can know really is the experience that is present to our consciousness. That means all knowledge is phenomenal. So, anything we know about God is a *reflection on our own experience*. Asking ourselves every year what we mean by God is a really deep mitzvah. Ask yourself, *What do I mean by God? What am I talking about?* It's not something that somebody else can tell you, because that's not really what *'emunah* ("faith") is. Someone else may try to tell you what you should believe. But no one can tell you what you really do believe.

11.17 Continue Struggling With Torah

What does it mean to experience the moment of Hoshana Rabbah, and really the whole period when we are ending Torah? We are coming to the end of one Torah cycle and the beginning of a new Torah cycle. This means we are going to struggle with the Torah for another year. That's basically what Moses, our teacher, is saying: *I'm not going to be here, but my Torah is here for you to struggle with. That's what I'm asking, for you to struggle with it.* Then we have to ask all these questions again. *What do we mean?*

11.18 Struggling With Your Own Questions

If you don't answer the question for yourself, you can't really get to the place of *simchah* ("joyousness"). You can't really be happy with this Torah unless you really believe it. The only way you can believe it is if you answer your own questions.

The whole Torah tradition is about people answering their own questions. There is a great joke. When a Jew asks a question, it doesn't mean they want you to answer; it means they want to tell you the answer to the question that they had. My old friend, God should bless him, Chananya Goodman said that "it's a culture of questioning." Judaism is a culture of questioning. I recall one time when Art Green and I were both in Israel, and he was being interviewed on the radio. The interviewer asked him: *What is it that you really believe in?* Art said, *I believe in my questions.*

11.19 Believe in Your Questions

I don't necessarily even believe in my answers, but the questions, I really believe these questions. I can't live without these questions. I can't feel real without these questions. That's how I get to be an Adam: by asking these questions. I have to ask myself, *What do I mean by God?* If I'm going to use the term, I should know what I mean. From that perspective, if this sounds blasphemous, it's because you're stuck in dualistic mind. Really, *there is no God that is always the same.* There is only the god that we can draw down into our consciousness that we can relate to, that we can really believe in. That may not even be the same from one day to the next.

11.20 Deep Inquiry as Torah Process

The process of deep inquiry is part of Torah itself. That's the way of Torah itself. It's not just repeating what somebody told you, but accepting the responsibility of *dor dor v'dorshav*, that each generation has and needs its interpreters. *Doresh* means to seek, to look for. It means to investigate deeply. That's what a real *drash* is, when somebody really has his or her heart and soul in focusing on the fundamentally mysterious and trying to draw something believable that connects us to it at least for that time. That's what's called being an Adam.

11.21 Primordial Torah Becoming Adam

Rebbe Nachman says the whole period from Rosh Hashanah to Simchat Torah is about the process of becoming a real Adam. That means, in the language of Torah, it's a *tiqqun chet Adam Rishon*, which means fixing the obscurations that were manifested by the limitations of Primordial Adam. It basically means making up for the limitations that we reached the previous year. We are doing a *tiqqun* of where we got the previous year. We attempt to correct the mistakes that we made last year, overcoming the limitations that obscured our access to the ever present reality, which is so difficult to grasp because it has no form. It has no color. It has no taste. It isn't accessible to the senses. Nevertheless, in the deepest sense, we know it. It knows us and we know it better than the things we think we know.

11.22 Primordial Points of Torah as Adam

To become an Adam, according to Rebbe Nachman, to become a real Adam, you have to be in a kind of state that is represented by the letter *Aleph*. What makes a person an Adam is not just being born into time and space, having a body and a mind—it has to be an *awakened mind*. To have an awakened mind is symbolized by the letter *Aleph*. The letter *Aleph* basically is composed to three marks as calligraphers know; it has a *Yud* above, then has a *Vav* and then has a *Yud* below. It has three marks. That's what an *Aleph* is. You can make the *Yud* as a dot. You could say it's like a *nekuda* above, a line in the middle, and a lower *nekuda*.

Rosh Hashanah is the upper *nekuda*; it's the upper point. You could call it the point of *bittul*: it's the point where the line is blurred between everything that is obscure and the clear reality that is present when the obscurations have been removed. It's a clear state that's called *bittul*. Sometimes it's called *Hokhmah*. To put it in theistic terms, it means that I'm so absorbed in God that I'm lost in God. Mystics talk about being lost in God. That's another way of ironically being clear. It's not the full degree of clarity. It's the degree of clarity that's represented by the upper point, the *nekuda elyonah*. Sometimes in the language of Kabbalah this is called *Hokhmah*—wisdom which is analogous, I think, to what the Buddhists call emptiness.

11.23 Traces of Light

Emptiness—you have become empty. It means you are empty of self. When you're truly empty of self, then that obscuration that's covering over the non-dual reality is eliminated. It's the experience of absorption in the *Or Ein Sof*, absorption in the divine light. There's no you there, only pure light.

That's the level of Rosh Hashanah, which is the source of new creation. Then you have a ten-day period of drawing what is called the *reshimu*, which is "the trace" or "what remains of that light" after Rosh Hashanah. It is being drawn down day by day for ten days until the mind gets its allotment. The amount of this light that one gets depends on how developed a particular mind is and how prepared it is as a vessel to retain that light. Then one can hold the *reshimu* that one got on Rosh Hashanah in their minds on Yom Kippur. That's the Yom Kippur experience.

When the *reshimu* is fully absorbed, that's its seal, and it's sealed in the mind. On Rosh Hashanah, you could still lose it. That's why you have to have ten days to form a vessel that can hold it. That's the process that leads to Yom Kippur. That's called the *chatimah*, "the sealing"—you've created a vessel that can contain that knowledge, the knowledge of the underlying reality. And it's the presence of that *reshimu* light that is the material out of which the new name YHVH can manifest. Because you have sealed the *reshimu*, you can bring a new YHVH into the world the four days after Yom Kippur.

11.24 Sealing Already There

It's already there. Then the question is how you complete the real "sealing" or *gemirah* required for bringing it into the heart. When you bring the *reshimu* to the level of the heart, it means that you can manifest that light. That's the process of Sukkot. I don't want to just know it. I want to be able to express it. I want to feel it and be able to show it. That's why you have these days. You have the seven days of Sukkot, each of which is devoted to manifesting one of the seven qualities which we call *sefirot* or spheres. That's why each day of Sukkot you invite one of the qualities into your sukkah. It's drawing it in, drawing it in. It's really manifesting. It's by manifesting *chesed* (compassion) and then *gevurah* (rigor) that you go through seven days and the seven spheres.

11.25 Sealing the Seal of Qualia

Hoshana Rabbah is *malchut*. Hoshana Rabbah means I'm going to manifest all the *sefirot* because *malchut* is the *sefirah* that holds all the qualities together. It doesn't have a new quality. Its quality is the sealing of the seal: sealing all of the qualities together. That is represented by the halakha of the willow branch. You have to have a certain number of them and a certain number of leaves and so forth.

11.26 Sweetening Primordial Earth Being

The *aravah* for Hoshana Rabbah—the key mitzvah of Hoshana Rabbah is that you take a willow branch, and you strike it against the earth five times.

That willow branch is not the same one that's included in the four species. It could be only one branch with one leaf because that's how simple it is. That's *malchut*. It's just one branch. It's one leaf. It contains everything. It's containing everything, and you bring it down to earth. You strike it against the earth. That's called sweetening. That's the *tiqqun* of Primordial Adam, the primordial earth being. When you take that willow branch and you strike it down on the earth on Hoshana Rabbah, that is the lower point of *Aleph* that you've then established.

When you establish the lower point of the *Aleph* on Hoshana Rabbah, you become a full Adam. The *Vav* is the whole process of connecting the upper point of Rosh Hashanah with the point of Hoshana Rabbah. You look in any of the sources, the really deep esoteric ones, and you'll see that Hoshana Rabbah and Rosh Hashanah are the same thing but on different levels. Rosh Hashanah is the upper point. Hoshana Rabbah is the lower point. That's why the completion comes only when you can draw down, not when you go up. When you go up in what's called the spiritual ascent, the *aliyat ha-neshama*, you can only draw the *reshimu* into your mind. You don't fully embody it until you pull it down to earth. You have to pull it into your body and find a place for it in your heart.

What sounds very abstract and obscure is exactly what Rebbe Nachman means when he says you should make every Torah a *Tefillah*! What you have received in your mind, you can meditate on. You can contemplate it. When you do, when you contemplate the teachings, think about a very deep Torah that you hear or you learned. You get it, and it can be, *Oh my god. That's blowing my mind*. It takes you somewhere. First, it's striking your mind, *but you really can't make anything out of it until you turn it into a prayer*. You have to change it from the intellectual to the affect level. You have to translate it from a teaching into a prayer. It has to become something aspirational.

11.27 Being Upper-point Adam

What are all of these prayers? They're all based on Torahs! If you don't have Torah, then the prayer is going to be meaningless. You have to have both points. To be an Adam, you have to have the upper point, which is the connecting to the source of Torah, and you have to have the process that connects the point above to the point below, which means it has to become meaningful to me. It has to become aspirational to me. For this Torah to really be important, I have to be able to turn it into a prayer. May it be your will that the understanding I get of the need to connect to the upper point, to really understand and ask my questions about what God is and what the Torah means, I should really want to do that. I should really take this seriously. I want to be reminded. I want to have reminders so I shouldn't forget to be seeking the meaning of God at every moment.

As Rebbe Nachman says, I want to be looking for *sekhel she-b'kol davar*, "a way to connect to God in every single moment and every single experience that I have." You make it into your own prayer. That's what Reb Natan of Nemirov was teaching us in one of his main books, *Liqqutei Tefillot*. Some people learn through them. They read and recite the prayers that he wrote. You can learn a lot from his prayers, but the main thing to learn is the process of making prayers of your own out of things that you learn because that's what it's really about. If you go deeper into the Breslov resources, you'd see that he's not the only one who wrote down his prayers. The people who were taking Rebbe Nachman's instruction seriously kept a kind of spiritual journal made of their prayers. This is one of the things you can do in a spiritual journal. *What's my prayer for today?* When you go into *what is my prayer for today*, the prayer mode, that's the way you engage your heart. This is the crucial thing, in order to become an Adam, to become a human being I have to be able to connect the mind and the heart together.

11.28 Heart Softening Earth

So, for Hoshana Rabbah, really the big thing is the heart, the heart, the heart. One of the great mysteries is how to be able to navigate the path that goes from tears to joy, *hazorim b'dima b'rina yikzoru.* "By sowing, you sow the ground with tears. Then you reap the produce with joy."[3] You have to soften up the earth. The earth is *malchut. Malchut* is the *sefirah* of Hoshana Rabbah. This is understood as far as the *usphizin*, holy guests, are concerned. You can, of course, invite in whomever you like, whoever you feel embodies a particular quality. But in the traditional iconography, King David is the one who is invited in. Hoshana Rabbah is the day of the master of prayer.

11.29 Heart Harvest

King David is supposed to be the master of prayer. The book of Psalms is attributed to David. You read the whole Torah, on the night of Hoshana Rabbah, and you read the whole book of Psalms on the day of Hoshana Rabbah. This connects Moses, our teacher, and David, the Sweet Singer of Israel. Moses, our teacher, is the upper point, and King David is the lower point. There's that lower point, the point of the heart connecting to the point of the mind. That is the imagination of sowing the Psalms; you're softening up the earth with your tears. Those who sow with the tears of Hoshana Rabbah will rejoice with joy, and so the harvest will come with joy. This harvest is *Simchat Torah.*

---

3. Psalm 126:5.

11.30 Vision of Beginning

I want to share this little piece from Rebbe Nachman[4] where he's connecting the beginning and the end of the Torah. This means connecting *Bereshith*, the first word of the Torah and the end of the Torah which is "before the eyes of all Israel."[5] "The eyes of all Israel" ends one Torah cycle. Immediately you go into *Bereshith*, the vision of the beginning. Rebbe Nachman says in this Torah that there are clouds that cover over the eyes. The clouds that cover over the eyes are the obscurations that prevent us from seeing the truth.

You could say, *"Okay, so what is seeing the truth?"* Well, one way that we in our tradition describe the truth is *Ein od milvado*, that "there's nothing but the One."[6] What isn't the truth? Seeing more than One. That means the two eyes are dualistic mind. The clouds are covering over the two eyes. That's the dualistic mind itself. When you see with the dualistic mind, you don't see that everything is "God" (the Oneness that can't be named). The amazing thing is you are seeing the same thing, but you just don't know what you're seeing because your experience is being filtered through dualistic mind. Because of the shortcomings of Primordial Adam, which is precisely what we have to fix, our view is obscured, as a result of eating the fruit of the Tree of Knowledge of Good and Evil. That's the dualistic mind. As soon as you realize that, you have the key to the Edenic view which is seeing "there's nothing but the unnamable Oneness."

11.31 Clear Visions via Tears

Rebbe Nachman is saying that there are clouds that cover over the eyes. They cover over our sight. Do these clouds come before or after the rain? Rebbe Nachman says what comes after the rain is called *Meor Einayim*, the clear sight. So, the light of the eyes means the clear vision that comes after weeping. Clear seeing only comes after tears. It's an interesting Torah. It's a deep and beautiful Torah. The paradox is that there's a sense in which *weeping itself is the clouding of vision*. But on another level, *weeping is the purification of the vision*. Until you can cry, you can't really see. In that sense, it's an incredibly deep psychological Torah. The clouds come after the rain. And yet the clear vision follows the weeping. The rabbis say in the Talmud that through crying your vision gets obscured. And yet it's called *Meor Einayim*.

---

4. Liqqutei Moharan Tinyana, no. 67.

5. ". . . and in all the mighty hand, and in all the great terror, which Moses wrought in the sight of all Israel" (Deuteronomy 34:12).

6. "Unto you it was shown, that thou might know that YHVH is God; there is none else beside the One" (Deuteronomy 4:35).

11.32 Conscious Suffering

What is the crying we are talking about? This weeping has two levels. On one level, it's the level of *teshuvah*, the *teshuvah* of the heart. The process of doing *teshuvah* means that you're really taking to heart how much you care about getting free of your obscurations. How deeply you feel the desire for liberation. That's a very crucial thing. Weeping is very important because if you don't really feel it, if you don't really get fed up with the pain of the experience, with the suffering that goes with the experience of the obscurations of living under the mediation of dualistic mind, you won't be able to restore your vision because the restoration of the vision comes through the tears itself. Then your suffering will not become *conscious suffering*.

11.33 Points in Conscious Suffering

Hoshana Rabbah is when the upper point and the lower point of *conscious suffering* are connected by the purified *Vav*, the inner channel. The *Vav* becomes clear enough so that through it the flow of the *Or Ein Sof* (in the form of the *reshimu*) can be transmitted to the Shekinah and from the Shekinah to all manifestation.

You might ask: *Why do we strike the willows on Hoshana Rabbah five times?* One explanation is that five is the numerical value of the letter *Heh*. The lower point is the lower *Heh* in the four letters, YHVH. So, striking five times is a symbol for the lower *Heh*, which reminds us of the importance of bringing the new light down to earth.

Dualistic mind is *Me'orai Esh* (a destructive form of light)—playing with fire. When I see things this way, I weep because I know that I'm playing a part in creating them. I'm creating them through my unskillful way of being. I'm playing a role in it.

There's a funny thing that Reb Natan says about doing *teshuvah*. One way to understand *teshuvah* is that by doing it we are restoring the temple. We are building the new temple. *I have to do teshuvah for what I might have done in an earlier* gilgul *or incarnation.* Just think of the image. It's very hard to think that you're responsible for something that was destroyed 2,000 years ago. We need a much more contemporary parable or *mashal* to really relate to it. Since we are transmitting the forms of Torah from generation to generation, here's a way that we may be able to connect to it. You can say how do you know that in a previous *gilgul* that you didn't contribute to the destruction of the temple? The *teshuvah* that you do now can not only be a *teshuvah* for something in the previous year, but also it could be a *teshuvah* for something in a previous life.

The point is not to take that too literally. I think it's to understand that the world that we don't like is at least in part the world that we create by

the type of consciousness that we are manifesting. Within that consciousness, we have a misconception of what is real. I don't say those things
are real. I say they're *not real*. What I'm weeping over is the fact that I'm
seeing things like that. I'm also praying for everyone else because I know
that everyone else is also creating and seeing things like that. Since we are
all seeing things like that, we are all freaked out and angry and upset and
defensive and going to war. This is all the consciousness of *Me'orai Esh*. I
see it as *Me'orai Esh*, as destructive vision.

11.34 Helping Others Heal Themselves

There is something that I constantly need to tell myself and that we have
to tell each other. You have to make *Tefillah* out of Torah. It comes down
the idea that you have to practice, and not just know things or think about
things. It's all about a certain transformation that is your own responsibility
that nobody is going to do for you. There isn't any deus ex machina outside
of our own consciousness that's going to come into a distorted mind that
isn't actually seeing things the way they are in the first place. We have to
heal ourselves first of all. We have to heal ourselves for altruistic motives.
That's what being a tzaddik-in-training or what the Buddhists call a bodhisattva means. Even though you're not completely healed, you're trying to
heal yourself and also encourage other people—to help other people to heal
themselves. That's what it's about.

11.35 Two Tasks for Restoration

The practice of restoring vision involves two kinds of things that we really
have to do. One has to do with the purification or the improving of *middot*, or spiritual qualia, or to improve our own behavior and really work on
personality traits. But that is not going to be effective because you can't
do it without recognizing the underlying reality. You have to also have a
practice that restores vision so that you can have knowledge when you're
dealing with the consciousness of *Me'orai Esh*. You need to be like somebody who is awake in a world of dreamers. This is like the image that Plato
gives of the one who got out of the Cave and is able to go back in. When
one returns to the Cave, she doesn't meet with a great reception. People
are not thrilled. It takes a lot of skill to deal with this situation. How do
you operate in that dream, in the dream-world? By dream-world, I mean a
world of beings whose consciousness is virtually determined by *Me'orai
Esh*. They believe that what dualistic consciousness is telling them is real
and they suffer as a result. Suffer is the operative term. So, you have to be
awake within the dream! That's what I think the Buddha meant. When he
was asked, *What are you?* he said, *I'm awake*. That's the bottom line. To
be awake, you have to practice being awake. That's also remembering the

world-that-is-coming.

We have to have some practice that takes us to clear presence, whether it's *Dzogchen* or Ramana Maharshi's *vicara*. We need a way to drop the identifying and attachments of the egocentric mind and to directly recognize that there is a clearer, purer state of consciousness. There is a consciousness that may include a sense of a separate self. Ramana Maharshi showed in the kind of *samadhi* that he could manifest, that there is a *samadhi* of clear presence, in which a person can function without having to be disconnected from sensory experience. That's also I think what it means to be an Adam, to be able to fully connect. You have the upper point connected with the lower point, or to put it in Rebbe Nachman's terms, to be above and below at the same time. In Sufi terms, this is to be in the world, but not of it. We all have to work very hard to be able to do this, as each tradition says in its own way. Rebbe Nachman says: *The whole world is just a narrow bridge, but the main thing is not to scare yourself.* It looks like a dangerous place. You have to walk a fine line. Be careful . . .

11.36 Restoring Unskillful Means

What we call our *het*, our unskillful actions or "unskillful attempts at being fully human," have the effect of reinforcing obscurations. They obscure our access to clear sight. This is represented in our tradition through the idea of the weeping of the Shekinah. There's a strong tradition, for example, that the Shekinah is weeping at the Western Wall. The Shekinah is present at the Western Wall in the Land of Israel and is weeping there. There are several accounts of kabbalists who had such a vision of Shekinah. They go to the Western Wall and got really deep into the connection there between the mind and the heart. Then they see a woman who is weeping. They recognize her as our matriarch, Rachel, weeping for her children.

11.37 Restoring Transparency

Rachel represents the Shekinah. Weeping for her children means that every time that we act unskillfully we create an obscuration that separates us from the underlying source, which is a state of transparent, perfect, shining clarity. It's really like there are three distinct levels to the construction of consciousness. On the deepest level, you have that upper point, *Hokhmah-Ayin* level. That's the empty level, the formless level, the pure light level that is indescribable, that has no characteristics except that it is inseparable from its other levels. It has a quality of *knowing*. It has a quality of awareness. There is a quality that is completely open and completely aware. The Shekinah is the "vessel" in which that awareness is located.

Then there is the level of manifestation that arises from it, so that every single thing that we know phenomenally is arising from that source in awareness. There's a whole system, a kind of cosmology, that attempts to trace the emergence of the four elements. Everything that takes form and can be experienced by the senses is manifesting through the energy of the Shekinah that emerges from the *Ein Sof*, which is the indescribable, deep ground of all that exists and all that can be experienced.

11.38 Restoring Purified Mind, Purified Light

If you have purified mind, which Rebbe Nachman used to refer to as *Me'orai Or*, it's like clear light. Pure light itself. When your consciousness is filled with pure light, then you are aware that "there's nothing but the Oneness." You're connected through and through. There's no obscuration, no separation: it is totally transparent. Your consciousness is the union of the light-energy-information of the Shekinah and the emptiness of the *Ein Sof*. Every single thing that arises is recognized as a manifestation and an emanation of that light.

The fall of Primordial Adam through the eating of the Tree of Knowledge of Good and Evil is the temptation to follow the allure and glamour of the dualistic mind. As soon as one does that, the Shekinah starts weeping. The weeping of the Shekinah is the obscuration of the true nature of consciousness and the reality of what is and who we really are. It's the natural state. It's the clear state of unobscured Oneness.

Thus, the vision that comes when the Shekinah is weeping is called *Me'orai Esh*, the destructive light, the light of fire. And *Me'orai Or* is pure light, which is healing, which is revealing, which is liberating. *Me'orai Esh* is a vision of destruction. You can see how it works out through the iconography of the story of the destruction of the temple. The temple is destroyed by the *Me'orai Esh*. It's destroyed by the kind of vision, the destructive vision that is rooted in dualistic mind, which isn't able to recognize *hashgachah peratit*, that everything is always inseparable from the totality of the Oneness itself.

In the Hasidic tradition, divine providence is no longer the earlier notion that there is a guardian angel that will intervene for you, and if you're good will make sure nothing bad happens to you. It's a deeper idea. It's the recognition that at every moment, regardless of how it may appear, there is no separation from that conscious source. Dualistic mind is the sense that we are somehow separate from it. That dualistic mind, because it isn't aware of the omnipresence of the underlying reality, generates all kinds of bad qualities, destructive qualities. Those destructive qualities are associated with this *Me'orai Esh*.

Reb Natan always turns Torah into prayer, and if you want to take this Torah and turn it into a prayer, we need to create our own prayers for the aspiration that we should be blessed with the *Me'orai Or* and that we should be able to rid ourselves of the bad habit of attachment to the *Me'orai Esh*, the destructive vision. We should be blessed with clear sight to be able to apply the remedies that we have, and with the wisdom to know how we can purify the vision of fire and destruction and restore for ourselves the vision of the new *Me'orai Or*.

In addition to how Reb Natan teaches us how to make a prayer out of a Torah, he also often adds pieces to the Torahs themselves to make them clearer and deeper. I'm going to share a little piece from his *Liqqutei Halakhot*, which is a brilliant work. One of the instructions Rebbe Nachman gave to Reb Natan is to go through the whole *Shulkhan Arukh*—the Jewish code of law legislated by Joseph Karo in sixteenth-century Safed—and connect the halakhot—the laws—with the Torahs that were coming through Rebbe Nachman. In this way, he used to teach the halakhot in a much deeper, personal, effective, and meaningful way. This is an example of the process of connecting it. The teaching has to become yours, something that's meaningful to each of us in order for Torah to continue and remain relevant.

11.39 Restoring Clear Vision via Four Species

Reb Natan in *Hilkhot Arbat haMinim*, on the laws regarding the four species, connects the first halakha with the state of clear vision. *Me'orei Or* is a state of consciousness whose energy can override the concealment of the glory. The glory is the condition of consciousness within which truth is unimpeded. This clarity is manifested by the tzaddik. This means that it's an Adam (a fully realized human) who embodies the consciousness of "there's nothing but the Oneness." The state of obscuration is called the concealment of the glory. The Shekinah's weeping covers over the clear vision, the clear sight, the *Me'orei Or*, the clear vision.

Rachel is weeping over her children. Therefore, the *tiqqun*, the remedy, is through the weeping of human beings. Human weeping is a form of spiritual homeopathy. Rachel's weeping means that human consciousness is in a condition of obscuration. It is not aware of the underlying reality. If the weeping of Rachel is itself the symptom of the concealment, then the homeopathic *tiqqun* comes through human weeping

Since the weeping of the Shekinah is the result of the unskillful actions of human beings. The cause of the weeping of the Shekinah is the unenlightened way that we have been acting. As a result, the clear vision, the pure light vanishes and the glory is hidden. *Teshuvah* is the remedy. You have to really be so deeply concerned, and care so much about your contribution to the weeping of the Shekinah, that such deep feeling in itself can fix this, through that weeping one can fix what one has harmed. The effect of this kind of *tiqqun* of sincere weeping can be very powerful, if it's done with this consciousness and the person knows why they're doing it and really understands the process. This is an indication of the responsibility that one has to take for one's own mind-stream.

The problem is that through a dualistic mind you're always looking for the cause and blame for something. Who did what to what, and who's the wrong one. But, that whole way of looking at our circumstances means that Shekinah is weeping. If you're doing that, the Shekinah is just weeping for us. So, the remedy is not to figure out who's wrong and to blame. The remedy is to figure out how am I contributing to the weeping of the Shekinah. That means that I have to clarify my own vision and restore the *Me'orei Or* and remove the *Me'orei Esh* from the way I'm seeing things.

11.40 Arousing Compassion via *Teshuvah*

When *teshuvah* is deep and sincere, it arouses compassion. The universe through its quantum field–like feedback loop responds with qualia that correspond to the feeling that you send out. If you put in sincere *teshuvah*, compassion has to be the response. It has to be the divine response. The feedback is going to be *rachmanut*, compassion. Rebbe Nachman says that "in the places of the ashes of destruction, the same letters of Torah can be rearranged." They don't have to be in the order that spells destruction. Through very skillful action, you can change the Torah. You can change the order of the letters of Torah from "ashes" (*Aleph Peh Resh*) to "glory" (*Peh Aleph Resh*), which means the glory will shine through. That is the power of the weeping.

11.41 Restoration of the Heart

Even though weeping initially has the effect of causing clear sight to depart, when we take it on ourselves to arouse this weeping as the form of sincere *teshuvah*, a compassionate response is all but guaranteed. This can be compared to how a loving parent deals with naughty children. As soon as they feel contrite, you have to forgive them right away. You know they're just little kids. If you are fully human with a heart, you're going to have to forgive them immediately. Anything less would be neurotic. All it really took is the contrition: waking up and caring, which is connecting to the heart, the restoration of the heart.

As a result of the weeping, there is a change from the destructive form of vision into the form within which one can see the glory of reality. It all depends on us. The rabbis had a saying that "the prisoner cannot release herself from the prison." Somebody has to come and let you out. If you're in prison and the door is locked, somebody has to come and release you. Therefore, the weeping of the Shekinah does not bring about the release. The Shekinah's tears are not going to redeem us. We have to redeem the Shekinah! That's the point.

11.42 Arousing Clear Insight for God

The key here is that the Shekinah's weeping is the *pega'*, the damage that has been done. We cause the weeping of the Shekinah, and this is responsible for the departure of the clear sight. Just as soon as we sincerely arouse ourselves through the purifying tears of *teshuvah* in the heart, immediately the divine compassion is aroused, and the *pega'* is fixed. The weeping of the Shekinah transforms ashes to splendor. So, when a child weeps, immediately one forgives him.

Here is one final point from Reb Natan. It's through this weeping and this *tiqqun* that we merit having the beautiful *etrog*. The mystery is that you can't see the beauty of the *etrog* until you do a real *teshuvah*. The whole point of the *etrog* is to see its beauty. The *etrog* is called the *peri 'etz hadar*, the fruit of the tree of glory. Being able to really see the beauty of the *etrog* means that you have healed the weeping of the Shekinah. You have played a part in restoring the *Me'orei Or*, the pure light of clear sight because the pure light of clear sight sees the *pe'er*, the glory. Then one can sees the beauty of "there's nothing but the Oneness."

11.43 Closing Intention

We should pray in the depth of our hearts. We should really do everything that we can to clear the sight of the Shekinah. The Shekinah should once again rejoice with Her children. That's Simchat Torah. All of us, we should have the Simchah of renewed Torah!

Chapter 12
Secrets of Hanukkah: Light One, Light Eight Candles

12.0 Hanukkah as Light of Prophecy

This is a particularly auspicious moment, coinciding with the culmination of Hanukkah, which is important for us. As *hevre RADLA*, we are dedicated to the Torah of the future. By *RADLA*, I refer to the mystical hypostasis or supreme level of consciousness that is beyond all conception. So, if you are open to receiving the light that flows from that level, you are connected to this group, this lineage, this *hevre*. This immediately suggests the function of prophecy. Even though there is big smokescreen about what Hanukkah is really about, in the esoteric tradition, Hanukah is really about working on the power of prophecy. This Hanukkah light is the light of prophecy, becoming perceptible, so that we can extend it.

12.1 Ways of Extending Light

Rabbi Yitzhak Maeir Morgenstern reminds us of a teaching from Reb Nachman,[1] that was delivered on Shabbat of Hanukkah. There is a famous disagreement between the Schools of Hillel and Shammai. The question is, does one start with one candle on the first night and add an additional candle each night until we have eight? Or, do we start with eight on the first night and go down from there to one on the final night? The halakha is to start with Hillel, starting with one going to eight. But in the Torah of the future, we will follow the School of Shammai, starting with eight and descending to one.

This controversy parallels a disagreement regarding tefillin or phylacteries. Do we use the tefillin of Rashi or Rabeinu Tam? Now what kind of tefillin, or phylacteries, does a devoted Hasid put on? The answer is: both. According to Reb Nachman's teaching, putting on tefillin is a kind of *Tiqqun Kelali*. It is a general practice that resets the entire system. Such a practice is of inestimable value, although we now have more effective ways of doing it than Reb Nachman's generation had. So, donning tefillin is a

---

1. Liqqutai Moharan, no. 54.

Tiqqun Kelali that resets existence to a mode of sanity.

If the Hasidim, in the case of tefillin, wear both sets each morning to honor the unresolved controversy between the two schools, perhaps during Hanukkah, we should be lighting two *menorot*, one according to Hillel and one according to Shammai. With the first night, you light one candle in one menorah, and with the other candelabra, you would light eight.

12.2 Light of One to Many

This may sound like a quaint scholastic matter. But it really alludes to something very deep. There are two ways to amplify light. One way is to increase all the potential light that is latently present in one light. And the other way is to increase the number of lights from moment to moment. And these two modalities of amplifying light correspond to "above and below." That is, the two directional flows of energy that form the circuit or feedback loop of existence. The flow from below to above (called *itaruta de-la tata*) goes from eight to one, from multiplicity to unity. From the perspective of the highest of the high, there is no distinction. So that flow starts with one candle and its path becomes multiplicity. But there is a mysterious sense in which the lowest of the low is the highest of the high and the highest of the high is the lowest of the low. So, in lighting two *menorot*, one going from one candle and increasing to eight and another going from eight and culminating with one, we attune ourselves to the mystery of how the highest of the high becomes the lowest of the low and the lowest of the low ascends to the highest of the high. And ultimately what separates "high" and "low" is transcended.

12.3 Miracle of Mystical Light

And that recognition would be the culmination of Hanukkah. Rabbi Yitzhak Maeir Morgenstern also explains how this issue is related to the Hanukkah legend of how the quantity of oil found after the Maccabean victory that was only sufficient for a single night managed to last for eight. What really was the nature of the miracle? Perhaps they took the oil and divided it into eight parts, so that each part was enough to last for each the subsequent seven days. Or perhaps they poured the light into the menorah, and as soon as they poured out all the oil it was miraculously refilled, so that the jar remained full for all eight days. If you look at this halakhic argument seeking its inner meaning, the question becomes whether the miracle occurs at the source of light which is never diminished or within the receiver of the light whose capacity to hold and distribute light increases incrementally. This question is also reflected in the different ways that Hayyim Vital and other students of Isaac Luria related Hanukkah to the *sefirot*. Vital held that Hanukkah was a function of the *sefirah* of *Hod*, whereas students of Vital's contemporary, Israel Sarug, understood Hanukah as a function of *Netzakh*. What does this really mean beyond an exercise in abstract thinking?

12.4 Eternity and Receptivity as Miracles of Mystical Light

Netzakh means eternity. Sarug understood Hanukkah from the perspective of a person who is an already perfect tzaddik, a fully realized being who like the light source is never diminished. In contrast, Vital was mainly focused on building vessels that could hold increasing light. So, he emphasized the vessels, and the issue for him is about receptivity and reflection of light which is represented by the function of *Hod*. Vital's perspective involves understanding the miracle as depending on what we do, the building of vessels with the capacity to hold and radiate more and more light. So, in his view, Hanukkah is about receptivity.

12.5 Tracing Mystical Light to Wisdom vs. Understanding

The dialectic can be traced back to *Hokhmah* and *Binah*. Does the miracle of Hanukah just come to me or do I have to have to do something in order to be able to receive it? *Binah* (Understanding) is the mind's capacity to draw out inferences from the undifferentiated source of inspiration called *Hokhmah* (Wisdom). The perspective that emphasizes the need to make an effort derives from *Binah*. On another level, the same dialectic is represented by the two spiritual archetypes, the tzaddik in essence, and the *Baal teshuvah*, or master of return. Recall that the Talmud teaches us that "a tzaddik in essence cannot stand in the place of a master of return." Although one might think that an already "perfect" being is superior to one who is still evolving, the Gemara tells us the opposite! The one who continues to aspire to further evolve is more praiseworthy. The *Baal teshuvah* embodies the function of the *sefirah Hod*.

12.6 Increasing Messianic Capacity to Receive and Transmit Light

So, the Baal Shem Tov teaches us about "*mashiach* consciousness," devotion toward the manifestation of new, more appropriate, and effective forms that can embody and amplify more of the eternally pure light. To achieve this, we need schools for tzaddikim in training that would support and enhance the yearning of masters of returning so that they can more effectively continue the process of evolution and also enable those on the level of tzaddik-in-essence to become masters of returning!

The tzaddik in essence is a person who "stands" in *Netzakh* from which perspective everything is seen as already "God," now and forever. The Ropshitzer Rebbe claimed that he never did *teshuvah*, because he was rooted in "God consciousness." For him everything was already sweet and nothing needed to be sweetened. But the archetype of *teshuvah* is King David, who was known for his unworthy misdeeds that mysteriously enabled him to do *teshuvah* and thus reach higher and higher levels—constantly increasing his capacity to receive and transmit light.

This dialectic is the difference between the *sefirot* of *Netzakh* and *Hod*, eternal light and periodic flashes that incrementally reveal more of the light. And these are also seen in the polarity of the two archetypes, the tzaddik in essence and the master of return. The Baal Shem Tov wanted to create more masters of return, but a person needs to be both a tzaddik in essence and a master of return. This is exemplified by lighting the two *menorot*, one according to School of Hillel and the other according to Shammai.

12.7 Be Something You Have Never Been Before

It is simple but important to remember Reb Nachman's teaching that when Hanukkah comes, I have to be something that I never was before.[2] If you are a real Hasid, you can never be old or the remain the same. There is no such thing as an old Hasid, which means that whenever you come to the same place on the calendar, it has to be different each year.

12.8 Remembering Torah of the Future

So, what are we working with in order to be fresh and new each day? Orienting ourselves according to the Torah of the future depends on remembrance: remembering where we come from and where we are going. This is the double meaning of *Olam ha-Ba*—which means both where we come from and where we are going. If we don't remember where we came from, we don't know where we are going. This is the plight of most of us on the planet today, insofar as we don't know where we are coming from and we don't really know who we are. Our confusion is largely due to identifying ourselves with the egocentric mind, which distorts who we really are. But to know who we really are demands knowing where we came from before we "became" who and what we think we are. In so knowing, we remember who we are, or real knowledge mysteriously remembers us. This places us in the state of *'emunah* ("faith").

How do we know that? We have occasional promptings. The sphere of *Hod* flashes and reminds us to be grateful. We could not be here if we did not have a little glimpse of where we come from and where we are going. But to have a real chance of re-membering, you have to be fortunate enough in your life to come across a transmission of wisdom that can motivate us to seek full re-membering.

12.9 Re-membering a Gateway Within

In the meantime, we may receive glimpses of what is beyond. Without the

---

2. Liqqutei Moharan, no. 54.

possibility of discovering a gateway within each and every one of us, it would not be possible to enter into the realm of consciousness that is "beyond," the real knowledge that is called gnosis. The level of real being that is beyond any stories or any garments, conceals itself in these lower worlds of consciousness. This light of real being is the consciousness of *Hokhmah*. *Hokhmah* (Primordial Wisdom) is associated with pure olive oil. That is why the best way to light the Hanukkah lights is with oil. Oil is a symbol of *Hokhmah*. When we kindle the Hanukkah lights with pure olive oil and contemplate that light, it reminds us of the light of pure consciousness. And precisely that light enables us to see and re-member who we really are and where we really come from. The point of kindling the oil, the light of *Hokhmah,* is to perfect our sight. And this may even lead to prophetic consciousness, seeing the sacredness in every single thing that comes into our sphere of experience.

12.10 Re-membering as a Degree of *Devekut*

The light of *Hokhmah* shines both above and below—it is not limited. There are certain moments of expanded consciousness when you are "in a higher world," experiencing an expansiveness within which the light is more evident. But that same light permeates all worlds and can be discerned by highly perfected beings like the Baal Shem Tov. Cultivating this abiding clarity in which we can recognize who we really are and where we really come from, always yields some form of the state of consciousness called *devekut* (holding it all together). Regardless of circumstances, whether I am in the heavens above or the inferno below, I'll still know who I am and where I came from. As long as I am re-membering, some degree of *devekut* will be present. But, if you do lose this sense, then we fall into the condition of death of the heart, that is, it is disheartening, for it seems as though we are separated in this world from the world-that-is- coming.

12.11 Full Immersion in Pure Light

Reb Nachman teaches that if a person keeps remembering the world-that-is-coming, the Reality that we never leave, we unify the divine names, *YHVH* and *Elohim*. When we light the Hanukkah lights, there are three things being brought into a continuum. One is *YHVH* (the Totality) with its aspect called *EHYH*; one is *YHVH* with its aspect called *Elohim*; and the third is *YHVH* with its aspect *Adonai*. There is integration on all three levels. But the middle level is the most important, because it is the one that integrates above and below. This issue here is that the higher level (*YHVH* with *EHYH*) represents the state called *bittul bimetziut* (full immersion of the pure light itself). In the form of *devekut* represented by the union of *YHVH* and *Adonai*, called *bittul ha-yesh*, the light is discerned even while fully immersed in phenomenality. But the crucial moment here is the unification of *YHVH* with *Elohim*.

The preparation for the mitzvah is greater than the act itself.

12.12 Preparing Pure God Consciousness

In order for a person to remember the world-that-is-coming even while seemingly immersed in this world, we need to gain the capacity to discern the presence of *ruchaniut* (spiritual energy) everywhere, especially in the "lower" world called *Assiyah*. In order to be able to do that in the course of your daily life, one has to become established in the experience of intimacy or *Atzilut* (the "world" of non-duality that is the ground on which all "lower worlds" [states of duality] depend). Without that experience, you will be unable to recognize the *ruchaniut* that is present as the energetic basis for dualistic experiences as well. Otherwise, you have no idea what it means and won't experience it. This state of pure god consciousness (*melo' kol ha-aretz kevodo*) requires preparation. If you have already re-membered who you are in the world-that-is-coming, beyond time and space, then it becomes apparent that *ruchaniut* is present in everything and is not merely "above." This is what is required in order to be able to kindle the Hanukkah lights.

12.13 Every Moment Is Illuminated

Moving ahead now—Reb Nachman teaches that Hanukkah is really about a sacred way of seeing. This means having a light that enables us to see what kinds of corrections are required and what forms of *ruchaniut* are present. The Hanukkah lights can help us shift our gaze from a constricted egocentric mind-set. That shift is *teshuvah*. This changes our perspective from *how can I take advantage of this* to *how can I restore the balance?*

Hanukkah is meant to teach us how to use our eyes in this way to see the world as it is. To be grateful, through a *tiqqun* of *Hod*, means I can accept the world as it is and I can access the light, so that every moment becomes be illuminated.

12.14 Sacred Forgetting vs. Remembering

Even though there is so much emphasis on remembering who we are and where we come from, paradoxically, there is also a need for sacred forgetting. Such sacred forgetting is even higher than sacred remembering.

12.15 Ever-changing Energy of Consciousness

Keep in mind this is all related to lighting candles. The root of *Hokhmah* (Wisdom) comes from the deepest level of *Atik* ("The Ancient One"). Where does that light come from? It emerges from a level that is preconscious. The ability to remember where we come from depends on accessing *Hokhmah*, which is represented by the oil of the menorah. But where does the oil itself come from? It comes from the olive. Something has to precede it. So, if you eat a lot of olives you will forget your learning.[3] But consuming olive oil causes you to remember! *RADLA* is a state of not-knowing, which is higher than knowing. *Hokhmah* (Wisdom) is a state of knowing, but it comes from the state of *RADLA*, the level of "unknowing" which is beyond knowing and remembering. Once you have the extension of the worlds, there is simultaneously the consciousness in which creation and its Source appear (as distinct). But in the very source itself, nothing is really created at all. Creation is a dynamic display of ever-changing patterns of energy that are intrinsic to the conscious source itself. The apparent separateness of creation from its source vanishes when its non-dual nature is recognized. This is the consciousness that is implied by the concept of sacred forgetting. It is not a condition of impaired memory. Rather, it implies dissolution of the dualistic state in order to gain access to the level of consciousness prior to differentiation.

12.16 Rebooting Consciousness to Bring Down the Light

To use an analogy that Reb Zalman loved, this is like when your computer gets stuck and needs to get rebooted. If you are a real computer maven, you might be able to get it to work without having to reboot, but sometimes you just have to shut down the whole thing, and then by some miracle it all gets fixed. Where does it get fixed then? Everything gets "fixed" in the level in which everything that was a certain way is completely forgotten. That level is prior to consciousness and its contents. It is essential to reach this state of sacred forgetting (the consciousness of *RADLA*) so that the light of *RADLA* can enter into *Hokhmah* (Wisdom). This is what enables us to bring the light down to *Hod* (gratitude) and to then see the *ruchaniut* in all things. To have this light in its purest form, you must go back to where the light actually originates from.

12.17 Immersion in Light of Limitless Luminosity *(RADLA)*

Without the immersion in the light of *RADLA*, something vital will be missing and the oil will not be pure. Even if you can merge fully with the level of *Hokhmah* (Wisdom), it won't be sufficient, because you will still be dependent on pleasure that is ecstatic. But in the sphere of *Keter* (Crown), which is higher and rooted in *RADLA*, the pure "dark" light is present even when there is no ecstatic experience of pleasure and light. And that "clarity" is still there even when life is not fun, when it is not inspired or illuminated. Such is the mystery of the light of *RADLA*—this is the most real

---

3. bHorayot 13b.

you can get. It means you are not going to go insane that easily. It is a tremendous paradox because you go insane because there is a piece missing. There is a kick and you cannot always get it. That is what confuses us. But there is something deeper than any "kick" or high. So, if you can recognize the level that precedes consciousness, then there is not anything that could possibly happen to you that could affect it.

12.18 Seeing Limitless Luminosity Everywhere

Reb Nachman is teaching that the entire practice of Hanukkah is to see divinity everywhere one goes and in everything that happens, and to stick with the oil. If you do this practice, it opens your heart. Opening the heart is precondition for the Torah of the future that comes through *Hokhmah*. This enables us to see *ruchaniut* everywhere, so that we can turn ourselves around and headed back in the direction that we came from.

12.19 Pure Limitless Luminosity

But be careful! We still need to make an effort not to be seeing things in a negative way. In order to accomplish this, one has to stick with the light of *RADLA,* the level of sacred forgetfulness. Otherwise you will not be able to deal with the vicissitudes of life. At the level of *RADLA*, there is no envy, jealousy, or competition, there is just the pure olive!

12.20 Sacred Seeing via *Hokhmah*

The other piece that is important here is sacred seeing—that is what prophecy is really about. If you want to see in a holy way, then kindle the light of *Hokhmah*. But in order to have the oil you have to go beyond the oil, to the state of sacred forgetting. Then always aspire to see things in a positive light. Be careful not to imagine things and to allow yourself to become deluded. Even being positive is not always enough—you could be creating illusions! Sanity and clarity are also required.

12.21 Going Beyond, Holy Darkness

There is a certain kind of inner path here to sanity and ultimate reality (*lev amiti*). It has to do with the ability to break through the sense of being defined by the egocentric mind. You break free of that by remembering who we are and where we come from. The first step is breaking out into a state of communion or intimacy (*Atzilut*), recognizing a deeper part of ourselves beyond the ego. For some of us, that is all we have gotten to so far. But there is further work to be done. *What is further than that?* You have to go to the place that is beyond even the light, that is, the holy darkness. It is the dark light, which is beyond the light of *Hokhmah* (Wisdom). One has to go to the level of the sacred forgetting. But that is also not the end. Those who end there will have reached the state of a tzaddik *ab initio*. But the Baal Shem Tov is saying that we have to teach the tzaddik *ab initio* to become a master of return. And the "master of return" (*Baal teshuvah*) represents a state that is more evolved than the complete tzaddik.

12.22 Integration of Wisdom and Understanding

The level of the perfect or complete tzaddik cannot really represent the totality of evolutionary consciousness. If that were so, and many err in believing this to be the case, there would be nothing left to do. But Rabbi Morgenstern is teaching that there is something even higher than *RADLA*. Beyond the sacred forgetting is "the hand" of the prophets, which reaches even further. Prophetic consciousness has the capacity to integrate the tzaddik *ab initio* with the master of return through the power of the sacred joy that enables this. The master of return has the *jouissance* which is beyond the tzaddik *ab initio*. That leads to the true seeing, beyond nonexistence, so that whatever appears to exist is radiating the light of the sacred. Reaching the level of *Hokhmah* (Wisdom) is not sufficient because *Hokhmah* is in a dialectical relationship with *Binah* and is always fluctuating. If I depend on the intimacy of *Hokhmah*, I am bound to be disappointed. I need to reach further to a more stable condition in which the dialectical poles of *Binah* and *Hokhmah* are integrated.

12.23 Asending Without Forgetting Who I Am

This ascent to higher integration means to be both above and below—to unite the conditions of the tzaddik *ab initio* and the master of return, without forgetting who I really am and where I come from. Then everything that is manifest is an extension of who I am and where I am coming from. That is the place that "the hand" of the prophet reaches. And this, according to the now emerging Torah of the future, is what Hanukkah is really about.

So, light two *menorot*—on one light, one flame and on the other light, eight. While lighting, focus especially on the unification on the names of YHVH and Elohim feeling your being become the hand of prophetic vision that reaches so far beyond all and everything that the entire universe becomes music.

12.24 Closing Intention

Let us all be the eyes of prophecy and then do the best you can. Never say I cannot do this. Just remember to try to recognize the ruchaniut that can show us the way to return or do teshuvah in each and every situation. That is how to light the menorah. Look into who you really are, and realize what Is before any form of I am, the prior to consciousness. But what is it prior to consciousness? It is the all and everything that there is. So, when I open my eyes, I see all of creation with the eyes of the prophet. Then my motivation is to be a master of return, following the light of emerging Torah that mysteriously leads asymptotically back and forward to the world-that is-coming where "there's nothing but that Oneness."[4]

---

4. Literally, "Unto you it was shown, that thou might know that YHVH is God; there is none else beside the One" (Deuteronomy 4:35).

Chapter 13
An Insider's Symposium: *Tu B'Shevat* Seder[1]

13.0 Appreciating the Wonders of Creation via *Tu B'Shevat* Seder

Jewish mysticism is not identical with philosophy, and yet Kabbalah cannot be what it is without a philosophical undergirding. This creative tension could not be more clear than with the case of the Insider's Symposium—*Tu B'Shevat*. The kabbalist's position is not identical to that of medieval religious philosophers, like Maimonides, who also viewed nature as a source for knowledge of God. In their view, the knowledge of the wondrous construction of nature and its laws led to an appreciation for its Creator. Here, at *Tu B'Shevat*, knowledge of God is theosophical. It regards nature as a symbolic representation of the hidden divine realm and not merely as an immaculately designed product of divine engineering. To understand this more deeply, let's consider the Insider's Symposium of *Tu B'Shevat*.

13.1 Brief History of *Tu B'Shevat* Seder as Kabbalistic Symposium

The kabbalistic symposium (seder) text known as *Peri Eitz Hadar* was originally popular in Sephardic (Spanish and Mediterranean) communities and unknown in the Ashkenazic (Eastern European) world. According to the author, this is due to the fact that in the Ashkenazic community, the eminent halakhic authority Jacob Emden (1697–1776) attributed *Peri Eitz Hadar* to Nathan of Gaza, a theologist who considered himself a prophet of Shabbetai Tzvi, the seventeenth-century pseudo-Messiah. Jewish authorities reviled Shabbetai Tzvi as a heretic because of his conversion to Islam. This material, therefore, was condemned by Emden as a heretical Sabbatean text.

While Emden was eager to discover Sabbatean influences in many works, modern scholarship does support his contention regarding *Hemdat Yamim*, the Sabbatean anthology that contains *Peri Eitz Hadar*. Nevertheless, this seder is a pure kabbalistic text of the Lurianic school, despite its

---

1. This chapter is excerpted and revised with permission of the author, see Miles Krassen, "Peri Eitz Hadar: A Kabbalist Tu B'Shevat Seder," in Trees, Earth, and Torah: A Tu B'Shevat Anthology, ed. Ari Elon, Naomi Mara Hyman, and Arthur Waskow (Philadelphia, PA: Jewish Publication Society), 135–53.

inclusion in the controversial anthology *Hemdat Yamim*.

The author goes on to state that in modern times, with the mutual influence of Ashkenazic and Sephardic communities—especially in Israel—many kabbalistic works, including *Peri Eitz Hadar*, have increased in popularity in Ashkenazic communities as well.

The notion of a *Tu B'Shevat* seder, that is, a ritual involving the eating of specific fruit, drinking wine, and studying or reciting specific selections from the sacred literature of Judaism, does not seem to have been known before the late seventeenth century. Until the sixteenth century, most kabbalist mystics were more concerned with providing mystical bases that would strengthen the motivation for observing the laws and traditions of classical Judaism than with creating new rituals. At that point, the kabbalists of Tzfat—the city of Safed—did create some new rituals, most notably the *Kabbalat Shabbat* service.

The kabbalistic *Tu B'Shevat* seder seems to have been created sometime later, in the wake of kabbalistic creativity in sixteenth-century Tzfat.

13.2 Insider's Book: *Peri Eitz Hadar*

The text of the seder, which has come to be known as *Peri Eitz Hadar*, is essentially the same as the section on *Tu B'Shevat* which appears in the Sabbatean-influenced anthology of kabbalistic customs, *Hemdat Yamim* (Izmir, 1731–32). Formally, *Peri Eitz Hadar* contains four basic sections. After an introduction that explains the basis for the *Tu B'Shevat* seder, there is a prayer to be said before the actual seder begins. This is followed by a description of the order of the fruit to be eaten and the way wine should be blended in each of the four cups. However, the bulk of the seder consists of selections from the Bible, early rabbinic texts, and the Zoharic (or kabbalistic) literature. In fact, the greatest portion of this material is taken from the Zohar, a mystical commentary on the Torah that is the major text of Jewish mysticism.

As a result, the *Peri Eitz Hadar* is essentially a kabbalistic work, meant to be read and applied by a reader thoroughly schooled in the outlook of the Kabbalah, particularly as it developed in the school of Isaac Luria. This fact renders the text, even in translation, virtually incomprehensible for a modern reader. This is due to several factors. First, the text does not explain the rather complex basic principles of Kabbalah as they developed since the late twelfth century. In particular, the text assumes that its reader is familiar and comfortable with the kabbalistic classic, *Sefer ha-Zohar,* an esoteric work characterized by obscure allusions and highly symbolic language.

In addition, the author's outlook involves certain fundamental notions about nature, the cosmos, and the spiritual role that human beings are meant to play, which may be unfamiliar and even strange to a contemporary reader. Such notions, moreover, are not defended or justified, but are implicit in the author's and the intended reader's worldview.

13.3 A Kabbalistic View of Nature

The *Tu B'Shevat* seder celebrates an important moment in the yearly cycle of nature, the appearance of fruit on trees. In the Land of Israel, this stage occurs during mid-winter. In order to understand how the *Peri Eitz Hadar* approaches this celebration, it is necessary to gain some understanding of how the kabbalists viewed nature. In general, the kabbalistic view shared many traits that were typical of other premodern cosmological systems, which tended to regard nature as in some sense sacred.

This approach to nature is in marked contrast to those that have become typical of the modern period. For the kabbalist, nature is neither a source to be exploited for utilitarian benefits nor a sentimental vestige of the past to be romanticized by poets and naturalists. It is rather an ultimate link in a chain of divine manifestation that directly emerges from the divine source of life.

Implicit here is a notion of sacred cosmology, which is not limited to material existence. The kabbalists' faith involves a hierarchy of worlds that are ontologically higher than the material world. These worlds are populated by angels and spiritual forces that span the ontological regions that separate humanity and the material world from God. Moreover, the forces in these worlds serve as conduits and sources for the divine energy that becomes manifest in nature and in Creation in general.

Although each world is characterized by an increasing degree of opacity that veils its divine root, all worlds share a common underlying structure. Thus, contemplation of any world can lead to knowledge of the structure of the ultimate theosophical realm. This realm is the world of the ten *sefirot* (emanations), which is composed of the ten divine qualities and aspects that constitute the inner life of God, insofar as it is accessible to human imagining. This principle is no less true of nature. Indeed, nature (along with the human body) is, in a sense, the most available arena of divine revelation, since the higher worlds are not apparent to the senses. As such, nature may serve as a mirror in which all of the mysteries of the concealed Godhead are reflected.

13.4 Nature as Torah

This fundamentally sacred view of nature renders it comparable to the Torah itself. For the kabbalist, the Torah is not merely an account of the sacred history of Israel and its divinely mandated laws. It is a primary manifestation of divine revelation. All of the secrets and mysteries of the cosmos and the inner workings of the Godhead are somehow contained within it.

However, it is a cipher, which only yields its concealed meanings to those who hold the keys of divine gnosis, the kabbalists, who through contemplation and mystical experience have gained access to the symbol system that opens the Torah's deeper levels of meaning.

13.5 Closing Intention

For the kabbalist, nature parallels the Torah—at this hour, when the planetary perspective is in such jeopardy, we might venture further to claim nature is Torah. Insofar as it can teach us secrets that are concealed within it, it is very much a kind of Torah. What I'm suggesting here is not a simplistic syncretism with paganism, but actually on a deeper level—the very same secrets that are concealed within the quintessential sacred text may be learned through directly contemplating aspects of nature. *May the structure of different kinds of fruit, the growing patterns of trees, the habits of birds, indeed all natural phenomena become again aspects of a divine epiphany that proclaims the truth of the Totality (YHVH).*

Chapter 14
Sweetening the Darkness around Midnight with *'Emunah* during *Shovevim*[1]

14.0 Affirming Convictions

'*A ni ma'amin b'emunah shleyma b'viat ha'mashiach, v'af al pi sh'yitmamei'a im kol zeh achakeh lo . . . I have firm conviction that* mashiach *consciousness evolves asymptotically, and will be faithful to its emergence forever . . .*

There is an amazing teaching of Reb Natan of Nemirov,[2] in the course of which he says that the very essence of working to be who we really are and in touch with reality in the deepest way—which is the meaning of "knowing God"—ultimately depends on *'emunah*. If Reb Natan claims that *'emunah* is so important, what could that mean for us? Moreover, what does this cluster of time called *Shovevim*[3] mean for us? Recall that *Shovevim* is actually a turning point of the year, a time for tricksters and mischief-makers and so it is also an acronym that distills tough time. We are concerned here with time. The reading of the Torah portions during the weeks of *Shovevim* fall within the two Hebrew months of Tevet and *Shevat*, a period considered auspicious for *tiqqun* and *teshuvah*.

Reading through the *40 Rules of Love*, written by the remarkable Turkish author, Elif Shafak, I have to admit that I am, at times, taken by the Sufi path. I became interested in her through reading one of Paul Theroux's travelogues. I like to read Theroux because he doesn't write for tourists, but

---

1. Shave l'kol Nefesh (Nahalat Shalom January 16, 2016).
2. Reb Natan of Nemirov, Liqquatai Halakhot, Hoshen Mishpat, halakha no. 5.
3. Shoveivim T"T is the full acronym for scriptural readings including for the weekly Torah portions in Exodus (Shemot, Vaera, Bo, Beshelah, Yitro, Mishpatim, Terumah, Tezaveh), and often there is a fast associated with the eight Thursdays of those Torah reading days. There are those who are dedicated to biweekly fasts of Monday–Thursday during this time period. These weekly Torah portions in Exodus themselves point to archetypal qualia that is the work of this period: (1) Shemot—revealed turning of teshuvah; (2) Vaera—returning the whole heart through truth; (3) Bo—devotion; (4) Beshelakh—prayer; (5) Yitro—receiving Torah; (6) Mishpatim—judgments; (7) Terumah—giving charity and social action from the heart; (8) Tezaveh—acts of lovingkindness. See Rabbi Isaiah Horowitz, Sheni Luchot baBerit, 306b.

rather for travelers. Travelers want to find out the truth about how people are actually living, not merely lose themselves in the glamor of a tourist's fantasy world. When Theroux traveled in Istanbul, he made a point of meeting with Elif Shafak and was struck by the fact that she was one of the most intelligent women he had ever met and one of the most strikingly beautiful. Shafak is a tremendous resource for travelers in Turkey in that she is quintessentially Turkish and at the same time so cosmopolitan. In order to help us get a deeper sense of what *'emunah* can mean, I'd like to call attention to one of her books, a novel called *40 Rules of Love*, which is the love story between Rumi and Shams of Tabriz. Let's consider the first two rules.

14.1 Rule #1: How We See God Is a Direct Reflection of How We See Ourselves

If God brings to mind too much fear and blame, then there is going to be much fear and blame inside us. If God brings to mind love, then we are filled with love. Most of the time, we don't believe that we are seeing God. Although we may have concepts of God that we believe in as something that is not seeable, that kind of belief is not real *'emunah*. Real *'emunah* (*'emunah sheleymah*) is when we *know* we are seeing God. The purpose of the work (*tachlis ha'avodah*) then is to cultivate real *'emunah* through realizing that if we don't like what we are seeing, it is partly because we don't even know that we are seeing God. It could be good, it could be bad, but whatever appears, it's different if you know that you are seeing God.

14.2 Rule #2: The Path to the Truth Is a Labor of the Heart, Not the Head

Make your heart your primary guide not your mind. Meet the challenge and ultimately prevail over your *nafs* with your heart leading your ego along the path to the knowledge of God.

14.3 From *Nafs* to *Nefesh*

To translate this into the language of Hasidism, the *nafs* is ego, which we call *nefesh*. So we call the path to clarity "fixing the *nefesh*" (*tiqqun ha'nefesh*). This means establishing the real "ground of being" (*malchut d'kedusha*) and seeing through and displacing the "Other Side" (*Sitra Achara*). This is a kind of qualified non-dualism or non-dual dualism. This kind of non-dual teaching is not quite a form of pure monism. Rather than putting the emphasis on reducing everything to One, it teaches us to recognize that the duality that we experience is really non-dual.

14.4 Cultivating Deeper Convictions

It reminds me of a story Shafak tells about Shams, who speaks about an encounter with a mercenary hired to murder him. Shams of Tabriz was Rumi's teacher who shook him out of his scholarly role, the way of the head, and taught him how to cultivate *'emunah shleymah*. There is something analogous in Reb Natan's teaching about the period of *Shovevim*, which can mean "backsliders" as well as "returners." The period of *Shovevim* is a kind of angle or turning point in the year that is difficult to navigate. It's a dangerous, tricky time, in which one may regress or leap forward. This recalls Yeats's concept of the gyre or spiral of time. Because time takes a spiral form, there are periods of the year that are like loops that spiral backward and forward at the same time. That is what makes them so challenging. There is a tendency to retrograde and we may feel that we are falling back or regressing while presented with the opportunity to advance and reach higher. So, when a planet is in retrograde, it's really just another sign that "the heavens are declaring the glory of the divine."

14.5 Inseparable from the Totality

At such times, it is especially important not to become absorbed by the *nafs*. The *Shovevim* practice is meant to loosen the grip of identification with an apparently separate self (*'ani hanifrad*). This appearance is a necessary part of the Totality, but the more strongly one identifies with it, the more the real ground of being (*malchut d'kedusha*) is hidden by *sitra Achara*. So there needs to be a conscious connection between the two "I"s, both the "I" of the apparent self and the "I" of transcendental consciousness that is inseparable from the Totality.

14.6 Is-that-is-not

When he was confronted by a person who had been sent to murder him, Shams was fearless because he saw everything with real *'emunah*, and he knew his place in the story that was unfolding. There are certainly times when it is right to resist injustice. But, if you are fighting because you want it your way, then you are firmly entranced in egoism, not in the way of the holy mind. Even though it may seem like it is taking forever for the time of *mashiach* consciousness to manifest, it is always and already the case that the only thing that truly exists is God and all that occurs is a display of Holy Power. So, I have to be prepared to wait forever. It is a practice for healing "I" of the path and not the timeless "I" of perfect knowledge, which needs no healing. Knowing reaches beyond the time and space that is "created" by *YHVH*, to that which never changes. The Rebbe RASHA"B calls it the "Is-that-Is-Not" (*Metziut sh'einu metziut*), that which can only be known by unknowing. When you have "real" *'emunah* you don't know, you don't see. What is the difference between *ge'ulah* (release) and *tiqqun* (fixing)?

Ge'ulah releases you from the constricted consciousness of egocentricity, but does not necessarily change anything. If you want to actually help "fix" something, an act of *tiqqun* is required. It requires *'emunah* to change it. Knowledge alone does not change anything. Shams recognized that he had to surrender to his murderer so that Rumi would be able to open up fully, to have the loss of Shams in his heart. Rumi already had knowledge, but he had not experienced loss requiring *'emunah.*

When Shams confronted his killer, he told him that he reminded him of someone who has a vision problem, someone who always sees double. There was once a merchant who had a servant with the same double-vision problem. The servant was sent for a bottle of wine. When he got to the wine house, he saw that there were two bottles there. He did not know which bottle to take. So, he asked the merchant which one he wanted. The merchant answered: Why don't you just break one, and you'll bring me the other one?

14.7 Break One, Broken Both

The purpose of this story is to teach us that non-duality is seeing double, but understanding that the two are inseparable. If we think that only one is true, then we shatter the other. It looks like there are two, but if you separate one from the other, you won't have anything. You break one, you've broken both of them!

Similarly, to be whole, you need to have both "knowledge" (*Da'at*) and "conviction" (*'emunah*). Knowledge may be liberating, but the work takes place in time and space. So, you need *'emunah* too to keep from being sucked into the egocentric reality trap. It's very hard to get out of there.

14.8 God Cannot Be Confined

Another rule: you can study God through everything in the universe, because God is not confined in a mosque, a synagogue, or a church. But if you are still in need of knowing where the divine abode is—it is in the heart of a true lover! The one who sees god at all times in every place. The problem is that we don't know what that means. You might think it means everything appears as peace and love. If you insist it always has to be the way you like it, then it is not real. The essence of the spiritual path is the cultivation of *'emunah*: it's always only "God," regardless of how things look! The lesson we have to learn is how much we need *'emunah* and how we are absolutely dependent upon it if we are to avoid getting lost in the egocentric states of anger, judgment, jealousy and competitiveness. It's a painful way of existing.

14.9 Names Enhancing Nature

In Rabbi Morgenstern's *De'ah Hokhmah L'Nafeshkha*,[4] the first Torah

---

4. R. Yitzchak Maeier Morgenstern, De'ah Hokhmah L'Nafeshkha, Seudah She-

in the period of "backsliding" and "returning" *Shovevim*, focuses on getting the sap to run upward for Jewish Arbor Day, *Tu B'Shevat* (the 15th of Shevat). According to the Torah myth, when the Israelites fell into the constricted state (*Mitzrayyim*), they were accompanied by Holy Names. According to ancient cosmology, letters are the fundamental building blocks of the entire cosmos. In this way, letters represent particular energies that can be combined in various ways to name and thus become all things. In the Israelite tradition, certain combinations of Hebrew letters form Holy Names which are especially potent. Such Names can be invoked in order to enhance natural processes with supernatural aid.

14.10 Backsliding into the Narrowness of Egypt

When the Israelites descended into Egypt, they were following the voice for God, that better part of our psyche that is seeking the way to the World-that-is-coming. Although they were looking for God in all places and all times, they fell into a tight spot called *Mitzrayyim*. The egocentric mind convinces us that this is the way the world is, and it can be very convincing and self-defeating. But because these Holy Names accompanied the Israelites into *Mitzrayyim*, there is a way out—"*Behold I (Anokhi) descends with you into Egypt, and the true I (Anokhi) am gets out of Egypt and beyond it with you as well.*"[5]

14.11 Exile as Pain and Suffering

The mystical tradition in the Zohar then teaches, regarding this verse, that when Jacob and his household went down to *Mitzrayyim*, 600,000 angels went with them. Rashbi teaches that if a person is used to bearing suffering, when a moment of suffering occurs, it's not so difficult to bear. As Sylvia Boorstein likes to say, "Pain is mandatory, but suffering is optional." But if a person is not used to suffering, when suffering comes they are likely to be overwhelmed by the pain. Then all one can do is cry. So, when the Israelites descended into *Mitzrayyim*, they were used to suffering already. Jacob's life had been a series of disappointments and suffering. He was used to it, having gone through those tests. That is why Jacob was able to bear exile as it should be borne in those moments when we find ourselves encompassed by the egocentric mind, that is, *Mitzrayyim*. The angels make it bearable.

But there is another kind of exile, called, the Babylonian Exile, which is virtually impossible to bear. Under such circumstances, there is weeping above and weeping below. What does the Babylonian exile mean? When does it occur? When we have had it too good, we lose the capacity for balance. As a result, we become hypersensitive and intolerant. Then ev-

lishith: Parshat Shemot (Jerusalem: Mechon Yam hHokhmah, 2016), 8b–9b.
    5. Exodus 3:6-10.

erything unsatisfactory seems like an existential threat. Someone wants to share space with you, and even that becomes too much to bear. You cannot handle the slightest bit of disappointment or challenge.

14.12 Divine Concealment vs. Divine Absence

Although in the Torah myth the terms "Egyptian (i.e., *Mitzrayyim*) Exile" and Babylonian Exile are used, these tropes represent spiritual states, not geophysical locations. "Egyptian exile" is a condition you can get out of through the work on *'emunah*. And that is why it (*yetziat Mitzrayyim*) is not considered to be a complete redemption. This form of liberation is *geulat da'at*—an awakening of consciousness which is beyond time and space. Someone who is attuned to it and can embody the message that there is God even when not apparent manifests the archetype of Moses. What is still there? It is called the *reshimu* or trace which remains in every condition of *tzimtzum*—states in which the ground of Real Being is concealed. This is why you have to think in terms of hiddenness and concealment rather than absence of the divine. Angels do abide with us there in the exile of *Mitzrayyim*. And they can also be called by Holy Names to come to our aid. Even in the place where everything looks so weak, for the person of *'emunah*, there are remedies available—which can be the 600,000 angels that descended into Egypt.

But the "Babylonian Exile" is different and provokes weeping above and below, because it's a hopeless and helpless state. Why? A spoiled person cannot handle the path. If you cannot take any suffering, you cannot make any progress. The prophetic act has to come from a place of "surrendering dering self" (*messirat nefesh*) and immersion in the "Is-that-Is-Not" (*bittul bimetziut*). Shams was capable of this and really had no interest in followers. When approached by someone who wanted to be his disciple, he told them, through the "I" that sees all, that they would be better off to go and be merchants. When the king tried to assert his authority by making a significant donation, everyone was shocked when Shams took the whole donation and pitched it back at the king, saying, this is not entertainment, we didn't do this for money, we did it for love! This is the highest level of *mesirat nefesh*, all is done for God, not trying to get anything out of it. All he wanted was someone who had the capacity to receive what he had to give. And that was Rumi.

14.13 Types of *Tiqqun*

Two things are necessary for the practice of *Shoveivim*. First, one has to give oneself over entirely to God (*messirat nefesh*) through the practice that is a complete remedy (*tiqqun haklali*). Such a healing sacrifice enables you to rewrite your story. This effectively resets your program entirely.

That makes you a new being. The great thing about a story is that it is only a story, and you can retell it in many different ways. When you think it's actually true, that's when you're stuck. That's why Moses said "around Midnight" and not "exactly at Midnight." He was introducing the practice of *Tiqqun Chatzot*. It is the most general, all-encompassing practice round midnight (*avodat hatzot*). Historically this practice of many traditional kabbalists was related to mourning for the Temple through *Tiqqun Leah* and *Tiqqun Rachel*, but these are really symbols.

Once you realize this, the "'Round Midnight" practice becomes a practice for total healing that can be done at any time. This is the way that you can achieve complete liberation. Situating ourselves within time and space, we are in the midnight hour in the iconography of Kabbalah, when we recognize the present moment as a crucial turning point. When things are darkest, it is the moment when something new may begin to emerge. Something can be revealed from that "Around Midnight" space. The Shekinah emerges from that space.

14.14 Black Is Beautiful as Shekinah

At that moment, when the crown of Sovereignty (*Keter* of *Malchut*) descends into the levels of *Beriyah, Yetzirah, Atzilut*, the Shekinah can form a vessel. What do these symbols mean? In order to form a vessel that can receive new light, you can change the story to the one that contains *'emunah*. That story is the one in which I "remember to find *YHVH* every place I look in the world."[6] But this descending sovereignty epitomizes darkness, as the Song of Songs states: "I am blackened."[7] But that is not the whole story. The *Vav* is connected to the light of *RADLA*, which descends by way of the "Around Midnight" state that illuminates by revealing the wisdom that there is no place devoid of the always present Reality. The "emptiness of the fullness" blesses us whenever we surrender to it by remembering the story of *'emunah*. Then the "Darkness" is sweetened, and the Shekinah can say, "I am blackened, and I am beautiful."

14.15 God Speaking to Itself Through "You"

If you have enough *'emunah* you can practice "Around Midnight" at any time and fix yourself through surrendering and remembering to place the divine in all places. The quality of the hidden wisdom is completely open—it is formless, or *'Ayin*. When you can bring down the crown of formlessness, that is beyond, so that the two bottles are not mistaken for one, then

---

6. Literally, "I have set the LORD always before me; surely He is at my right hand, I shall not be moved" (Psalm 16:8).

7. Literally, "I am black, but comely, O ye daughters of Jerusalem, as the tents of Kedar, as the curtains of Solomon" (Song of Songs 1:5).

you can get to the place where you can say "You" (*Atha*), everywhere I look I am saying "You!" Then I see God as present before me, and that is the practice of *'emunah*. This is why the practice of retreat (*hitbodedut*), deep isolation so that nothing is there but God, is so important. But the innovation of Reb Nachman was that deep isolation (*hitbodedut*) has to be recited out loud. It is so easy to do it inside, but it is so hard to open your mouth. If you want to bring down the quality of *Keter*, that is of the two is *not two*, beyond the mistake of *this or that*, which bottle is the real one? That is when you can pray out loud, because everything is God, every single piece. It is then only God speaking to itself, but God has to reverberate through the field of all existence.

14.16 Closing Intention

Let us merit to have such 'emunah *to open our mouths, regardless of what we are suffering, and may we profit from our suffering, so that none of us should be condemned to suffering that is nothing but weeping. May we have the joy of those who weep for Jerusalem, such a person will merit rejoicing. Jerusalem is the rebuilding of the heart. May we be the witnesses of* Atah, *and when we can see, we should merit knowing that what we need is* 'emunah. *We should turn around and rise with the sap that ascends with the Tree . . .*

About Face:
Holding onto a Vanishing Path

by Miles Krassen

At the very Heart of Existence, there may be a force that in the old-paradigm terminology of Kabbalah is called *ratzon* or "divine will." This intuition is shared by old-paradigm monotheistic kabbalists and modern Western philosophers like Blessed Spinoza and the great Schopenhauer. However, in distinction to the liberating insights of Spinoza and Schopenhauer, the idea which Judeo-Christian tradition established within medieval Western thought was accompanied by another idea, probably imported from ancient Zoroastrians, which would have it that such a "divine will" is purposive and driving humans, at least, if not the entire cosmos, toward some better end.

As an unconscious (later awakening) effect of forces in the noosphere during the years of my development, for a period of many decades, I believed in the dream of this mode of wishful thinking ("optimism"). Yet, as Reb Nachman slyly hides in plain sight in his Tale of a Lost Princess, there is a goal that will eventually be attained, but it is absolutely not possible to tell you how that happens—because in fact it does not happen—ever. It is always aspirational.

But, quite ironically, through following this dream in a manner suggested by the pathways that underlie the methodology of the teachings in this brief work and taking advantage of the increasing possibilities for seeing reality more clearly and objectively, something unexpected may happen. I have found that if the path is followed faithfully enough, it may (and perhaps must needs) become a cause for its own dissolution. Religious paths are meant to continue forever, although they may promise some ultimate reward elsewhere. More "spiritual" (often called "mystical") paths are meant to cancel themselves out. If we are fortunate enough to find our way to such a path, it may enable us to eventually outgrow our dependency on it.

In such a moment of abrupt "about face," it is understood that "paths" are not "eternally true" or eternally necessary, but something more like bridges constructed of elements dependent on and determined by particular circumstances of time, space, and causality. More importantly, paths, being strategies for moving through time, are only important when and where there is time to move in.

Our problem as human beings at this particular moment is that we are running out of time. And if Peter Russell is correct in his essential essay "The Blindspot" (and I think there is a fairly high probability that he is), we are running out of time at an ever-increasing rate of acceleration! So there is (probably) even a lot less time (left) to work with than we think.

This presents us with a dilemma, a kind of updated form of Pascal's wager. Perhaps we want to (continue to) bet that some mythic deus ex machina can and will save us. Reliance on such "salvation" may involve a form of monotheistic deity or its agent or in its update as faith in the power of materialist scientific knowledge. While the latter is surely a more rational belief, how rational is it to believe that (even) science will have enough time to save us from the impending sixth extinction and concurrent melting-down of all systems upon which the present form of human life depends?

Many optimists can only believe that time is endless. For such people, paths of all types are still valuable and even necessary. For, to paraphrase the remarkable G. I. Gurdjieff, if such people were to suddenly realize what is actually occurring, the ensuing panic itself would be catastrophic. So, for the possible benefit of such "souls," as still find solace and meaning in adhering to some form of historical Judaism and those who remain committed to investing in its transformation and survival, I am allowing the dissemination of this modest offering of *The Vanishing Path*. As long as there is still some time remaining, however much or little that may be, people will certainly be better off following a newly emerging path rather than continuing on the entrenched forms of "spirituality" and religion that, ironically, through supporting dogmatic beliefs and triumphalism, only serve to "hasten a coming 'War of Gog and Magog,'" which in their folly they imagine will lead to the promised end. How ironic that such an end may indeed be The End.

Our emerging path does not anticipate or "hasten the coming of a Messianic Age," which indeed never does come. But it subtly and gently guides and nudges us asymptotically toward a point of clarity and realization in which the path gradually overtakes itself and becomes superfluous. This goal is desirable, on one level, precisely because all previously defined paths strengthen a sense of identification and alterity which is not sustainable on an earth populated by almost eight billion humans. Although, such identification and self-serving aspirations have always led to conflict, in the past there was sufficient time and space for them to also yield some apparent benefits. However, now that sufficient time and space are so rapidly diminishing with the impending drastic undermining and depletion of most if not all supports for human as well as most other forms of life on Earth, the identifications that were meaningful in the past are becoming artifacts of a "world-that-is-going." Cleaving to them may be suicidal.

On the other hand, if the conventional sources of hope and optimism are suicidal, what option remains? Although we are certainly not suggesting that any presently existing tradition adequately models reality, there do seem to be certain reflections available within already existing sources of "Wisdom" that may prove useful to the construction of a path that may enhance our chances for survival. Such a path could not be an "orthodox" extension of artifacts from a "world-that-is-going." But it might be based in a synthesis of salvageable treasures that may be recovered, transported, and combined with new elements into the context of a "world-that-is-coming."

Let us consider, for example, the Lurianic notion of cosmic catastrophe and reformation (*shevirat ha-kelim* and *tiqqun*). If the present construction of systems and identities cannot withstand the implications of its own built-in but no longer adequate components (*sefirot*), the reformation and emergence of new systems, based on mutual support and cooperation (*partzu-fim*), might. Practically speaking, that means we need paths that support cooperative rather than self-centered efforts to form new systems. Such paths, in order to be sustainable and have a chance at surviving, could not privilege any of the obsolete modes of identification based in "race," ethnicity, nationality, gender, wealth, class, appearance, or "religion." Each brings to the "Great Work" whatever materials one has to offer. A path leading to a "world-that-is-coming" would have to be inclusive, planetary, and emerging through the process of discovering itself in response to the various contributions of salvageable material from all possible sources, volunteers, and benefactors that may prove helpful. And, if the AR"I was "right," it will require an entirely "new light" or vision in order to integrate all of the necessary sparks. Such an emerging world would be an *Olam ha-Tiqqun*, a microscosmic model of Totality that is sustainable at least insofar as that is presently foreseeable and constructed out of the viable remnants of the "world-that-is-going" along with the newly emerging "lights."

I resist characterizing this vision as "optimistic" insofar as conventional usages of this term tend to lure us into further degrees of enchantment. Optimism in preserving the models of reality that form an aging old-paradigm of the "world-that-is-going" would deny us the precious and unique opportunity afforded by recognizing the very terror of our present situation. Ironically, it may be precisely the shock of recognition that can provide us with the energy necessary for dispelling complacency.

So our steps are leading us to an orientation to life that calls on each facet of the Totality to recognize itself as such and in so doing gain the capacity to consciously play its own given role of deployment (*tafqid*)in the mutual and "reciprocal maintenance" of what Spinoza and others would be happy to call the "Divine Body," particularly insofar as that "great work" worships and supports the Glory of the entire earth, that cosmic jewel of which we are presently mostly unwitting facets.

This vision does not rely on old-paradigm "virtues" such as "faith," "hope," and "charity." It is not merely a matter of refurbishing a vehicle that has long outlived its usefulness. To make the jump from perishing within the dire straits (*mitzrayyim*) of a "world-that-is-going," we need "virtues" that are more expansive and immediate. That means our mode of being has to be rooted in a direct and intuitive Gnosis of Reality as Totality—the All that really is One; and other than which there IS no Other.

For us, "virtues" are refinements of the capacities of each microcosmic "facet" to consciously participate in the splendor of continuous creation (*Ma'aseh Vereishit*). The attainment of such virtues is not a matter of obedience to the demands of some external authority that threatens us and whom we must obey "or else." Rather, it is a matter of potentially avoiding extinction through skillfully balancing and integrating our body/minds (*Ma'aseh Merkavah*) through recognition of our own presence as microcosmic facet moving with and moved by the spontaneously manifesting expression of the macrocosmic forces of the Totality.

We do not accept any external authority's notions of "ought versus is," making impossible demands that we can never meet. Rather, we understand and directly sense our good fortune and capacity to receive guiding influences and insight that are available to us through the grace of the Totality (*ahavah rabbah ahavtanu*) as aspects of our own minds, however submerged in unconsciousness. Indeed, worship for us is essentially and precisely a "balancing act"; an "about face" which releases us (*havdalah*) from enslavement to limiting, unbalanced, and deluded, merely microcosmic perceptions of separation (*tzimtzum*), after recognizing (*hakhna'ah*) and surrendering to the very necessity for our participation in the all-inclusive panoply of the Totality's splendor (*gadlut YHVH*). This subtle act of balancing ourselves through nonjudgmental surrender and alignment to Reality is inherently meaningful, satisfying, and blissful (*hamtakqah*).[1] By this means and mode of being ourselves as given, we become "free" to function as "co-creators" (*hamlakhah*) of a "world-that-is-coming."

But what if time does run out? Indeed, time always runs out. Moses never actually enters the promised state that is always aspirational. The Viceroy never actually "finds" and ultimately restores the Princess. And the tale of the seventh beggar is never told. Why then bother taking steps

---

1. To appreciate this innovative revision of the Beshtian devotional triad of hakhna'ah-havdalah-hamtakqah, see Baal Shem Tov, The Pillar of Prayer, #95:113–14;#96:119; #143.1:178; #148.9:198–99.

along a path to a "world-that-is-(always)-coming," but never actually comes? One answer is that a path that leads to its own dissolution removes the "optimistic" delusion that there is some particular future that has to be reached. As such, to paraphrase Rebbe Nachman, there is no despair (*asur le-hitya'esh*), precisely because despair is an effect of deluded and frustrated optimism. On our path, we recognize with increasing clarity that we are always "there" exactly where we are meant "to be." And the more that we can cultivate the "virtues" that align us with wherever the Totality moves us, the more meaningful, joyful, and real our lives become. Regardless of what may happen or when it may occur, this Torah of a "world-that-is-coming" is the Torah of Moses.

May it help us to reach that place of constant prayer which is beyond all aspiration. And may we, too, live to see what Moses saw when "that time" comes (*ba-yom ha-hu*). *Amen, keyn yehi RATZON.*

Completed on the day in which we read: "If you will only pay careful attention to these steps and keep doing them, The Totality (*YHVH*) will constantly empower you as co-creator and shower you with love as has been assured" (Deut. 7:12).

No Face:
Emptiness at the Heart of Spiritual Practice

by Norman Fischer

Miles Krassen is of course absolutely correct that in our urgent times (and what times, for human beings, have not been urgent!) we have no choice but to drop our previous claims to exclusive metaphysical truth and literalistic teaching and recognize that spiritual paths though absolutely different from one another, and therefore not reducible to generic "perennial wisdom," are at the same time mutually supportive and mutually necessary. In fact, as Reb Miles points out, it is obvious that though rational objective physical solutions to our global problems are necessary, they cannot be sufficient. Spiritual transformation is the crucial ingredient for human survival and flourishing ("survival" means surviving as long as we survive). In short, there can only be an inspiring human future when human beings are inspired.

Reb Miles's teachings touch the clear pivot point: time. We can no longer aspire to a future we project from the standpoint of the dualistic world-that-is-going, but rather embrace a hope that is embedded in a fuller, grander, and more profound understanding of what time and being actually already are. All of time is always here, in existence as we can live it. As he teaches, we must go beyond optimism and pessimism. Both are dead ends, built on a concept of time that is outmoded.

In Zen Buddhism, this sense of time as inherently redemptive is embedded in the emptiness teachings. "Emptiness" sounds like a bleak concept. We want a "somethingness," a "fullness," maybe even a "God-ness." But emptiness doesn't violate any of these hopeful aspirations—instead it shifts the ground on which they rest. If we understand the emptiness of time, we see that our hopes for the future are realized right now, that our longing to cleave to God is already effected in our truly being who and what we are.

Since any explanation of emptiness would necessarily be misleading, Zen talks are usually paradoxical, if not entirely silent. There's story about this: One day the Buddha ascended the ceremonial dharma seat to speak. Manjushri, the bodhisattva of emptiness, struck the gavel to formally open the talk. He said, "Clearly observe: the dharma of the dharma king is thus!" The Buddha then got down from the seat.

In saying nothing at all, the Buddha gave an ideal Zen talk. The message of such a talk is—whatever you can say and know is partial and will lead to more partiality and suffering. (The sentence you have just read is such a partial and therefore incorrect and damaging statement.) In fact, nothing is partial. Everything is important; everything is crucial and complete. Everything as it is expresses the dharma if you can really be there for it.

When I give a Zen talk, I usually use some words. But I always tell people not to think there is some special truth in my words. Instead, my words are supposed to turn listeners back around, away from looking for something later and elsewhere, and back toward themselves, to the ground where they are right now standing. We are always in the midst of enlightenment, perfection, God-ness, though we think there is something else we need.

Prajna is the wisdom that cognizes emptiness. Usually the word prajna is translated as "wisdom," but lately I have been translating it as understanding because in English understanding means empathy. Practicing prajna makes you an understanding, an empathetic, person. You understand that everything is unexplained, everything is complete. You understand that what you think you know you don't really know. You have an open feeling about life which gives you a great empathy, sympathy, and compassion for others because you know that others are empty of others, self is empty of self. We are all sad and magnificent together as one.

Technically, emptiness means that things lack "own-being." Things exist, but not as we think they do—as solid, graspable, separate. The practice of Zen meditation—sitting in silence without trying to do anything but be there as fully as possible—is meant to help us to appreciate this. Practicing Zen meditation usually gives you some composure even when things are tough, because you know things simply come and go and are not real in the conventional sense. This is quite relieving. It usually makes you more relaxed and more kind. At Makor Or, our Jewish meditation center in San Francisco, Rabbi Lew and I applied this simple yet radical Zen technique to Torah. We understood sitting in the present ineffable moment as sitting in the midst of *Yod Heh Vav Heh*, Reb Miles's world-that-is-coming.

Such sitting is elusive. Even more elusive are words to describe it. All religious teachings are true in one sense, but not true in another sense. As Rabbi Miles teaches, all paths are meant to be discarded once they are fully practiced. Once you discard them you may continue to practice them, but in a new sense—in a world-that-is-coming-and-is-here sense. You see that the meaning of your practice and of the sacred teachings that support and propose to describe it is, simply, love. This is old and new news that we need now to seize as our one and only collective human truth.

Though we cannot fully know or even conceptualize *Ein Sof*, the endless nothingness that is the ultimate source of divinity, we can imitate and manifest it in our lives as humility. To fully embrace *Ein Sof* is to appreciate the emptiness of all things and the nothingness at the heart of the human soul. This embrace makes you a truly humble person. You know you have no truth to hold onto and that the practice you are doing, that you have perhaps devoted your life to, is nothing more or less than what anyone is already doing anyway. So there is no source of pride.

You might think that being humble in this way is disappointing (one wants after all something important and special!), but it is exactly the opposite. To be humble is to be innocent, open, interested, curious, amazed. To always see possibility. Limitless possibility.

Norman Fischer, Zen priest and poet, founder of the Everyday Zen Foundation (www.everydayzen.org), and cofounder, with Rabbi Alan Lew of blessed memory, of Makor Or, a Jewish Meditation Center in San Francisco. Author of *Experience: Thinking, Writing, Language and Religion.*

Original Face:
Face(t)s of Totality Coming and Going

by Zvi Ish-Shalom

In his essay "About Face," Miles Krassen reminds us that time may well be running out. As such, he wisely calls upon us to not waste time hoping to attain the always aspirational (and thus, unattainable) goals of the "world-that-is-going," but encourages us to take an "about-face"—a turn toward an emerging paradigm of spiritual paths that can more effectively guide us (through their own self-erasure in time) to the timeless source of the "world-that-is-coming."

In the view of *Kedumah*, which represents one such new-paradigm path, this "about-face" from the optimistic directionality of the "world-that-is-going" is not so much a "turning" as it is a "re-turning" to our primordial face, the timeless and dimensionless nature of our being, freed from the conceptual rigidities accrued from lifetimes displayed through the dimensions of time and space.

Since conventional time may be running out, it is surely "about-time" that we return to our original face. Indeed, it is ultimately all "about-face": that is, the "inter-face" between inner and outer, beyond and within, before and after. The Hebrew word *panim*, which means both "face" and "inside," also—through shared etymology—points to the possibility of "turning" (*ponim*) toward our true "inner face" (*panim*), that which is "prior-in-time" (*lifnei*), yet is "in the presence of" (*bifnei*) and "within" (*bifnim*) each and every moment in time.

This "about-face" turns us toward an experiential principle found in ancient texts that describes a *Torah Kedumah*—a "primordial teaching"—that existed before the creation of the world. Since the dimensions of time and space are expressions of the created realm, the *Torah Kedumah* is therefore prior to—and not bound by—time and space. In this sense, the *Kedumah* principle does not mean ancient or primordial in relation to space and time. Rather, it points to reality *as it is*, that which is more fundamental than the creation of the world of our concepts, including the concepts of time and space.

As such, *Kedumah* turns us toward that which is always-already existing, to the most basic reality and truth that eternally abides as *what is* before

215

our mind reifies our experience into conceptual categories and labels. If we can learn how to follow Krassen's vanishing path, if we can take an "about-face" and return to our primordial nature, to our original face, then we may come to appreciate more fully that we are fundamentally not bound to the dimensions of time and space.

This primordial freedom is realized by penetrating the truth of our experience in the here and now. The Hebrew word for "truth" (*emet*) reflects this process, since according to a well-known rabbinic teaching, the word *emet* is not only equated with the dynamism of Being (*yhvh eloheichem emet*), but also, since it is constituted by the first (*aleph*), middle (*mem*), and last (*tav*) letters of the Hebrew alphabet, it embodies the totality of time—past (*aleph*), present (*mem*), and future (*tav*).

The essence of truth (the letter *mem* at the center of the word *emet*, whose numerical value is forty), thus represents the process of re-turning (*teshuvah*) to our primordial nature in both time (forty days of *teshuvah* between *rosh chodesh elul* and *yom kippur*, etc.) as well as in space (the volume of a *mikvah* must contain forty *se'ah*, etc.). The essence of truth—the letter *mem* which represents the present moment as well as the number forty—thus re-turns us not to some ancient point in space or time, but leads us in an "about-face" into the present moment—to the inner nature of our being that is bound neither by space nor time.

Only from the ground of this timeless realization is it possible to authentically formulate the new-paradigm paths that we need to guide us through the end of time to the endlessness of being. These paths will guide us to this end(lessness) not by leading us to some imagined point in space or time, but by leading us on an "about face" into the depths of the present moment, which effectively takes us to the end of time and to the always beginning timeless and dimensionless ground from which the Torah for the "world-that-is-coming" is being revealed.

On the Kedumah path we articulate five stages or journeys in the about face process: contraction (*malchut*), expansion (*tiferet*), wholeness (*binah*), vastness (*chochmah*), and freedom (*keter/ein sof*). Each one of these journeys represents a particular experiential juncture that integrates progressively deeper and subtler face(t)s of our being. Like a Torah scroll, the human being is constituted by layers of conceptual narratives that can be deconstructed through contemplative inquiry, ultimately exposing the blank parchment that constitutes the primordial ground of our being. The realization of the blank parchment of our soul correlates in our system with the journey of vastness, the timeless ground and source of wisdom upon which new letters, words, narratives, and teachings are inscribed.

However, while experiential access to the journey of vastness is necessary to articulate the emerging Torah of the world-that-is-coming, it also serves as a portal to an even more radical truth. The journey of freedom, the fifth journey in the *Kedumah* teachings, represents the all-inclusive totality of the scroll: the words (*contraction*), letters (*expansion*), ink (*wholeness*), and parchment (*vastness*). When we view reality through the lens of the journey of freedom, all the forms of manifestation—both hidden and re-vealed—are included as equalized face(t)s of a singular scroll.

The journey of freedom, which correlates with the principle of totality, is rooted in our understanding of *Ein Sof*, which is the realization of the truth that transcends and includes the concepts of infinite and finite. Since this radical nondirectional, nondimensional, and multi-perspectival reality includes everything and nothing at all, it is possible for multiple and even contradictory truths to interpenetrate and coexist without friction (*elu v'elu divrei elohim chayyim*). This mode of non-binary perception underscores how the spiritual hierarchies and identities that have governed the "world that is going" are based on a limited view of the total nature of reality.

Therefore, the Torah for the world-that-is-coming not only must return us through an "about-face" to our true interface—our primordial nature that is always-already abiding in the hidden depths of the present moment—but, like Miles Krassen so beautifully teaches us, it also must be a Torah of totality, one that is inclusive, planetary, and that shows us how to inter-face with each other in cooperative, participatory, and evolutionary ways: a Torah that celebrates the unending display of letters refracted through its living parchment as individual human face(t)s of the totality, collectively co-creating the emerging scrolls of the world that is beyond (and includes) the concepts of coming and going.

Rabbi Dr. Zvi Ish-Shalom is an associate professor at Naropa University, founder of the Kedumah Institute, and author *of The Kedumah Experience*.